Praise for *Echolands*

'Jump back in time for a moment – Duncan Mackay effortlessly weaves history and archaeology together in this masterly evocation of the bloodiest year in British history'

Professor Alice Roberts

'I found *Echolands* hard to put down! Mackay's scholarship is laced with a vividness of imagination'

Professor Miranda Aldhouse-Green

'Mackay unravels the story of Boudica's revolt, expertly patching together the written sources with the archaeological evidence and modern recollections . . . *Echolands* brilliantly reminds us how to locate the past in the present'

Dr Cat Jarman

'An engaged, informed companion for the armchair time traveller . . . captures the thrill and the difficulties of interpreting the past'

TLS

'Duncan has written a masterpiece – a journey and an investigation that fuses landscape and history, chasing the echoes of Boudica's rebellion and finding its physical traces that still surround us today'

Nicholas Crane

'A brilliant imagining of the past. Mackay's knowledge is profound, but lightly worn, his writing elegant and witty, and his enthusiasm infectious. A joy to read'

Dr Harry Sidebottom, author of *The Mad Emperor*

Echolands

A Journey in Search of Boudica

DUNCAN MACKAY

HODDER &
STOUGHTON

First published in Great Britain in 2023 by Hodder & Stoughton Limited
An Hachette UK company

The authorised representative in the EEA is Hachette Ireland, 8 Castlecourt
Centre, Dublin 15, D15 XTP3, Ireland (email: info@hbgi.ie)

This paperback edition published in 2024

4

Picture acknowledgements:
p. 1 (above) © Chris Rudd Ltd, www.celticcoins.om; (below) engraving from G.F.
Raymond, *History of England* (c. 1786); p. 4 (above) engraving from D. Hume and
W.C. Stafford, *The History of England* (c. 1868); p. 5 (below) postcard, Rotary
Photographic Series (pre-1920); p. 6 (above) Alfieri Picture Service, reproduced by
the *Daily Telegraph* on 23 April 1937; p. 7 (above) © The Trustees of the British
Museum; (below) engraving, c. 1870s. All other images © Duncan Mackay.

A CIP catalogue record for this title is available from the British Library

Paperback ISBN 978 1 399 71414 3
ebook ISBN 978 1 399 71412 9

Typeset in Sabon MT by Hewer Text UK Ltd, Edinburgh
Printed and bound in Great Britain by Clays Ltd, Elcograf S.p.A.

Hodder & Stoughton policy is to use papers that are natural, renewable
and recyclable products and made from wood grown in sustainable
forests. The logging and manufacturing processes are expected to
conform to the environmental regulations of the country of origin.

Hodder & Stoughton Limited
Carmelite House
50 Victoria Embankment
London EC4Y 0DZ

www.hodder.co.uk

For Clare, Tristan and Jojo,
who sometimes jumped back with me

I'll go with you, then,
since you must play this game of ghosts . . .

Siegfried Sassoon

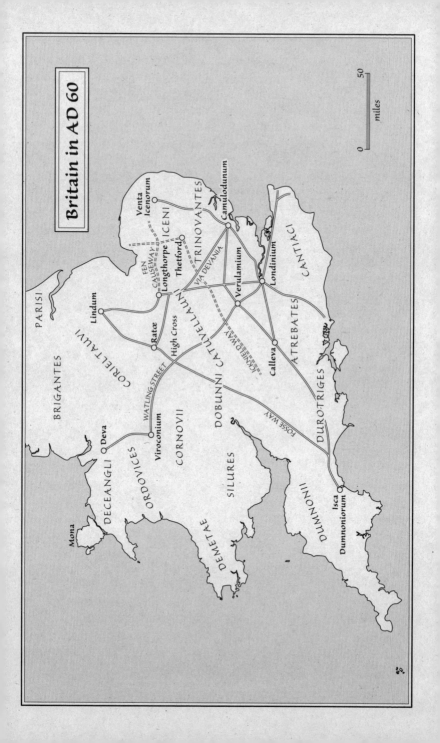

Contents

Significant Historical Figures

Romans

Agricola – Staff officer in AD 60, later governor of Britain and father-in-law of Tacitus.

Augustus – Emperor, 27 BC–AD 14.

Aulus Plautius – General tasked with invading Britain in AD 43.

Cassius Dio – Roman historian, late second century AD.

Catus Decianus – Procurator of Britain in AD 60, a sort of Chancellor of the Exchequer.

Claudius – Emperor, AD 41–54.

Julius Caesar – Governor of Gaul, later dictator. Led expeditions to Britain in 55 and 54 BC.

Nero – Emperor, AD 54–68.

Ostorius Scapula – Second governor of Britain, AD 47–52.

Seneca – Roman philosopher and statesman, advisor to Nero.

Suetonius Paulinus – Governor of Britain, AD 58–61, senior commander confronting Boudica.

Tacitus – Son-in-law of Agricola, Roman historian, late first and early second century AD.

Britons

Boudica – Wife and queen/consort of King Prasutagus of the Iceni.

Caratacus – Prince of the Catuvellauni, and British resistance leader.

Cartimandua – Queen of the Brigantes, Roman client monarch.

Cunobelin – King of the Catuvellauni, died c.AD 40.

Prasutagus – King of the Iceni, husband of Boudica, Roman client monarch.

Togidubnus – King based near Chichester, probably of the Atrebates; Roman client monarch.

Togodumnus – Prince of the Catuvellauni, British war leader.

Preface
AD 60 and All That

A Game of Ghosts

*But you are wrong to say that we cannot move about in Time.
For instance, if I am recalling an incident very vividly, I go
back to the instant of its occurrence: I become absent-minded,
as you say. I jump back for a moment.*

H.G. Wells, *The Time Machine*

One fateful day in 1919, Rik Mortimer Wheeler, a demobbed artillery officer fresh home from the trauma of the Great War, was exploring the dungeons beneath the dishevelled Norman keep of Colchester Castle. Still only twenty-nine years old, Wheeler was already an experienced archaeologist and decorated soldier, and had conducted excavations in Colchester during the war whilst waiting to go overseas. Blinking through the cold, claustrophobic gloom at the vaulting arches of gravelly mortar around him, Wheeler gazed into the eyes of his companion. By his own admission, peering out of the gloom, he must have looked like an owl.

'Dungeons,' he murmured, 'dungeons be damned.'

Where his guide saw the cellars and dungeons of a medieval castle, Wheeler saw the hard concrete underbelly of Roman foundations, and not just any foundations, but those of a temple. And in that city, with those foundations, they could only be for one building. The Temple of Claudius.[1]

Rik Mortimer Wheeler, later Sir Mortimer Wheeler, one of the most famous, colourful and controversial characters ever to emerge from British archaeology, had stumbled across a site of monumental importance. The Temple of Claudius, the centre of the Imperial cult, was the most prestigious building in the Roman province of Britannia at the time of its construction. More than that, it had the rare distinction of being specifically mentioned in the scant histories of Roman Britain, and was central to one of the most terrible tragedies related in them.

In AD 60, when Queen Boudica's rebel army surged across the south-east of Britain, destroying all in its path, Colchester, then Camulodunum, had been its first objective. Undefended by ramparts or much of a garrison, the city had fallen in a frenzy of slaughter and fire. *All else was plundered or fired in the onslaught;* wrote Tacitus, *the temple where the soldiers had assembled, was stormed after a two days' siege.*[2]

The foundations of that temple, now known as the Vaults, can be visited today. The arching walls of rough concrete embedded with gravel, which seem purposely designed to scalp anyone unfortunate enough to trip and bang their head against them, are, for me, the most remarkable Roman remains in Britain. What the place lacks in architecture, art and colour, it makes up for incomparably with a less tangible commodity – atmosphere.

The enclosing gloom is no less oppressive than in Wheeler's day, and if you are able to linger alone for a moment, when the rest of the tour party stoops through the small doorway hacked through the concrete into the next vault, I know of nowhere else in which the imagination can run quite so rampant. It is one of those rare places that forms a direct link with a specific event so long ago that almost all other traces of it have been erased.

Experiencing archaeological and historical sites in person inevitably requires some sort of input from the visitor if we are to see more than a bit of old wall, a ditch full of its famously dull water, or simply an empty field. Rik Mortimer Wheeler, as an older man, observed that 'the archaeologist is digging up, not things, but people,'[3] encapsulating the need to repopulate those ancient sites with real human beings, and all the noise, smell and colour, passions, joys and woes accompanying them; in short, to bring it all back to life.

Archaeologists dig up people, and stories. Sometimes those stories are great, sweeping changes on a landscape scale, or the evolution of a single town or farm over centuries. For the individual excavator, at trowel level, those stories can be more intimate, exposing the physical residue of single moments; of individuals and their lives. Excavating a grave, perhaps, is the ultimate example of literally digging up people, but there are stories to be teased out from soil layers and scraps of pottery that open equally vivid, astonishing little windows.

But brushing up against the past, and glancing momentarily backwards, is not just the privilege and preserve of the excavator. Those windows and links to the past surround us every day, wherever we are; we simply have to notice them, and allow them to tell their story. The examples I would like to share, for they really inspired this book and are crucial to understanding the journey we are making, have nothing whatsoever to do with Boudica, but they condense the sheer wonder that seeing the history around you can inspire. We are not going back much more than a hundred years, but to pay lip-service to the Great Queen in her own book, I will start the story with her.

From Boadicea's statue beside Westminster Bridge, if you walk north along the Victoria Embankment for ten minutes, you come to Cleopatra's Needle, all at once magnificent, understated and completely out of place. The needle itself is impressive enough, but it is the sphinxes to either side that catch my attention, lying like bored guard dogs waiting for some sort of pharaonic Scooby Snack that never materialises. From across the road there is not much to choose between the sphinxes, identical mirror images of cast bronze placed equidistantly from the needle.

But not quite. The one on the right has dark mottling on the stone pedestal, and a small plaque. You cross the road. The dark mottling is actually pitting, as if someone has taken a hammer to the stone, blackened now by pollution, and there are irregular holes in the bronze arm of the sphinx. The plaque reveals all:

> The scars that disfigure the pedestal of the obelisk, the bases
> of the sphinxes and the right-hand sphinx, were caused by
> fragments of a bomb dropped in the roadway close to this spot,
> in the first raid on London by German aeroplanes a few minutes
> before midnight on Tuesday 4th September 1917.

September *1917*?

I'm guessing most of us were expecting a date closer to 1940, but London, and other cities, were heavily bombed in the First World War. The first raids on London were by Zeppelins, sleek, 650-foot-long airships. Next came the Gothas, huge biplane bombers, and even Staaken Giants, a biplane so monstrous that only one Second World War bomber matched its vast wingspan. The Giants would fly sorties over London beginning that same September, but the plane that dropped the bomb by Cleopatra's Needle was a Gotha, and the sign is incorrect – it was the first *night* raid by aeroplanes.

Night-time on the Embankment. It is a fine, cool September evening. The moon is almost full, and only light cloud litters the sky. You cannot quite see Big Ben, for its bright face, like a guiding lighthouse, has been put out to comply with the blackout, and is likewise silenced. It is fifteen minutes before midnight, but no thunderous chimes echo along the Thames.

However, all is not quiet on the Victoria Embankment. Trams and taxis, both horse-drawn and motorised, are still plying their trade, and dawdling couples walk arm in arm through the late summer night. Along the Thames to the east are the familiar searchlights of Chatham and Gravesend fingering the sky for Zeppelins, and the distant *pop, pop, pop* suggest the anti-aircraft gunners have spotted one, or are unusually jumpy tonight. You are not concerned.

The Zepps haven't broken through central London's defences for nearly a year, and the Gothas only raid in daylight.

But then the bombs start falling. Distant at first, and then the drone of the bombers can be heard, drowned out momentarily by the clatter of a passing tram, and then a deafening roar and blinding flash as the road erupts before you. Knocked flat, winded, deafened and momentarily blind, your senses return as the smoke slowly clears from the scene ahead. The tram has stopped, the windows all blown out, the driver slumped at the front, the two passengers silent somewhere in the wreckage; another figure staggers like a drunk. Some passers-by are screaming. Others are sprawled across the pavement. The Needle is still standing, miraculously, but bomb fragments have cut through the bronze arm of the sphinx like pebbles plopping into foreshore mud.

I put my finger into one of the holes. School kids with iPhones take selfies behind me. Whenever I stand near the needle those same events play through my mind and *I jump back for a moment*, as Wells says at the beginning of this chapter. The driver of the tram and his two passengers were killed and eight pedestrians injured by the 50-kilogram bomb that pockmarks the sphinx; the conductor lived to tell the tale. And every time I look at those holes, the archaeologist in me can't help but think, Is the shrapnel still inside there?

I walk a few yards back and hold up a picture; a photograph taken the next day that shows the terrible damage.[4] With the advent of photography, and moving film, we can visit such places and stand at the exact viewpoint of a photographer or filmmaker, hold up the picture, or footage, and gaze across the decades like time travellers.

I have done this on the Somme battlefield of Beaumont Hamel in northern France, standing on the exact spot where Geoffrey Malins, the official British cinematographer stood on 1 July 1916, filming men shortly to go over the top in that catastrophic first attack of the battle. In August 2014, I had taken a copy of the footage to the battlefield, tracked down a couple of exact filming locations, lined up the miniature screen horizon with the real one, and simply sat back open-mouthed to watch real ghosts wage their long-finished war, of young soldiers standing beside me, bayonets fixed, some smiling, some wretchedly scared, their hundred-year-exhaled cigarette smoke almost drifting out of the screen around me, sixty minutes before most dashed to their deaths or disablement.

I watched the quiet, wooded hilltop beyond erupt like a volcano in front of me as 40,000 pounds of secretly laid high-explosive did its work, throwing half the hill itself and all who stood on it thousands of feet into the air. Panning the DVD screen to my right-front, just as Malins had done with his camera, I watched the first men scrambling across no-man's-land at zero hour and, almost unnoticed, I watched the first of those tiny, grey-scale figures falling as the machine guns opened up on them, able to glance across the few hundred yards and identify the exact spot where their crumpled bodies lay; perhaps where they still lie. Living, breathing human beings to archaeological deposits in the flickering of a cine film cell.[5]

The sense of the past happening before my eyes, of *jumping back*, was so remarkable that it returned to me time and again in the weeks and months to come. This was the artist's reconstruction drawing, *from where you stand now*, writ large, that transported you momentarily back. Having spent the better part of two decades in professional archaeology, I was used to moments of connection with the past, of excavating a skeleton and being the first person to have any dealings with that forgotten individual for thousands of years; of being the first to see a 6000-year-old flint blade emerge from the soil, as perfect as the day it went in, and carelessly slicing my finger open on the still razor-sharp edge.

I remember one humid August afternoon on a fenland gravel quarry in 1996, being absorbed in the fragile task of lifting several Bronze Age cremation urns from their long interment, whilst dark clouds gathered above us. As the first fat raindrops spat up the dust like bullets, someone quipped that we must have triggered an ancient protective curse, that lightning would strike down anyone disturbing the graves. There was a chuckle, but I remember the second observation, said in a slightly quieter, more reverent tone, a spoken thought, that after 3500 years, perhaps that curse was simply too old now to do more than rain on us.

Archaeologists, of course, do not believe in curses, but I have never forgotten the poignancy of the statement, nor the way it somehow expressed the enormity of the time span that separated us from those burials, at the same moment as emphasising the intimacy of our very real, if fleeting, part in their story.

None of this, however, had inspired the sense of the past happening before my eyes as had watching that century-old battle footage from the footprints of the cameraman. I began to wonder if such a sense of immediacy could ever be achieved for the pre-film era; as an archaeologist I inevitably wondered if, by combining the various strands of evidence, it could even be achieved in any small way in an *ancient* context?

How far can we do this with Boudica? The Romans did not have cinematographers, but they did have historians, and two of them, Cornelius Tacitus and Cassius Dio, recorded the events of AD 60 for us in three surviving texts, Tacitus's *The Annals* and *The Agricola*, and Dio's *History*, of which only the *Annals* provides enough detail to recreate the events meaningfully. All were written long after the war, Tacitus in the late-first and early-second centuries, Dio in the late second century, and their sources are unknown, although they undoubtedly included official dispatches, not to mention now-lost memoirs, perhaps even of the Roman commander, Suetonius Paulinus himself.

It is also surely worth mentioning, as it so often is, that Tacitus was married to the daughter of Julius Agricola, who had served on Paulinus's staff during Boudica's war, and went on to become the governor of Britannia two decades later. Tacitus undoubtedly discussed the event with his father-in-law, although both of his accounts, especially the *Annals*, were written long after Agricola's death. As such, both authors are tantalisingly close to the events they describe by using primary sources, but far enough removed that they are confused and contradictory, sometimes clearly fabricated, and shamelessly dramatised for their audience.

But Tacitus and Dio are not our only sources for this war. They are the only *written* sources. The other great document we possess is the landscape upon which we live, with its hills, lakes and bogs, farmland, building sites, towns and museums. Beneath some of those towns lie the bloody scars that show Boudica once passed that way. The ploughsoil hides the post-holes, ditches and pits of lost villages, towns and forts. Garden soil might yield the coins and pottery that whisper of the ghosts of the soldiers or tribespeople who once shared that ground. Museums hold objects that cry out to be heard, to lend their own stories to this remarkable odyssey.

What I hope to show you is how we can pull together those separate strands – history, archaeology, landscape, conjecture, artefacts, deduction and good old-fashioned imagination – to weave the tapestry of Boudica's war, and to find that the land upon which she lived, alien, brutal, and sometimes familiar, lies only a few inches beneath your own feet.

This, then, is not a conventional retelling of Boudica's story, but an unashamedly personal journey through a lost landscape, and an intimate reimagining of events; an experiment in jumping back.

I trust the reader will forgive me for switching between ancient and modern place names with seeming impunity, but I will inevitably discuss the ancient and modern in the same breath, and for our purposes, they are pretty much the same thing, so Camulodunum and Colchester will be fairly interchangeable. Likewise, the use of Wales and Welsh – completely incorrect in an ancient context – are useful locators for the modern reader. Besides, if you can inadvertently refer to London as Londinium without meaning to, you'll already have one foot firmly planted in Boudica's Britain. In no time at all you'll be catching the scent of its smoke on the breeze as well.

1

A Far-Flung Isle

How the Romans Did For Us

The Roman Conquest was, however, a Good Thing,
since the Britons were only natives at that time.
R.C. Sellar and R.J. Yeatman, *1066 and All That*

I have before me a picture of Queen Boadicea drawn by an eight-year-old boy. She is mounted in a chariot, wears a green dress belted at the waist, and a red crown pokes out of the top of her waist-length black hair. She holds an enormously long spear aloft in one hand, and the reins of a horse with the other. The kid has skilfully avoided the difficulty of drawing the galloping horses by having them beyond the edge of the page, and if the rendition of the rear-end of the one horse just visible is anything to go by, it was a wise move. The chariot has a strange, stepping crenellation, like a miniature fort, and the wheel has the obligatory scythe on the hub.

My favourite figure is a warrior standing on the ground beside her, bronze sword raised to the sky, with horned helmet and elongated shield, heavily bearded, blobs of blue woad, basically an Airfix toy Ancient Briton. All in all, it's an awful picture, but I am rather fond of it in a sentimental sort of way, for it wasn't my own son who drew it, nor one of the children from a local school where I talk about archaeology and history from time to time; I'm allowed to be mean about it because I drew it in the second year of junior school back in 1978.

My wonderful teacher that year, Mrs Milner, has ticked the page in red biro, and then added the crowning glory beneath it:

'Tried.'

Not 'Good', or 'Well done', which I could now show to my son, not 'Hasn't tried', which would have a certain devil-may-care rebellious cool to it. 'Tried' is the charitable consolation prize meaning 'Rubbish, despite having tried.'

So much for my first attempt to tell Boudica's story.

The Roman conquest of Britain was apocalyptic. In the forty years it took the legions to campaign from the beaches of Kent to the Highlands of Scotland in the first century AD, a quarter of a million Britons may have been killed. A similar figure might be proposed for those taken into slavery, and these losses do not begin to quantify the wounded, displaced and press-ganged, nor those who starved in the resulting famines.[1] From a population that perhaps numbered only two million souls, it is not implausible that between half a million and a million Britons became casualties of the invasion or disappeared forever from their tribes.

Of those who resisted this conquest, Boudica of the Iceni, from the region of modern Norfolk and Suffolk, is surely the most famous, but she can be problematic as a heroine. 'Was Boudica a War Criminal?' asked *BBC History* magazine on the front cover of its June 2017 edition, and two of our best-known modern Roman historians have recently dismissed her as a 'dinosaur'[2] and a 'brutal terrorist'.[3]

In December 2000, the *Observer* ran a story entitled, 'Dig Uncovers Boudicca's Brutal Streak'.[4] Drawing on recent archaeological work in Colchester, which confirmed that the Roman city had been comprehensively razed in AD 60, the story concluded, 'The new evidence of Boudicca's brutality will dismay many. For 150 years the woman who led the Iceni tribe from its base in Norfolk against the Roman invaders has been viewed as an icon of national resistance.' The archaeology was well worth reporting, but had it changed our perception of Boudica?

Tacitus and Dio were certainly unambiguous on one point – the rebellion had been bloody and ruthless. Even my beloved *Ladybird Book of Roman Britain*, published in 1959 for the under-ten market, clearly stated that the towns captured by Boudica, 'were all burned to the ground, and everyone in them massacred.' Was the *Observer* telling us anything more? Had erasing the principal settlement of an invading power from the face of the Earth somehow gone beyond the acceptable remit of 'an icon of national resistance'?

It can be difficult to be neutral in studying the story of Boudica and, love or hate the Romans, it would be disingenuous to claim that the first two decades of their rule in Britain were anything except brutally mismanaged – certainly the Romans never refuted it. I don't deny that for many years my heart lay in Boudica's camp, but in the pages to come I have tried to be more understanding of the many motivations and rock-and-a-hard-place decisions of the different people caught up in this conflict. What I am invariably trying to find is the human experience of the moment, whoever that human may have been.

In the final analysis it is impossible not to sympathise with the disinherited queen, flogged and brutalised, who has witnessed her daughters and people being raped, enslaved and plundered by an invading army. But we are missing a trick, or at least a good many essential other human stories, if we don't sometimes look through the eyes of those young men of the imperial Roman army, the sandals on the ground, doing an unenviable job at the behest of a distant authority. Likewise, the retired veterans of that army settling as colonists, on whom so much of the blame for this cataclysm has to lie, must be understood at the level of their prejudices and why they held them. Their wives, many of whom might have been British ex-slaves, and their kids, who suffered the devastation of Boudica's war as surely as anyone else, all have their stories to tell and their own sufferings to relate.

Boudica's war has been all things to all people. It was a war of resistance, freedom and liberation, and one of plunder and murder. It was a rebellion, a revolution and a mutiny; for both sides, a fight for survival. It was a civil war and a tribal war, naked barbarism against civilisation, and the stand of a proud indigenous people against plundering conquistadors. It was a war *of* terror and a war *on* terror, and a war of cultural, if not genetic, cleansing.

It is all too easy to forget, however, that this war was the closing act of Boudica's life. She had lived her entire adulthood under the mantle of Rome, but had grown up in an independent tribal kingdom, an independence maintained in a nominal way until the death of her husband in AD 60. Hers was a society of the Late Iron Age, and, to use an academically troublesome term, a Celtic society.

The Iron Age feels deceptively familiar. I have seen so many artists' reconstructions of the homes, villages and people, that when I see the pictures, or walk through a reconstructed settlement like Butser Ancient Farm, I feel an absurd sense of homeliness, that this is something I know, something familiar, like a dim memory of childhood. Of course it is not something I know or can ever know, but the dim childhood memory is appropriate enough. Where Ladybird books and Airfix Ancient Britons left off, popular culture took over, informing my childhood mental landscape of late prehistory and classical civilisation's rude interruption of it.

In the same year that I drew Boadicea seeing off the Romans with a miniature plastic army, the BBC aired *Living in the Past*,[5] the original, and incomparably best, fly-on-the-wall social experiment, in which a group of volunteers lived for thirteen months on a reconstructed Iron Age farm, cut off from the modern world except for weekly visits by the camera crew.

The project's visionary founder and producer, John Percival, did not throw in nightmare eccentrics or explosive personality cocktails for the pleasure of the watching mob. The participants were chosen for qualities that would benefit the group and lead to the least chance of conflict, and were ultimately self-selected by the shortlisted participants. The final group, six couples and three young children, then camped whilst they built the entire Iron Age farm by hand. Provided with authentic clothes, tools, animals and a four-month stock of basic Iron Age provisions, the time travellers were left to fend for themselves.

Their achievements were huge. They harvested their crops, and trained their cows to pull a plough, slaughtered their livestock and processed every bit of them. They made their pots, spun wool, wove clothes, worked iron, built a cart, endlessly ground corn, drew their water from a well, and mastered a thousand other tasks and skills. The tragedy was that the project lasted for only thirteen months, for there was a clear consensus at the end that they were leaving just as they had acquired the skills to be truly self-sufficient. Their failures, and they were few enough, had been born of inexperience. Their year in the past had corrected that, and they really could have lived in the Iron Age now if they chose to.[6]

It is important not to confuse *Living in the Past* with another BBC project aired in 2001, called *Surviving the Iron Age*. Inspired entirely by the original, and, as a nice touch, taking on some of the grown-up children of the original participants, the new experiment was hurried in its planning and far too short, at a little over six weeks long. The obsession with reality television had just started with a bang, with the first hugely successful series of Channel 4's *Big Brother* coming to an end only one day before filming began on *Surviving the Iron Age*. The volunteers arrived without training and moved straight into the pre-existing Iron Age village of Castell Henllys hillfort in Pembrokeshire.[7]

The results were predictable enough. After a few days they had given themselves food poisoning, major rows flared up, and within a fortnight five of the seventeen volunteers had gone home. The water standpipe was moved from the nearby river to the village to save the labour of carrying buckets, and most of the volunteers ditched their Iron Age shoes for green wellington boots, on health and safety grounds. The younger members smuggled in cash and sneaked off to the pub, and the group received regular 'time challenges', such as making beer or constructing a wicker man for a sacrificial burning.

The whole atmosphere was far less *Living in the Past* than *Big Brother BC*, and lacked any of the charm, commitment or worth of the 1970s original. The volunteers had been sold a dead duck, and small blame to some for admitting halfway through that they wanted to go home.[8] The first valiant soul to jump ship, after less than a week, would have been a distant second to me by at least five days.

But there is, perhaps, one crucial lesson to be drawn from all of this, and the participants of these experiments might unwittingly have been far more authentic in their weaknesses than we have given them credit for. Just as the members of *Living in the Past* desired hot baths and a less restricted diet, and those of *Surviving the Iron Age* wanted water on tap, gumboots, and the bright lights and drinks of a modern pub, so the inhabitants of southern Britain in the late Iron Age wanted Roman wine, delicacies, high-class tableware and prestige goods.

Step by step they were led to things which dispose to vice, the lounge, the bath, the elegant banquet, wrote Tacitus. *All this in their ignorance, they called civilisation, when it was but a part of their servitude.*[9]

For the status-conscious elites of Ancient Britain, Rome was a seductive brand.

Julius Caesar came to Iron Age Britain twice, in 55 and 54 BC, as a glory-stealing interlude during his conquest of Gaul. By any account, except his own, both expeditions were little short of disastrous, but they succeeded in transforming Caesar himself into an almost mythical hero who had crossed the ocean defining the edge of the world, and gone beyond it into *terra incognita*.

Disasters or not, both expeditions were extraordinary achievements, and if they returned only by the grace of the gods, return they did, which was all that really mattered to SPQR, *Senatus Populusque Romanus*, the Senate and the People of Rome.

Narrowly averted disasters they might have been, but Caesar left Britain with many submissions, promises of tribute, and hostages. He may also have had the first recorded contact with, and submission of, a tribe that would become one of Rome's bitterest enemies, a people he recorded as the *Cenimagni*, effectively the *Great Ceni* – presumed, reasonably enough, to be the Great *Iceni*.

The following hundred years formed a buffer between these inquisitive forays and full invasion, and also between prehistory and history – protohistory – in which a society is historically recorded externally by others but not by itself. Whilst Caesar crossed the Rubicon and marched on Rome, which drifted through civil war from republic to dictatorship to monarchy in all but name, the powerplay of the southern British tribes, particularly the warlike Catuvellauni of modern Hertfordshire, had resulted in the dominance of that tribe from east to west.

For their monarch of those final decades before the conquest, King Cunobelin, this effectively monopolised control over the lucrative flow of slaves and other commodities from the interior of Britain to the channel ports and thence to the markets of the classical world.

There was clearly much contact across the Channel in these years, and some tribes may have acknowledged Roman suzerainty. We must remember that all those hostages taken by Caesar, scions of the kings and nobles, were not destined for the slave markets. They probably ended up in Rome to be raised and educated as little Romans, before returning home as members of the tribal aristocracies, a tradition they may have continued with their own children – it is little wonder that they nurtured a taste for Roman luxury goods, or minted coins with classical motifs.[10]

It is likewise unsurprising that a succession of aggrieved British royals felt at ease seeking Roman assistance in their dynastic struggles. Britons were not an uncommon sight in Rome in the hundred years after Caesar – Strabo describes the British teenagers wandering around as being lanky,[11] although their land beyond the edge of the world never lost its dark mist of dread.

The territory of the Iceni lay immediately north of the eastern expansion of the Catuvellauni, which had assimilated the Trinovantes of Essex. Archaeologically, the Iceni were materially wealthy and culturally distinct, being much less seduced by the wheel-thrown pottery, wine consumption and continental funerary rites encroaching south and west of them.[12] They were also extrinsically more isolated, half of their tribal boundary being North Sea coastline, and a good third or more of the remainder being the impenetrable morass of the Fens.

Whether this strong tribal identity, wealth and limited access made them too formidable a foe, or if they negotiated a mutually beneficial peace is unknown, but there is little to suggest that the Catuvellauni played overlords to them,[13] except for one intriguing detail of potential lip-service.

During this era of protohistory, in which classical authors might mention Britain but tell us little of what was going on within, the tribes of southern Britain did a remarkable thing – they produced large numbers of coins, sophisticated, beautiful, remarkably consistent in weight and tribally distinct, and some of them had writing on them. In the century prior to the Roman conquest, the Britons themselves tell us far more about their tribal dynasties, territories and politics than contemporary Roman historians, often in Latin, but sometimes in the native tongue, some of which on the coins of the Iceni could be Germanic in origin,[14] the result of their North Sea-facing coast.

Also, uniquely for any British tribe, we possibly have coins on which the proud Iceni might be attempting to write their own name – *ECEN* – as well as the name of Boudica's ruling husband, Prasutagus, rendered as *PRASTO*, but both of these interpretations, like so many details of Ancient British coins, are hugely contentious.[15]

We need hardly be surprised at the interesting spellings adopted in antiquity, and there are hints (not least the Icknield Way, which *might* be an echo of the tribal name) that *Iceni* – commonly pronounced as *eye-see-knee* – should more correctly be pronounced as *ee-kee-knee* or *ee-kay-knee*. Likewise, the traditional rendition of the queen's name as *Boadicea* is a Renaissance spelling mistake; Tacitus spelt the name *Boudicca*, and a tired scribe has miscopied the *u* as an *a*, and the second *c* as an *e*. Modern Celtic scholars have suggested that *Boudica* would be the more correct spelling, and pronounced 'Bowdeekah',[16] although I freely confess to sticking to the far less breathy pronunciation of 'Boodika' myself. The name means something broadly equating to 'Victorious'.

Professor Mary Beard refers to the spelling of the queen's name as 'a strange academic obsession, since one certainty in the whole story is that Boadicea/Boudic(c)a herself could neither read nor write, let alone spell.'[17] This is a moot point. Going back to the coin evidence and their numerous snippets of text, for all that the meanings of the words are not always obvious to us, their appearance at all does beg the question – who was the writing for?

Although they undoubtedly had a fundamental trade use, coins were not small change for the illiterate majority to use at market. They were likely part of a complex system of exchange and reward, as well as ritual, sacrificial tokens of supernatural reciprocity. If the writing was not understood by at least a portion of the religious, royal and aristocratic elites, why was it there at all?[18] There is a sense here of being 'part of the club' if you can issue coins with text and decipher them, and instant superiority over those who know it means *something* but no idea what.

If Boudica was unlikely to sit down of an evening and chuckle over the description of Britons in a borrowed scroll of Caesar's *Gallic War*, she may well have been able to interpret the names stamped on coins, and if her own name is not one of those represented numismatically, she may indeed have known how to write it.

Ancient British coin experts have suggested that certain motifs on Icenian coins infer an alliance with the Catuvellauni, originating in the latter half of the first century BC, and continuing to the Roman conquest.[19] These designs, including crescent moons and ears of corn, seem to have been copied from Catuvellaunian issues, and may hint that the Iceni accepted client status under King Cunobelin – the approximate date of his accession coincided with the Iceni ceasing production of gold coins, and issuing more standardised silver units with back-to-back crescent moons dominating the artwork.[20] The coinage can also be used to attempt to name some of the rulers otherwise unknown from history and to reconstruct the political framework of these pre-Roman societies, fascinating insights derived from these little tablets of silver and gold.

The coins suggest that the Iceni were a confederacy of several smaller tribal groups, each with its own leader. The names of these rulers, all appearing on coins in the last three decades before the Roman conquest, are Antedios, Ecen (if not the tribal name), Cani Duro, Saenu, Aesu, Ale Scavo, and Esuprasto, or Prasto, and some must have ruled concurrently.[21] If such a list is highly speculative, it would certainly explain how King Prasutagus was able to rule after a minor rebellion of the Iceni in AD 47 – presumably another ruler led the anti-Roman faction and Prasutagus remained loyal to the Romans. It is also quite plausible that Boudica was the daughter of one of these other coin-named monarchs.

The hunt for Boudica in her own tribal territory is frustratingly vague, more intuitive and ephemeral than anywhere else associated with her story. To anyone interested in Iron Age Norfolk, certain place names leap off the page – Snettisham, Saham Toney, Ashill, Fison Way, all sites of enormous archaeological importance, and yet many of us who can rattle off their names have never been to them. The reason for this is that there is nothing there to see, no earthworks to walk around, rarely an information board and little access to the sites themselves. If we are lucky a road passes near them, but they are part of a working landscape, and are often little enough understood even by archaeologists.

I have driven past all of these sites, seen signs that made my ears prick up, places of importance to the Iceni, and yet I never pull over to see what I can discover. It is a mistake, for they are indelible presences in their landscapes, and it is impossible to appreciate any of them fully without seeing them within their physical context.

At a distance, from the seaward side, Ken Hill looks like a long, dark eyebrow rising from the salt-marsh. To the west lie the mudflats and vast grey bay of the Wash, the far shore – the coast of Lincolnshire – invisible to the naked eye even on this cool, clear day. For all that some of the ground is still frozen after a recent cold snap, and the wind blows directly from the north, the day is sunny and surprisingly warm. About as far out as I can see is some sort of ship, but that stark black slug of Ken Hill would be clearly visible to them. It is a subtle enough landmark, but in a flat landscape it stands proud.

I follow the public footpath towards the hill a mile or so away. My black Labrador, Jojo, tail down and panting, is unaccountably spooked by something, probably a car door being slammed half a mile away. Turning off the serpentine bank of the sea defences to the flats below, the footpath is flooded, and my walking boots are quickly breached as I sink up to my shins in foul-smelling, stagnant water. Jojo perks up a little; he rather likes stagnant water, and, clearly weighing up the pleasure of splashing around in it against the bollocking he'll get, promptly leaps into the deepest bit and drags me with him.

I squelch on until the ground rises, passing a farm as I begin climbing the hill proper, all forty-two metres of it, wooded and muddy. From the highest point on the footpath I turn to look back over the Wash, but the tree cover is too thick, and from that moment on, my eyes are helplessly glued to the floor. This is a place where it is difficult to glance at the rich orange-brown soil without longing for the glint of gold.

In November 1948, a lavender field on the slopes of Ken Hill, just north of Snettisham, was being ploughed in preparation for sowing with barley. The plough was set to twelve inches, a good five inches deeper than ever before, and the tractor driver, Ray Williamson, set to work on 12 November. On the first day he ploughed up several metallic loops, and the following day ploughed up more from another spot. Assuming them to be bits of an old brass bedstead, he paid them no attention,[22] and on the third day ploughed up yet more loops and scrap from a third spot.

The heaps of shiny metal lay for a full week on top of the furrows, clearly visible from the busy King's Lynn to Hunstanton road at the edge of the field. Only when the dumbfounded contractor arrived on site was the metal recognised as gold. The loops were Iron Age torcs, great Celtic neck rings of gold and silver, along with coins and gold scrap.

R. Rainbird Clarke of Norwich Castle Museum excavated the sites of the three hoards that same December and recovered more artefacts, but only limited work was done. Ray Williamson did rather well out of his three days of heavy ploughing. He received £400 from the resulting 'treasure trove' inquest at a time when the average weekly wage was a good deal less than ten pounds.

In the autumn of 1950 another tractor driver, Tom Rout, was ploughing the same field, this time to a depth of thirteen inches. Well aware of the rewards attached to finding new material, he was watching carefully, and promptly ploughed up a gold torc and ring from yet another hoard and immediately reported the fact. An inquest declared the new finds to be treasure trove, and within another twenty-four hours Tom had ploughed up the most spectacular hoard of the lot, containing what would become known as the Great Torc, one of the most sumptuous masterpieces of European prehistoric art.[23] Mr Rout did rather well out of his tractor driving, too. His extra inch of ploughing had earned him a pay-out of £1850, about the average value of a house in 1950.

The owners of the newly christened Gold Field were left in peace to farm the land. Although the plough occasionally dragged new treasures to the surface, it was not until 1989 that a local metal detectorist, Cecil 'Charles' Hodder, secured permission to search the field to see if any scraps had been missed. He found a few oddments that were duly reported to the museum, but the following year he dug down on a signal and found another hoard, a pit of scrap gold containing pieces of torc. He knew it was a job for the archaeologists, but worried about leaving the treasure in-situ over a long Bank Holiday weekend, he excavated the lot and took them home. His wife, less keen on metal detecting, made him keep the nine-kilogram haul of muddy gold in the garage.[24]

This time the archaeological community acted in earnest. Dr Ian Stead of the British Museum was on site by November 1990 with Charles Hodder as part of the team, and large-scale stripping of the topsoil ensued over three successive seasons. Another five hoards were discovered, bringing the total to at least eleven, and possibly as many as thirteen.[25] These excavations revealed undisturbed 'nests' of torcs, lying neatly stacked in circular holes. One torc had been compressed to fit in its hole, and as it was removed, even after two millennia under tension, it sprung back into shape.

The November 1990 excavation alone had uncovered a further sixty-three torcs, nine of gold, fifteen of gold/silver alloy (electrum), fourteen of silver, and twenty-five of bronze. In total, the field had yielded seventy-five more or less complete torcs, and fragments of another hundred, over 100 ingot rings and bracelets and 170 coins.[26]

In addition, the team became aware that thieves, so-called 'nighthawks', had metal-detected another hoard in 1991, consisting of the most important deposit of late Icenian coins ever found, estimated at around 6000 silver coins, all contained in a silver bowl, with about 500 gold coins and ingots buried beneath it.

Archaeologists found out about the theft by rumour, and were able to piece together some of the evidence from antiquities dealers, but it was a tragic loss. Two other coin hoards are also suspected to have been stolen from the site.[27]

There are a lot of Snettisham artefacts out there in the ether now, dispersed and gone, their significance lost forever and their provenance unrecoverable, but occasionally a more innocent relic of the site crops up. When I was first researching Snettisham for this book, I was hunting for obscure reference material on the internet. I came across a postcard on eBay, evidently some decades old, of the magnificent decorative village sign for Snettisham, consisting of two smugglers flanked by a pair of giant sea-horses, all surmounted by a beautiful Iron Age golden torc. It was a couple of pounds and I bought it.

It was one of those little serendipities that often assail you when you are doing research, for when my postcard arrived I looked at the back and saw that it had originally been posted exactly twenty-five years before, in November 1991. It was a message from an archaeologist involved in the Snettisham excavations:

> Dear Ian,
> Hope you are better. I'm having a pleasant month
> digging up Iron Age stuff with the British Museum.
> Hotel nice, weather good, soil brown, sea wet, etc.
> Ian

Another little artefact in the Snettisham story. How archaeology *becomes* archaeology.

Jojo and I walk along the verge of the busy main road, past a gruesome menagerie of roadkill, to the edge of the Gold Field. No footpaths go anywhere near the place, but the King's Lynn to

Hunstanton road still runs along its eastern edge. Had I stood beside this hedge seventy years before, those piles of ploughed-up torcs might still have been visible in the furrows. Had I stood here two thousand years ago, who can begin to imagine what I might have seen?

In 1997 Barry Cunliffe, then Professor of European Archaeology at Oxford, wondered if Snettisham represented a 'natural' sacred place, a clearing in a forest, protected by its sanctity alone, a sacred *grove*, dare I say it?[28] It is certainly an unremarkable enough place now, a field of rough grass backed by a solid black wall of conifer woods, but two thousand years ago, one way or another, this must have been a spot of enormous power and significance, a natural promontory with views right across the Wash, and impregnated with offerings of gold, silver and bronze. Just what did this accumulation of staggering wealth represent, why was it buried, and why was it never recovered?

In his report of 1954, Rainbird Clarke had speculated that the hoards were the result of a single event, the work of hours, and represented the stock-in-trade of a metalworker.[29] The artefacts seemed to belong to the earlier half of the first century BC, and nothing fell uncomfortably outside of that date range. Convinced that a votive offering wouldn't contain so many partial and broken pieces, the stock of a jobbing goldsmith, buried for safety in several pits, was as good an explanation as any.

The richness of the 1990 discoveries, however, made the goldsmith hypothesis less likely, and Ian Stead[30] suggested that the combined hoards represented a treasury of some sort, supported by the fact that some of the more precious torcs had been hidden beneath less valuable items to confound thieves – thieves, it has to be said, without the benefit of metal detectors. Coins found with the hoards had begun to widen the date range away from a likely single event,[31] and the so-called Bowl Hoard that had been stolen appeared to date to the time of Boudica's war,[32] well over a hundred years later than the earliest hoards, or more.[33] If Snettisham was the treasury of the Iceni, it was a bank that took deposits for numerous generations without a withdrawal ever being made.

In 2004, metal detectorists with permission to search the woods at the edge of the Gold Field reported finding a wall. Excavation exposed a rough stone structure interpreted as a Romano-Celtic temple, which appeared to lie within a *temenos*, or sacred precinct, that encompassed the Gold Field[34] – not only was this spot a sacred place in the Iron Age, but that sense of reverence continued through the era of Roman occupation. The knowledge of the gold deposits may have been forgotten, indeed, may only ever have been known to a privileged few, but the site retained its aura of local importance for generations after the last precious metals were interred there. Perhaps Ian Stead had been right, in essence; this was indeed a treasury, not of the Icenian Royal House, but of the gods and goddesses they worshipped.[35]

This sense that the Snettisham Treasure was placed in the ground with no intention to recover it, as a gift to the deities, is the more common interpretation now,[36] and the layering of the hoards, separating certain types and colours of metal from others by layers of soil, that Stead saw as protection against theft, may be the physical remainder of complex ritual.

They weren't alone; this corner of west and north-west Norfolk was, figuratively speaking, stuffed with these hoards, at Sedgeford a couple of miles behind me, at Bawsey a few miles south, at North Creake and Marham, running in an arc around the Fen Edge and the Wash, surrounded by contemporary earthworks, with Snettisham at the epicentre.[37] The excavators of nearby Sedgeford saw the Iron Age settlement and ritual deposits there as part of the same landscape-wide sprawl of activity, and even wondered if Ken Hill is an echo of the tribal name as pronounced with a hard *c* – I*ken*i.[38]

The detail and colour of this mindset, of the religion and ritual behind it, is lost to us. We might speak of that enigmatic priestly caste of the Druids, or of deliberately damaging or 'killing' votive objects before burial, hence all the broken torcs, but there is ultimately nothing to illuminate our visual picture of what happened here; unless, that is, we allow ourselves to peer through a handful of tiny little portals. It was not only torcs that were found here, remember – a significant element of the haul was coins, and if anything can shine a tiny light back to those times, it is these forgotten little witnesses of the Snettisham story.

The coinage of Iron Age Britain owes much of its artwork to the coins of Philip of Macedon, showing the head of Apollo on the obverse and a charioteer on the reverse, that made their way across Europe and into Gaul in the fourth century BC. Some of the most bizarre designs on British coins are vestigial echoes of the artwork on Philip's coins, and a marvellous evolutionary chain can be constructed showing the gradual distorting of the crisp, classical original to the mesmerising abstract of its Celtic descendant.

These coins are astonishing miniature works of art. Generally less than twenty millimetres diameter in gold and ten millimetres in silver, they contain not only the obvious images of crescent moons, wild boar, horses and faces in profile, but so-called 'hidden faces', obscure combinations of dots and rings that combine with other elements to leap out as the coin is turned and contemplated. Even more astonishing, particular coins are clearly meant to be viewed obliquely; held at an angle, some lose their rather one-dimensional side-profile face to take on a disturbingly sinister and animated three-dimensional aspect,[39] a complete transformation of an image already believed by some writers to be the Icenian goddess of war, Andraste.[40]

On other coins, disparate elements combine edge-on to form another obvious image, both examples of anamorphosis. Discovered by Geraldine Chimirri-Russell in 2003[41] on Gaulish coins, these complex optical illusions now bear her name as the Chimirri-Russell effect, but it was Iron Age coin expert John Talbot who applied the oblique viewpoint to Icenian coins, and was astounded by what he found.[42] In another example, a silver Icenian coin with a rather ugly, fat face surrounded by confusing imagery transforms obliquely into a haunting, thin, howling face[43] reminiscent of Edvard Munch's *The Scream*.

These optical anamorphisms are clearly intentional, and their tiny size aside, are made all the more remarkable because they utilise the slight convexity of the coins' profile. There may be a whole world of such hidden imagery permanently lost to us, the specific cultural lens they required to view them perhaps rare enough even in their own time, for if we cannot always make sense of the more overt artwork, we can hardly expect to appreciate skilfully obfuscated representations that might have leapt out to a few Iron Age eyes, but probably not to all.

Being able to truly *see through* a Celtic coin may have been a much greater privilege than owning one,[44] and a much more esoteric skill than simply reading its stumbling script. It is still a privilege, and there is something indefinable about the detail of the coins that provides an insight into the visual mindset of the Iron Age absent in the potsherds, postholes and ditches we excavate, for all that they represent the actual physical and visual landscape of most people's lives.

What I think the coins might help us to do is to see that landscape through different eyes; eyes that saw a wild boar and expressed its form as a headless, bristle-backed shrimp, or glimpsed a wolf and reproduced it as an emaciated, beak-jawed, spike-eared and spindle-limbed creature that must have moved more like a spider than anything mammalian, beneath a moon and star-studded sky, and with a bird almost always on its back.

A remarkable interpretation of this scene draws on Norse mythology that might represent a more general prehistoric tradition, and remembering that some of the text on Icenian coins appears to be Germanic. This convincing narrative is based around stories of the pursuit and capture of the moon by a cosmic wolf, which splatters the sky with blood at the crack of Doom and consumes all heavenly bodies before it, played out in the sky in the form of lunar and solar eclipses.[45] In the Norse versions, the wolf is known as *Fenrir* (fen-dweller), or *Fenriswolf*; the birds perched on the back of the Icenian wolf have been convincingly identified as lapwings, bitterns and avocets,[46] all birds of the fenland, marking the miniature wolf on that tiny coin too as a fen-dweller.

A wolf only appears on the coin of one other British tribe, the Corieltauvi,[47] neighbours and possible allies of the Iceni, with whom they clearly shared some cultural affinity. The wolf is otherwise mostly absent from the artistic menagerie of Iron Age Britain, dominated by boars, horses, bovines and birds.[48] The imagery is all the more intriguing because the wolf would have been a rare sight in Icenian lands when the coin was produced, already a fugitive inhabiting upland and marginal lands;[49] a shy and dreaded denizen of both myth and fen alike.

Standing by the Gold Field, where numerous examples of this coin have been found, there is one more chilling detail to contemplate. The miniature artwork portrays the wolf standing on ground littered with torcs and coins, indeed, the beast itself inhabits the ground surface, dotted with coins, with more coins and torcs *beneath it*, as if buried. The excavators of Sedgeford note that the slope of the Gold Field faces east, towards the rising sun, and imagine, literally, a field of gold displayed to catch the first golden rays of dawn,[50] a fusion of earthly and heavenly treasure.

Is Ken Hill, with its echo of the tribal name, the very spot denoted on wolf coins that depict ground strewn and stuffed with gold?[51] Did this terrifying wolf-creature stand guard at this place in the minds of those who came here to worship; this fen-dweller, here, overlooking the very entrance to the Fens? Was the imagery a warning to those who might come here with less reverent intentions, or does it hint at what deity was worshipped here?

Imagining that emaciated, ghoulish wolf prowling the dark treeline across the field, I can't help but think of the persistent local legends of Black Shuck, the spectral black dog that haunts the hinterland of this Norfolk coastline, and *Chrom Dubh*, 'Black Crooked One', a dark, evil creature of famine and cold recorded in twelfth-century Ireland[52] that must surely hark back to a universal denizen of pre-Christian Celtic nightmare, as Fenrir was to the Norse. *Unfettered will roam the Fenris Wolf and devour the world of men.*[53]

If the coins themselves might have been seen by only a narrow section of society, the images they contain could have been everywhere, a true worldview. I imagine these coin images painted on roundhouse walls and shields, tattooed on naked torsos, embroidered on banners, and scratched in the dirt by kids. By far the most common metal artefact recovered from Iron Age Norfolk, coins are frequently excluded from surveys of Celtic and prehistoric art.[54] What an insight we might be missing.

Iron Age coins are incredibly tactile things, little tabs of hallucinatory braille, if only our fingers could fathom their meaning. Indeed, archaeologist John Creighton has speculated whether much of this bizarre imagery is a physical rendition of shamanic hallucinatory experience,[55] and the evidence is compelling. But when we see those gorgeously stylised horses, boars and wolves, particularly of the Iceni and Corieltauvi tribes, what we are looking at, hallucinogenic or not, is a purely Celtic, insular manifestation of the spirit of those creatures in perfect miniature, something subconscious and elemental. To glance into the universally homogeneous imagery of hallucination experience is one thing; I am far more haunted, when I hold an Ancient British coin in my hand, to wonder if we are simply peering into Iron Age dreams.

As I drive home through the dark woods of the Sandringham Estate about three miles south of Snettisham, the imagery of Norfolk Wolf gold coins still playing on my mind, my very own stinky, domesticated Black Shuck asleep in the back, and my feet still wet from the salt-marsh of the Wash, I chuckle as I see a sign for the fortuitously and evocatively named village of Wolferton. Glancing along the minor road that leads there, I see the silhouette of a very large and disturbingly dark deer, standing in the middle of the wooded lane. The falling sun is still bright, but at dusk, in fading light, with the flickering form of that black deer taking flight and disappearing into the trees, I wonder what my brain would make of that dark blur of fur and limbs caught in the peripheral glow of the headlights.

The following week I have the chance to visit Norwich Castle for an hour. This wonderful museum used to be a home-from-home, when my son Tristan was little and always wanted to run through the natural history galleries, pressing interactive buttons and trying to creep past the Bengal tiger without activating its motion-sensor roar.

Our membership cards are rarely used now, but my wife Clare and I can't quite commit to giving them up. We tell ourselves that they are still useful, but in truth we don't want to admit that the happy days of popping in to carry a little bucket of plastic animals around the displays, followed by coffee, juice, cake and tantrums in the restaurant, are now irretrievably behind us. And it's good to still have the card; if I have half an hour to kill in town before school pick-up, I can come along and stare at Iceni gold.

The Snettisham treasure, or a small portion of it, is one of the first displays in the Boudica Gallery. There is a selection of original material, mostly the 1948 finds, as after that date the British Museum acquired most of the new artefacts. In pride of place are the three fat tubular torcs of gold foil ploughed up by Ray Williamson, that decorated the furrows of Ken Hill for a week. Looking at them now, having been to Snettisham, they have acquired a new significance and awe, and imagining them sticking out of the orange-brown ploughsoil, seeing daylight for the first time in two thousand years, it is easy to forgive Williamson for assuming a previous farmer had dumped his old brass bed there.

If there is one thing that is striking about torcs other than their beauty and craftsmanship, it is the inescapable assumption that they must have been thoroughly unpleasant to wear. I have spent several hours wearing a brass reproduction of a twisted two-strand torc on my naked neck (in the privacy of my own home, I hasten to add). It is typical of many of the Snettisham torcs, copper-alloy being a significant but less glamorous component of the assemblage. Ignoring the initial coldness, because it soon warms to skin temperature, it doesn't rattle around half as much as you might expect, and after a little while I really did almost forget I was wearing it.

We have no idea how much they were worn, whether martial or ceremonial, but certainly the Greeks and Romans portrayed them being sported by warriors in combat. It has been argued that such items would have been unknown to Boudica, predating her by over a hundred years, the artwork out of fashion with first-century style.[56] A torc might have been used for generations, however, and any left over from Boudica's time would have ended up as Roman plunder, melted into ingots and dispersed, invisible in the local archaeological record. They certainly appear to be depicted on Icenian coins in Boudica's lifetime, including those of her probable husband Prasto.

In the corner of the Snettisham cabinet is a selection of gold coins. One is a bronzy hue compared to the radiant gold of the rest, having been alloyed with copper, and I can guess by its obverse that it is a Norfolk Wolf stater. Over time the Wolf stater became increasingly debased, the artwork less crisp, and the production can appear a little careless, the head of the wolf often being absent, all of which are true here.

The crying shame is that the wolf cannot be seen, face down, out of sight, whilst the abstract chaos of the side on display, a vestigial echo of the head of Apollo, is pretty much meaningless to modern eyes. But he is here, at least, that forlorn little wolf, all fifteen millimetres of him, still standing guard over his stolen treasure, no longer just an image on a pretty coin, but the narrative of a dark, fen-dwelling sentinel played out above a field of buried torcs in the Iron Age subconscious. Another Norfolk Wolf, in the coin section behind me, is also displayed wolf-down,

Apollo-up; the forgotten Fenriswolf has been condemned to pad the aisles of the Boudica gallery unseen.

I move on to a cabinet beside a reconstructed Iron Age chariot, studying the beautiful bronze horse and chariot fittings recovered from the fields of Saham Toney. Whilst such items are rare in some other parts of the country,[57] it seems that horses and chariots really were a major part of Icenian life; associated items – harness rings, bits, linchpins – make up a quarter of the Iron Age finds in the museum collection,[58] and no fewer than 97 per cent of Icenian coins depict horses.[59]

Horses must have represented great wealth and prestige in Iron Age society,[60] which, together with the Iceni's obvious gold ownership, lends weight to Tacitus's description of Prasutagus as a man of *renowned prosperity*. It is entirely fitting, therefore, that Boudica should traditionally be shown mounted on her chariot, however contrived the classical reference to the scene might be.

Admittedly, these are the pieces that have made it into the museum display, and torcs, coins, chariots and swords were the accessories of only a sliver of Iron Age society, but there is so little here that is purely utilitarian; terret rings – loops of bronze that fed the reins to the chariot horses – are stunning pieces of workmanship, clearly recognisable as expressions of the classic, late Iron Age *La Tène* style of art, many coloured with swirling tendrils of enamel, for which a plain and simple iron ring would have sufficed. Even the linchpins that held the wheels in place were tipped with enamelled knobs and curving tails of bronze.

In all of these objects there are hidden meanings, hidden faces, hidden stories; if there are esoteric narratives woven into horse tack and axle pins, are we really to believe that it was Romanisation that civilised and sophisticated these people? Sir Cyril Fox viewed the detail of Icenian coins 'indefensible', showing 'little art', proof that 'East Anglia was culturally backward despite its wealth in goldwork.'[61]

In her extraordinary children's novel *The Eagle of the Ninth*, Rosemary Sutcliff has a British slave, Esca, explain the difference in their artistic souls to his master, Marcus. Picking up a Roman dagger-sheath, he points out the symmetrical back-to-back curves with a stiff little flower in between, 'and then it is all repeated here, and here, and here again. It is beautiful, yes,' he concedes, 'but to me it is as meaningless as an unlit lamp.'

Then he picks up a decorated British shield and points to the boss, the metal handguard that rears from the centre. 'See the bulging curves that flow from each other as water flows from water and wind from wind, as the stars turn in the heaven and blown sand drifts into dunes. These are the curves of life; and the man who traced them had in him knowledge of things that your people have lost the key to – if they ever had it.'

Sutcliff has him pause before he makes his final point. 'You cannot expect the man who made this shield to live easily under the rule of the man who worked the sheath of this dagger.'[62]

You only have to look at the coins, torcs and terret rings in Norwich Castle to know the truth of it.

The deserted Roman town of *Venta Icenorum*, literally Market Place of the Iceni, lies in the shallow vale of the Tas at Caistor St Edmund, a couple of miles upstream from the tri-confluence of the Wensum, Tas, and Yare rivers. This conflux of navigable waters, flowing east towards the rising sun and draining into the vast coastal inlet now occupied by the Norfolk Broads, must have been a place of significance to the Iceni. It represented both a junction of inland river routes coming in from the four corners of the tribal territory at their junction with the sea, and a merging or blurring of the perceived spiritual presences embodied by the water – the name of the pan-Celtic deity Condatis literally means 'where waters meet'.[63]

Upstream along the Tas lies the forgotten Roman town, a sad place I always feel, the long-suspected Iron Age precursor still lost save for a scatter of high-status artefacts, despite ongoing excavation at the site, and the Roman town never really blossoming in the post-rebellion backwater of the old Icenian tribal lands.[64] The Iceni of the last decades before the conquest lived in unenclosed settlements – no ditch, bank or palisade normally surrounded their farms and villages, as they did in much of the rest of the country, which makes them very difficult to spot archaeologically, and troublesome to define their extent.

Many would have been little more than farmsteads, but artefact scatters suggest that much larger areas of dispersed settlement clearly existed, like Saham Toney, and perhaps Caistor, not towns in the modern or even Roman sense, but loose concentrations and zones of activity spread over a significant piece of landscape.

Archaeologists have given these the imaginative name of 'splurgy' landscapes, settlements appearing as amorphous blobs on distribution maps rather than the deceptively logical dots of neatly enclosed farms and settlements, so-called 'spotty' landscapes.[65] So far only a possible pre-Roman religious site has been identified in the vicinity of the Roman town, but further zones of activity may yet be identified further afield. It seems the vale of the Tas held not a village or a town, but a *splurge*.

The gentle bluffs of the Tas rise to either side of the river, with the ruined walls of the town beginning to emerge from the darkness as I watch from the high ground to the south-west at dawn. A couple of red-lit radio masts stand tall on the far side of the vale. Norwich, only a mile away, is surprisingly absent save for a couple of bright lights and a slight orange glow above the northern horizon.

The normally busy A140, the Ipswich Road, immediately beyond the railway line at my back, is silent. It is itself a Roman road, but at this point has meandered from its true course, long-gone now, which lies below me in the darkness. The thoroughly modern A47 dual-carriageway three-quarters of a mile away is never quiet, but is mostly invisible from hereabouts. It all conspires, at six o'clock on a February morning, to give the place a sense of ancient isolation.

The winter sun is coming up just to the right of the Roman town, casting it into deep shadow as the first light bathes the western side of the vale around me, not with warmth, it has to be said, but with a pale, almost ghostly, illumination. Without knowing exactly where to look, it would be easy to miss the Roman walls hidden in the darkness, and denied the benefit of the inhabitants themselves stirring, stoking their hearths and lighting their little pottery oil-lamps, you must stare hard at the black lines of the hedges and field boundaries.

As I do so, a white figure emerges from the darkness near the river, and beats a deliberate course uphill in my direction; a bird, and a big one, at first I think it must be some sort of gull, but as it wings by ten yards away I recognise the fat, moth-like form of an owl. I involuntarily shiver. I had hoped the morning would be clear and crisp with a wisp of a mist to lie along the river, but it is cloudy and damp, though still very cold.

It is probably the wrong day to have cycled to *Venta Icenorum* in the chill pre-dawn. The moon, a couple of days past full, is still bright in the clear, black sky behind me, but the blue of the dawn ahead is darkening again with clouds speeding in from the north-east. As they clump together over the ruins of the Roman town, they look like a gathering hurricane and their underside takes on the smoky, feather-edge of distant rain falling. The temperature is dropping as the sky darkens again. This is dawn happening in reverse.

The wind picks up and the temperature continues to fall, at least with wind-chill. The storm slowly passes along the eastern edge of the vale, the sky brightening behind it, lighting up the Roman town, but there is no chance now of seeing what I have come to see. The light is flat, an artist or a skier might say; there is no shadow or definition anywhere.

Sometimes, when a low light glances across the countryside at dawn or dusk, or if snow falls, or when the vegetation is parched in prolonged dry weather, an ancient map emerges from the land. The subtlest of sub-surface features can become visible as hints of shadow and light, or different growths of vegetation.

They are best seen from the air, but on the high ground to the west of Caistor St Edmund it is sometimes possible to see the streets of the Roman town laid out, crisscrossing what is now a featureless, grassy field. It can be like putting on a pair of X-ray specs and suddenly seeing what lies beneath. But even though those streets were laid out in the half century or so after Boudica's war, and enclosed by the surrounding walls about two hundred years later, it is not these features that I come time and again to try to glimpse.

In the fields surrounding the walls lies a system of enigmatic earlier features, three parallel ditches. They can only be seen in aerial photographs and geophysical survey, and are now recognised as forming a huge, kite-shaped enclosure completely encompassing the later town walls and an area about twice as large, with a perimeter of nearly two-and-a-half kilometres. They predate the walls, and could be the earliest town defences.[66]

One enduring suggestion has always been that they demarcate an early military site[67] suitable for housing a Roman legion in the era of Boudica's war when the army, in unforgiving mood, arrived to stamp out the embers of dissent. However, more recent excavation has suggested that they date to around AD 100,[68] making a military origin much less likely. Whatever they represent, they are unusual and, considering the labour required to create them versus the small size of the settlement at the time, strangely over the top. Military or civil, they are some of the earliest Roman features of the site. I have never seen them, and I do not see them this day. It is too cold to sit any longer, and as I head back along the path towards the road and my bicycle, a light sleet begins to fall.

In 1913, a young archaeologist and little-known poet called H. Lang Jones published a slim volume of poems called *Songs of a Buried City*.[69] They are all musings of an archaeological nature, with such names as 'The City Under the Corn', 'Down the Roman Road', and presciently, considering what would happen the following year, 'In the Trenches'. Lang Jones was not one of the great twentieth-century poets, to be sure, but there are moments of beauty and vision in this meditation upon the ability of the archaeological imagination to illuminate the past around us.

In a disjointed poem called 'The Dry Bones', he ponders the ability of any of us to see beyond 'cold interpretation':

'Beyond our powers,' we say, and drop our hands.
Beyond our powers! And yet I think – I think –
That I have sometimes trembled on the verge
Of vision; and the veil may yet be raised . . .
It may be on some breathless summer's eve,
The twilight deepening to the shades of night,
I shall be leaning on my favourite gate,
Gazing across the fields to where he stands,
The Wall, lone relic of the mighty past,
When I shall see, all swift and silently,
His brother-walls rise up, and take their place,
And others here, and there, and everywhere –
Ay, all the City start up from her tomb,
With halls and temples, baths and colonnades,
Great mansions, meaner tenements, and shops,
And streets that run this way and that, whereon
Are men and women faring to and fro.

This is the way we must hunt for Boudica's war in Norfolk. Her world is all around us, in upstanding earthworks such as Warham and Thetford, or buried beneath the artefact-rich soil of Caistor St Edmund, Saham Toney and Snettisham, but identifying the actual event of her war is almost impossible within the county, that grim process of annihilation, subjugation and occupation, of which but little trace exists beyond the ghostly hint of ditches in the sleet. The jagged wall of the Roman town, 'lone relic of the mighty past', stands as our proof that the Iceni were brought to heel here, and the invisible ditches I continue to hunt for show us how it was done.

But in AD 43 all that was still away, unsuspected, in the future. One evening in the early summer of that year, there must have been people of the Iceni at this place momentarily distracted by a flash of light crossing high in the sky from east to west. They may have taken it as an omen, for good or ill we will never know. Probably only the Druids could interpret such a thing.

Over a hundred miles away, being blown off course in a black and terrifying sea, 40,000 legionaries and auxiliaries of the imperial Roman army, according to Dio, watched that same falling star scud west over the black hulk of Britannia. Only just brought back from the edge of mutiny at the prospect of crossing the forbidding waters of the Channel, and shamed into boarding the transport ships, they took the shooting star as a good omen. As they staggered and swayed unhappily, vomited and willed the wind to turn back, perhaps they did so a little less anxiously than they had before the star fall.

As the Iceni huddled beneath their blankets for the night, perhaps some still pondered the meaning of the passing star. They could not know that a distant army cheered into the darkness as their ships were caught by a landward breeze, and that a great eagle riding the sea wind had spread its wings to land.

The Eagle Has Landed

First Blood

> *I tell you, I know these people.*
> *It means war, Catus; war. And we are few.*
> *There's but a handful of old soldiers left*
> *At Camelodun. Suetonius has marched,*
> *Is far in the North by now. You'll start a fire*
> *You cannot quench so easily.*
>
> Laurence Binyon, *Boadicea*, 1927

If Britannia in AD 43 seems a place of mist, myth and mystery to us, it was more so to the Roman army, with the added horror of a night sea-crossing in crammed, leaking troopships awash with vomit and urine. If they were not fated to drown *en route* or be snatched by submerged leviathans, a land of hurricanes, were-creatures and head-hunters awaited them. Not for nothing had the legions refused to board the transports. Having been exhorted to embark by one of the emperor's aides, an ex-slave, the appalled legionaries made reference to the feast of Saturnalia, when slaves exchanged clothes with their masters, and were shamed into compliance. Boarding the hundreds of waiting transports at Boulogne under an offshore breeze, the wind had changed mid-Channel, in the darkness.

It is difficult to imagine a greater horror for the troops. All knew the story of Germanicus, twenty-seven years before, sailing his legions from Germania to winter quarters in Gaul. Tacitus recorded the story:

At first the calm waters merely sounded with the oars of a thou-
sand vessels or were ruffled by the sailing ships. Soon, a hailstorm
bursting from a black mass of clouds, while the waves rolled hither
and thither under tempestuous gales from every quarter, rendered
clear sight impossible, and the steering difficult.[1]

Germanicus's fleet was pounded and scattered to the four winds.
In their terror the soldiers had thrown everything overboard –
horses, baggage and weapons, but many ships were sunk, and
men stranded far and wide, on enemy shores and barren islands.
Some were forced to eat the rotting horses that washed up behind
them, many were ransomed back by hostile tribes, and others
were undoubtedly kept as slaves, sacrifices and pets, never to be
seen again.

Some had even been tossed onto the shores of Britannia. The
British tribes had returned the men unharmed, it was true, but,
every one, as he returned from some far-distant region, told of
wonders, of violent hurricanes, and unknown birds, of monsters
of the sea, of forms half-human, half beast-like, things they had
really seen or in their terror believed.[2]

These were surely the events fixed in the mind of every man as
the wind turned that night. Crossing from Boulogne would have
taken the fleet northwards, never much more than ten miles from
land, and for much of it the dark line of Britannia would have
loomed up from the west. Making a sluggish three knots,[3] at best
the contrary breeze meant longer spilling their guts on the transports; at worst, the fate of Germanicus loomed with every dark
cloud and crosswind.

It was then that a meteor had lit the sky, racing west towards the
enemy coast. *In their voyage across they first became discouraged*
because they were driven back in their course, wrote Dio, *and then*
plucked up courage because a flash of light rising in the east shot
across to the west, the direction in which they were sailing.[4]

This was surely a sign from Jupiter himself.[5] The oarsmen
toiled afresh and the wind must have dropped or turned. Dio

suggests that the fleet, perhaps as many as a thousand ships,[6] crossed in three groups to be sure of securing a landing, potentially as a three-pronged assault against separate beaches,[7] or a single landing in three waves. Richborough, on the east Kent coast has long been the favoured spot,[8] but a convincing case can also be made for West Sussex and Hampshire.[9]

Either way, the crossing was completed without reported loss, and the landing was miraculously unopposed. As the soldiers set to work consolidating their beachheads and stockpiling the unloaded stores, they must have done so in buoyant mood. Jupiter himself had guided their passage, and not a single bestial savage had stood in their way.

By the first century AD, the Roman army was an entirely professional, full-time military force. The primary strength was the legions, numbered units with a strong regimental identity. Recruited entirely from citizens, legionaries could expect to serve twenty-five years of hard active service under punishing conditions and brutally enforced discipline, after which they would be pensioned off with money and a farm. In recompense for the discomforts of service, they were guaranteed regular meals and pay, excellent medical care, a secure old-age, and the manifold spoils of war.

The legionary was a heavy infantryman, armoured from shoulders to crotch by either a mail shirt or, more commonly in this era, a flexible cuirass of segmented iron strips. He wore a helmet of iron or bronze, with cheek flaps and flaring neck protection, and carried a large rectangular shield. He wielded one or two javelins designed to penetrate deeply shields and armour, and a short-sword, intended for stabbing underarm. He wore a short-sleeved tunic to the thighs, a hooded cloak in foul weather, and open-work, iron-shod all-terrain boots. In short, he was the best armed, armoured, equipped, trained and disciplined soldier of the ancient world, the lowest ranker more richly adorned than the wealthiest individuals of the warrior elites he might come up against.

Each legionary was part of an eight-man section, a *contubernium*, who shared a tent or rooms in barracks. Ten *contubernia* made up a century of eighty men, led by a centurion, risen from the ranks and singled out for his courage and leadership, whose staff of office, a vine stick, was actively wielded to instil discipline. Six centuries formed a cohort of 480 men, and ten cohorts comprised a legion. However, the prestigious First Cohort may have been composed of five double-strength centuries, totalling 800 men, and each legion also fielded a unit of 120 cavalry.

A legion therefore numbered well over 5000 soldiers, but allowing for dead or time-expired men yet to be replaced, the wounded, sick and men on detached duties, most would fall somewhat short of this theoretical strength. In overall command was a *legatus legionis*, or legionary legate, a man of senatorial rank, normally in his early thirties.

The second component of the army was the *auxilia*, non-citizen soldiers recruited from the provinces and fringes of empire. With broadly similar terms of service, an auxiliary would receive citizenship at the end of his career, but was very much the inferior of the legionary and far more expendable. Not much less encumbered than the legionaries, the auxiliary soldier was nonetheless more of a light infantryman or cavalryman, at least in spirit, skilled in skirmishing, reconnoitring and pursuit. It was upon the *auxilia* that the army relied for its main cavalry strength.

Although diverse in their origins, the *auxilia* seem to have achieved some uniformity in appearance by the mid-first century. Mail shirts, bronze helmets, oval shields, spears and swords were the standard basis of their equipment, but the affectations and strengths of individual tribal or ethnic groupings were not necessarily ironed out. Levies raised from people naturally skilled in the use of bows or slings, for example, provided useful specialist units, and the Batavians, from the Rhine delta, were famous for swimming rivers fully armed and armoured. Recruited from peoples where only a king or warlord might boast a mail shirt and helmet or never go hungry, the trappings and regular meals of the *auxilia* must have been a great lure to many, and a consolation to those forced into it.

Four legions and probably a similar number of auxiliaries, totalling around 40,000 men, are thought to have landed on the south coast that day in AD 43, under the overall command of Aulus Plautius. Dio does not name or enumerate them, but the near certainty is that they were the *II Augusta*, *IX Hispana*, *XIV Gemina* and *XX Valeria Victrix*. Legions were generally identified by both their number and a name, usually awarded by the emperor. *Augusta* may refer to the Second having been raised under Augustus, or winning him a great victory, and *Hispana* to distinguished service in Spain.[10] *Gemina* denotes a combining of two older units, and *Valeria Victrix*, 'Valiant and Victorious', clearly a prestigious battle honour, seems not to have been awarded to the Twentieth Legion until after Boudica's war.[11]

It was a substantial expeditionary force that should, in theory, have been able to overcome anything it came up against. As the jubilation of surviving the sea-crossing and establishing a beachhead unmolested wore off, however, the troops would have been acutely aware that their backs were to the sea. The ghost of Quinctilius Varus, whose three entire legions had been massacred almost to a man in the dark forests of Germania three decades before, fighting tribesmen not dissimilar to the Britons, would have been the personal demon of every man.

The tribal army that finally barred the progress of Aulus Plautius had been caught napping. The ruling princes of the Catuvellauni, Caratacus and Togodumnus, knew well enough that an armada was assembling to cross the Channel, but they also knew of the mutiny. The food and forage demands of a warband numbering in the tens of thousands would quickly exhaust all local pasture and grain stores. It needed to keep moving, or disperse. Not a single warrior therefore had been present to oppose the landing, and as Plautius's great army began to forge inland, the call went out for the warriors to reassemble.

The tribes opposing Plautius were the Catuvellauni and Trinovantes, the latter a subservient vassal of the former,[12] and others under Catuvellaunian control, willing or not. No doubt such a tribally disparate army took time to recall, perhaps with some groups reluctant to fight, and initially the Romans were subjected to a wearing guerrilla campaign instead of a head-on fight:

> And even when they did assemble, they would not come to close
> quarters with the Romans, but took refuge in the swamps and
> the forests, hoping to wear out the invaders in fruitless effort, so
> that, just as in the days of Julius Caesar, they should sail back
> with nothing accomplished.[13]

But Plautius continued undaunted, and was finally brought to a halt by a great army gathering on the far bank of a wide river. This has traditionally been identified as the Medway, somewhere between Rochester and Snodland in Kent, but this is based on the 'Kent Landing Theory', and is much debated now. We do not know the size of the British army, presumably at least equal to the Roman force, but fighting a guerrilla campaign before blocking the advance from behind a large river might suggest that they were yet to reach full strength.[14]

Either way the Britons were surprised by the amphibious Batavian auxiliaries, who secretly crossed upstream and hamstrung the British chariot and cavalry horses. A hard-fought two-day battle resulted in the defeat of the Britons, who fell back across the next major barrier, the Thames.

Once more the riparian Batavian units crossed unseen in full armour, allowing crossings from other points, and once more the Britons were routed in a fight that proved costly to both sides. Prince Togodumnus had been killed, and Caratacus made good his escape westwards to the hill tribes of Wales. As the remaining

Britons steeled themselves to resist the next advance, or offer their submissions, the Romans unaccountably stopped, dug-in, and advanced no more.

Unknown to the Britons, the invasion of their lands and whole-sale slaughter of their warriors was little more than a propaganda stunt for the new emperor Claudius, and it had long been arranged that he would personally lead the final, victorious entry into the settlement that Rome saw as the regional powerbase – Camulodunon, *Fortress of Camulos*, the God of War. Encompassing the present city of Colchester in Essex, and later Romanised as Camulodun*um*, the capture of the settlement had been the military objective of Plautius all along, to dismantle the paramountcy of the Catuvallaunian–Trinovantian alliance, simultaneously ending resistance in the south-east.

Having seen off the worst of British resistance, messengers raced south to alert Claudius in Rome, and it probably took the emperor, mostly travelling by boat, about a month to land in Britain. Whether the resulting 'battle' was anything more than a stage-managed sham we will never know, but Claudius had his victory.[15] The great *oppidum* of Camulodunon, once the principal settlement of the Trinovantes, and then of the Catuvellauni, was finally entered by the emperor of Rome.

It would be wrong to think of Camulodunon as some sort of Celtic metropolis or densely settled hillfort. The eminent Roman archaeologist Sheppard Frere, who was not usually given to being uncharitable towards the Britons, was perhaps being a little harsh when he described King Cunobelin's old capital as 'an amorphous collection of round huts and unorganised squalor',[16] but we can appreciate the point he was making.

Camulodunon, the settlement the Romans saw as the capital of the Britons and the keystone on which to anchor their toehold, justifying the triumphal entry of the emperor himself, with elephants, was more of an extensive *splurge* defended by errati-cally laid-out defensive dykes, a landscape of dispersed *foci* of activity. Claudius's impression of the place is not recorded; it was probably not too dissimilar to Frere's. Although he was only in Britain for sixteen days, Claudius must have spent a good few of them at Camulodunon, receiving tribute, hostages, and, most importantly, submissions. According to a surviving fragment of Claudius's triumphal arch in Rome, eleven British kings submitted to him.

We do not know for certain where Claudius's encampment was, but archaeologists Christopher Hawkes and Philip Crummy have made a convincing case for a spot tucked neatly into the Iron Age and Roman dyke system by Lexden, on the outskirts of Colchester, surrounded by defensive dykes and the river Colne.[17]

Based on this, and if we assume for the sake of fancy that Claudius entertained the British kings close to the *principia* or headquarters of the fortress, the eleven compliant tribal leaders submitted to the Roman emperor Tiberius Claudius Caesar Augustus Germanicus somewhere in the present-day vicinity of the Lexden Crown public house at the triple junction of Cymbeline Way with London and Lexden Roads. Prasutagus may well have been among them. It was here, perhaps, somewhere beneath the chatting diners of the brightly lit gastropub, that the Iceni irrecoverably mortgaged their future, and from where the eleven British kings returned to their tribes, a little less kingly than they had left them. The pub itself, or the pretty parkland behind it, is a pleasant spot to contemplate the monumental shift of fortune and sovereignty that might have been enacted there.

And so, Claudius, *deprived the conquered of their arms and handed them over to Plautius, bidding him also subjugate the remaining districts.*[18] The emperor was gone, and Plautius given *carte blanche* to get on with his campaign. Having been delayed in getting his troops embarked, and then waiting weeks for the emperor to earn his triumph, he wasn't going to kick his heels any longer. He constructed a permanent base to herald the New Order, a fifty-acre legionary fortress that seared the brand of Rome indelibly into the earth.

On a commanding hilltop the Twentieth Legion built their new base, a vast rectangular fortress with a ditch two and a half metres deep and four metres wide, with high earth and timber ramparts, topped with palisades and gatehouses.[19] Not only does this fortress from the first days of the conquest now lie directly beneath the modern city centre of Colchester, it still defines much of the modern layout.

The Twentieth Legion would garrison and consolidate this heart of the fledgling province, whilst the Second, Fourteenth and Ninth would march south-west, west and north respectively. It would be Legio II Augusta under the future emperor Vespasian that had the most fighting to do as it pacified the south-west, where, *he fought thirty battles with the enemy, reduced to subjection two powerful nations, more than twenty towns, and the Isle of Wight*.[20] The IX Hispana, skirting the western edge of Icenian territory, pushed into the east Midlands, and the XIV Gemina into the west Midlands.

By AD 47, when Plautius came to the end of his tenure, the army had pacified and occupied Britain from the Humber in the north-east to the Exe in the south-west, broadly lying behind the rivers Severn and Trent, with, by and large, friendly buffer states beyond. The line of the Fosse Way, an early road running almost straight from end to end of this line, effectively delineated this provincial zone, as well as lowland Britain and the extent of the major coin-producing tribes.

The idea that this road, the modern A46, formed an actual military frontier has long been frowned upon, out of kilter with the expansionist outlook of the conquest period,[21] but whatever the Fosse represented, its presence must have been a real enough physical and psychological boundary to soldier and native alike, bisecting the kingdoms it crossed. Beyond lay tribes with which the Romans were far less familiar, and who had a brooding suspicion of them in return.

It was Plautius's departure that heralded a change of the wind. The fugitive prince of the Catuvellauni, Caratacus, had not retired to live in peace elsewhere, but had spent four years fomenting resistance amongst the hill tribes of Wales. In the autumn of AD 47, war bands flooded into the territory of the allied buffer tribes at the very moment of changeover to the new Roman governor, Ostorius Scapula.

Stepping into this province of only recently conquered barbarians, with war erupting on a rambling frontier he had yet even to inspect, Scapula had no intention of treading softly with the natives. He would go west and smash those hill tribes, but not with fully armed, independent tribal territories at his back. These supposedly friendly tribes in his rear provided no buffer role, and lived within the province – if they meant no trouble they had no need of their arms. Hunting spears might be essential for men still living in tribal lands, but none could have legitimate use for a sword.

We have no British voice to tell us what the confiscation of a sword would mean to a warrior undefeated in battle, but it is easy enough to imagine it being deeply shameful and offensive, humiliating beyond endurance and an affront to almost everything warriorship stood for. In the ancient Irish sagas weapons are often given personal names and have, by extension, personalities; if we must be cautious in dragging such details across both the Irish Sea and many centuries, it is a whisper of how appalling the prospect of mass disarmament was to the client tribes.

As defeated enemies, the Catuvellauni and Trinovantes might already have been disarmed, and of the tribes of the southern hinterland, we do not know. We do know, for Tacitus tells us, that the Iceni had not been disarmed – for when the time came, they were:

> the first to resist. At their instigation the surrounding nations chose as a battlefield a spot walled in by a rude barrier, with a narrow approach, impenetrable to cavalry. Through these defences the Roman general, though he had with him only the allied troops, without the strength of the legions, attempted to break, and having assigned their positions to his cohorts, he equipped even his cavalry for the work of infantry.[22]

This *rude barrier* is hardly a description likely to lead to a conviction, and many suspects have been named in the past. I have visited most of them at one time or another, but there is one name that has started to recur in recent times more than any other, and it is the one that I have, until now, failed to visit.

The so-called hillfort of Stonea Camp, occupying the southern tip of what was once a small island in the Cambridgeshire Fens near Wimblington, is approached by a bumpy, tarmac farm road, as straight and narrow as it is flat in this flattest of British landscapes. It is stretching credulity a little far to describe this place as a *hill*fort, for the site it occupies is a giddying two metres above sea level, almost a sort of vertigo in reverse, and it is not the height of the ground that is unnerving here; it is the vastness of the sky.

There is a commonly quoted fear of the Celts, made famous in the Asterix cartoons, that they feared the sky falling. It stems from the Greek historian Arrian, who recorded that in 335 BC the Celts of the Adriatic pointedly told Alexander the Great, 'We fear nothing except that the sky might fall on us,' inferring that whatever else they might fear, it certainly wasn't him.

Whether this phobia was widespread beyond that particular tribe we do not know, but it would be easy to imagine that it originated here, where the span of the sky completes a 180-degree arc in all directions, from horizontal to horizontal, just that vast, endless, overpowering firmament. It is beautiful, there is no denying it, but one can become oppressed by the sheer, endless weight of it. This place, beneath one of the heaviest skies in the world, is a fitting spot to recall the legend, not least because for the rebels of AD 47, this may indeed have been where their sky came crashing down.

After three days of iron-grey clouds and pelting rain in Norwich, it is a shock to reach this spot about fifty miles west. Surrounded by an azure sky, the only clouds lie low on the northern horizon, looking like a distant mountain range, or the edge of a vast prehistoric ice-sheet. The sun is warm through a chilly breeze, and I realise that it is May Day, Beltane in the ancient Celtic world.

This day was the gateway of summer when, we are told, the herds would be driven between two great purifying bonfires, and once the rituals woven through with the death of winter, the rebirth of spring, and the fecundity of gods, goddesses, fields, beasts and humans alike were done with, and perhaps the odd sacrifice, great feasting and licentious carousing would ensue.[23] It is, I fear, an inappropriate image of gaiety to conjure at Stonea; apart from the sacrifices, perhaps.

What you can see at Stonea are several phases of Iron Age ditch and bank earthworks that were mostly reconstructed in 1992, to show not what the site looked like in the Iron Age, but how it appeared early in the twentieth century, before much of it was flattened in the 1960s, believe it or not, with bulldozers.[24] It is sensitively done, manipulating only the unstratified topsoils to recreate its character as an ancient monument without disturbing the underlying dead, of which there are many.

The raised banks are low, some no more than a couple of feet, and the ditches shallow, often watery, hollows. There are, thankfully, several information boards around the perimeter with *you are here* icons, but it is very difficult at ground level to get any sense of what the humps and bumps all mean.

In brief, entering the site from the south-east corner, where there is a tiny car park, a single ditch and bank run straight away to your left. This denotes the old edge of Stonea island; all the land to the left of it would have been fen. Beyond is a double ditch and bank that sweeps round from end to end of that southern boundary in a great curving arc. This probably forms the enclosure that stood here in AD 47, looking, in plan, like a capital D. Beyond all of that is another earthwork representing an earlier phase.[25]

The site today still gives a good impression of its bleak isolation, but around is a sea of farmland, as far as the eye can see in every direction, long drained and cultivated, with not much to hint at its ancient setting. A densely wooded island of oak and birch continued beyond the curving earthworks, all surrounded by sodden fen, standing water reflecting the vastness of the sky, punctuated by endless swathes of tall reed, lapping right up to the ditch of the southernmost boundary.[26] You must also vastly increase the scale of the earthworks; many of the ditches were five metres wide and two metres deep, with banks seven metres wide and far higher than now, topped with a palisade.

An Iron Age settlement lay just to the north, but the Camp was separate, a place apart. Like many Iron Age so-called forts, its role is ambiguous, clearly not simply an enclosure of defence or habitation. Whatever else it was, the little evidence hints that this was a sacred, wooded place, a grove,[27] perhaps where funerary rites were enacted,[28] but lacking the artefacts to suggest gatherings or feasts.[29] Human remains, both complete and fragmentary, were the dominant component of the limited excavations conducted here, and there are reports of more brought to light during agricultural work.[30] In every way, and by any interpretation, Stonea Camp is a place of the dead.

Fittingly, for Beltane, I unintentionally walk the top of the low bank in a clockwise, or *sun*wise direction, *deosil*, as derived from the Gaelic. The inner line of the curving defences, more substantial than the rest, are still the original earthworks, the only ones to survive the twentieth century without being flattened. I am completely alone, a privilege indeed on such a beautiful spring day, at such an important Iron Age site, and on a famous Celtic festival day to boot – I half expected there to be a cloaked neo-pagan or two wandering around.

This is the first time in the story of the Iceni that we have a detailed account of a specific event, and a possible location in which to place it. Stonea Camp is by no means the only candidate for the site of this rebellious last stand – Borough Fen fort, just north of Peterborough, is the other one that shouts out to me, approached across a narrow neck of land jutting out into the fen, *a narrow approach, impenetrable to cavalry* that fits Tacitus like a kid glove.

There are 'forts' right across East Anglia that could be shoe-horned to fit, and suggestions range from Holkham on the north Norfolk coast[31] to Wandlebury near Cambridge,[32] but so far it is Stonea that effortlessly slips into place, close to the border of Icenian territory with the Corieltauvi, long suspected as one of the *surrounding nations* mentioned by Tacitus who joined in the fight.

Although there is no evidence at all for habitation within the earthworks, there is a single, brief flurry of occupation at the right time, in the mid-first century AD, with pottery and brooches scattered across the site. Excavations sited over these artefact concentrations found no building or settlement features at all,[33] consistent with a brief occupation utilising temporary shelters.

The skull of a three- or four-year-old child that has suffered two sword cuts, one of which neatly bisected it from the top of the crown to the back of the jaw, was found dumped, or placed, at the bottom of the southern ditch, along with more bones of a toddler and an adult.[34] After weaving the radiocarbon dating into the archaeological sequence of the site, these have an almost certain date of between 210 BC to AD 60,[35] a helpful window on a site so devoid of dating material, but an impossibly wide span of nearly three hundred years in which to identify an exactly dated event. A complete skeleton of a man, dumped into the top of the outermost circuit of ditch, although of the same era, was deemed unlikely to be of exactly the same date.[36]

Neither group of bones therefore need be the work of the Romans, but theoretically either could be, and they surely represent only a small sample of the human remains present. In short, what looks like the detritus of a massacre may be episodes of Iron Age ritual or burial, Roman pacification, or even inter-tribal warfare, but we simply can't be sure.

Most of all, the narrow approach we require is very real at Stonea, surrounded by fen, where access across, whether by sodden ground or constructed causeway, would be difficult terrain for horsemen. It is just possible that this wooded islet in the middle of the Fens, such a natural bolt-hole for the survivors of a failed rebellion, was the location of the final massacre of its participants:

> *Then at a given signal, they forced the barrier, routing the enemy who were entangled in their own defences. The rebels, conscious of their guilt, and finding escape barred, performed many noble feats. In this battle, Marcus Ostorius, the general's son, won the award for saving a citizen's life.*[37]

The rebels, trapped by earthwork and fen, must have known they were done for. Most agonising of all must have been the comparatively small numbers that had flocked to the fight whilst the remainder of their people stood by. Scapula did not even feel obliged to move a cohort of legionaries to stiffen his attack. He was confident of success with his auxiliary troops alone.

Unless another earthwork yields positive evidence of such a fight, Stonea is as good a screen as any on which to project our mental footage of the *auxilia* bursting through the defences on the curving, northern side that faced out onto the island, and here too the bull-necked Marcus winning his equivalent of the Victoria Cross in saving the life of a citizen, presumably a fellow officer of the non-citizen *auxilia*, from the spears and swords of the screaming natives.

His glory would outlive his favour. This Roman hero, *of huge bodily strength and skill in arms*, would later die unflinchingly by his own hand, disdaining execution in the paranoid bloodlettings of Nero in AD 66. *That fortitude which he had often shown in fighting the enemy Ostorius now turned against himself.*[38] It must also be here, tight up against the south-western ramparts, that the desperate final struggle took place, no further retreat being possible for the Britons, *entangled in their own defences*.

I sit on the low bank of this southern boundary, about

two-thirds of the way along, approximately where the sword-cleaved skull of the four-year-old kid, described above, was found in the ditch, an artefact so wrenchingly at odds with our world, it has to make us wonder if we can ever, or would ever want to, enter the mindset of the past. It could be the result of a war massacre, of which our own times can provide enough sad parallels, but kids' bones are not infrequent finds on Iron Age sites, sometimes in contexts that force questions about sacrifice, or at least the superstitious manipulation and dismemberment of corpses.

There is no point being misty-eyed and wistful about the Celts. However rich and sophisticated the cultures of Late Iron Age Britain, they had hard lives. Inter-tribal warfare was probably endemic,[39] with constant cross-border raiding for livestock, portable wealth, and slaves. Slave-chains have been found across Britain, indicating not only indigenous slave ownership, but a lucrative trade with the hungry European markets.

Most lived within a fragile subsistence economy that may often enough have produced a surplus, but a bad harvest could spell unimaginable hardship and starvation. To mitigate against these uncertainties and misfortunes, there is strong evidence that human sacrifice was resorted to, but whether this levy of the gods was administered as an annual prophylactic or an occasional desperate remedy, a rare cry for appeasement in times of dire need, we cannot know.

If Stonea is the rustic earthwork of Tacitus, then here by this ditch on the islet's edge is undoubtedly the stage of those terrible last moments in which man, woman and child were indiscriminately cut down; but to Iron Age eyes, this was also a transitional, liminal spot, a threshold between the island and the wetland. It is impossible to overstate how spiritually and ritually significant that might have been in prehistory, an ambiguous space straddling the worlds of the subterranean chthonic and subaqueous fen deities; a place where we might expect human bone to be ritually deposited. Either way, the carrion crows that rise in a swarm from the trees on the northern ramparts in noisy intimidation of a passing gull are appropriate guardians of this field of the ancient dead.

We can never know for sure how the tribal balance of power hung for the Iceni in AD 47, who it was that led the rebellion, or why Scapula chose to allow continued independence. He did the same with the Brigantes in the north, bolstering another Roman client monarch, Queen Cartimandua, against anti-Roman factions, but Brigantia was a vast buffer state the army could ill-afford to subdue and occupy; by acting as a prop to Cartimandua's powerbase, the army was saved from opening a draining second front.

Icenia, however, buffered no one. It was practically an independent tribal island, and Scapula must have been hugely tempted to simply annexe the kingdom. Prasutagus clearly had no hand in the revolt, indeed, it has been suggested that it was raised against him and his willingness to kowtow as much as it was against the Romans themselves.[40] It could have been at this point that he was able to seize sole kingship, or clung on to his teetering throne by the skin of his teeth. Whichever it was, it must have suited Ostorius Scapula or the kingdom would have vanished.

A reason for this stay of execution is not hard to find. Scapula was planning the invasion of Wales, a monumental undertaking, at the same time as balancing a precarious peace in the vastness of Cartimandua's Brigantia. If Prasutagus could control his people, then it prevented Scapula's hard-pressed legions from having to do so, and he could turn back and absorb the Iceni once the west was won.

Fortunately for Prasutagus, the war in the west dragged on, and on. Caratacus was finally captured in AD 51, his army broken, but defeat only stiffened the resistance of the hillfolk as the war intensified. If Scapula had intended to absorb Icenia once he could spare the men, it was forgotten when he died a year later, exhausted by his duties, and by successive governors as each was faced with hurling fresh troops into the crucible of the western hills to replace the rapidly accumulating losses.

To the tribes of the eastern seaboard, the fighting in the west would have been a distant thunder indeed. The Romans would hardly have advertised that other Britons were fighting for every rock and tree of their homeland, and holding the army back season after season, but news would have filtered through from travellers and merchants, and snatched conversations with slaves taken in the fighting. The Iceni would have known full well why three legions were in the west, with only the Ninth legion on the edge of their lands.

They would also, sharing a long border with the Trinovantes, have seen the full horror and shame of occupation. The Twentieth Legion had treated the Trinovantes as slaves, appropriated their grain and livestock, and run riot through their lands. In AD 49, Scapula had marched them west to bloody their swords, but if the Trinovantes prayed that their troubles had marched with them, they were to be sorely disappointed.

Many of the soldiers that had marched and fought through Britain were no longer young men. They had served their legions for the better part of twenty-five years, and the deserted fortress at Camulodunum could serve a dual purpose. As well as becoming the first city in Britain, advertising the glory and benefits of Roman life, in bathhouses, temples, shops and monuments, the place could act as a *colonia*, literally a colony, for retiring soldiers to settle and claim their farms.

It also, as Tacitus was quick to point out, provided a tough, trained and presumably still-armed militia in the heart of the province to guard against rebellion:

> *a colony of a strong body of veterans was established at Camulodunum on the conquered lands, as a defence against rebels, and as a means of imbuing the allies with respect for our laws.*[41]

It was a civilising mission that would go catastrophically wrong.

All armies have pejorative nicknames for the enemy, ranging from the mildly mocking to the deeply offensive. We know of one used in the invasion of Britain, *Britunculi*, recorded on the Vindolanda tablets in northern Britain later in the century. Literally translated as 'little Britons', which has an almost endearing quality to it, it was an insulting, diminutive word that would have been spat out derisively as racist names are today – a translation into modern usage might more realistically have it prefixed with a strong expletive, something in the order of 'fucking little Britons'.[42]

The veterans returning from the vicious guerrilla war on the Welsh front, where Tacitus tells us a policy of near-genocide was being enacted, were not bringing with them a respectful appreciation of British culture and customs. Traumatised, surly and belligerent, they were used to taking what they wanted at the point of the sword, and may have seen little difference between Britons in the east and Britons in the west. *Britunculi* were *Britunculi*, and where the veterans had come from, the only good one was a dead one.

It is not difficult to imagine the emerging culture of the fledgling *colonia*. These were hard men who had, by modern standards, led lives of unimaginable hardship and spent their entire adult lives in an all-male environment glued together by brutal military discipline and homicidal aggression to outsiders. Coming from the nightmare of the Welsh front, the men would mostly have hated the Britons, seeing them all as potential slaves and commandeering many as such, an attitude encouraged by their betters and peers alike. We have to remind ourselves that these men were not being integrated back into a civilian society; they themselves were founding the city in which they would live and which other veterans would join.

The evolving ethos of Camulodunum was a distillation of those prejudices and grievances. Tacitus is quite explicit about this:

> *For these new settlers in the colony of Camulodunum drove people out of their houses, ejected them from their farms, called them captives and slaves, and the lawlessness of the veterans was encouraged by the soldiers, who lived a similar life and hoped for similar licence.*[43]

The retired veterans, arriving in droves, moved into the abandoned fortress, levelled the ramparts, infilled the ditches and began a programme of development. They surveyed huge tracts of the surrounding land to cultivate as their farms, each man entitled to his generous acreage. They began erecting a great temple to the imperial cult, a theatre, and government buildings. They named the new city *Colonia Victricensis*, the City of Victory,[44] and raised a monumental arch at the entrance to the town to commemorate its capture.

On the surface, this show home of Roman life was progressing well, but it was Trinovantian slaves who provided the labour, Trinovantian money that paid for the amenities, and Trinovantian lands that the new colonists were allotted as their farms and retirement properties.

A stark illustration of the relationship existing between the veterans and local natives was found in the 1970s during the construction of the Balkerne Lane ring road in Colchester. The ditches of the legionary fortress were exposed at the site of the main gatehouse, now the Balkerne Gate. In the transition from fortress to city, the old wooden gatehouse was replaced with a monumental arch, and human remains were deposited in the ditch, consisting of six full or partial skulls and a variety of other bones. Two of the skulls showed evidence of extreme violence, one with a depressed fracture caused by a heavy blow, another with a sword or axe cut clearly meant to decapitate.

These represent the bodies, and particularly heads, of execution victims displayed in all their horrific detail as they slowly rotted away and fell apart into the ditch. The bones all represent young men of seventeen to twenty-five years, apart from one piece of skull, which might be that of a woman.[45] The likelihood, surely, is that they were Trinovantians, executed and spiked onto stakes, their decomposing bodies fitting decorative baubles for the monumental arch of Victory, to express the spirit of the times.

Many of the veterans would settle down and marry. The wives of some might have been incomers, the daughters and widows of foreign merchants, but in the time-honoured tradition of soldiers overseas, many wives were undoubtedly local women, not just barbarians, but *Britunculi*. After a life largely starved of female company and performing every mundane task for himself, from cleaning his equipment and mending clothes to grinding corn and cooking his own food, many must have favoured women as house slaves, their abuse in the bedroom as much a part of their expected duties as the cooking and cleaning.

British slaves were mostly illiterate, rough and backward to Roman eyes. A hundred years before, during Caesar's expeditions, the great orator Cicero had snobbishly brayed in a letter to his friend Atticus that in Britain, . . . *there isn't a pennyweight of silver in that island, nor any hope of booty except slaves, among whom I don't suppose you can expect any instructed in literature or music.*[46]

It was true, as far as the refined Roman upper classes who desired such slaves were concerned, and most Britons must have been at the lower end of that market, fit for hard manual labour, sex, or the arena. For housekeepers the unsophisticated veterans merely required someone who could light a fire, bake bread, keep house, and lie compliantly on the bed when required. It was surely not uncommon for the veteran to become attached to the woman most frequently singled out for the latter duty, who would quickly begin producing children. To legitimise those children, he might free the woman and then marry her, instantaneously conferring citizenship on their offspring.

The very thought that a freed slave would willingly marry her former owner might be anathema to us, but it was not uncommon in the Roman world. These were brutal times and choices could be bleak indeed. This might not have been the life she would have chosen, but her sudden transformation from abused slave to Roman matron was little less than resurrection from the dead. We must forgive her if she thought less about her former life in the smoky half-light of a British roundhouse than she did about running her new household, and the future prospects of her children as Roman citizens in colonial society.

This experience of the Trinovantes was epitomised in a life-size frieze 1600 miles away, in a Roman city called Aphrodisias, a carving that specifically represents the conquest of Britannia by Claudius. Now in Turkey, Aphrodisias was a Greek city that had fallen under Roman dominion, but the frieze originally featured in a temple of the imperial cult, the *Sebasteion*, a stark celebration of the power of imperial Rome.

The carving has become a common stop for documentary makers who want to make a hard-hitting point about the realities of Roman annexation – Mary Beard, David Dimbleby and Bettany Hughes have all said their pieces before it.[47] The frieze shows a well-muscled Claudius, naked but for a cloak and helmet, straddling Britannia in the guise of a prone woman, tunic torn away to expose her breasts and barely covering her thighs. He grips her by the hair or scruff of the neck with his left hand, and raises his right to deliver a blow with a now missing weapon. There is no ambiguity about the scene; there is more than one sort of conquest going on here.

Britannia's upraised, pleading right arm conveniently covers Claudius's crotch, as if the ubiquitous flaccidity of Roman statuary would detract from the obvious sexual violence – the virile Claudius has more on his mind than mere submission; the final act of dominance, of victor over conquered, or master over slave, is about to be enacted. As the weapon Claudius was once grasping is missing, we cannot tell if this is the prelude to rape or post-coital murder, but I doubt that the ultimate aim is to kill her, for there is much more to this scene than immediately meets the eye.

The most sobering aspect of the Aphrodisias relief is not the inherent violence of the scene, or that we are watching rape, but that we are meant to approve. The viewer was not intended to recoil, or pity the prone and pleading Britannia; the Roman or provincial Greek man was meant to feel pride and vindication, perhaps the desire to slip on Claudius's helmet and cloak and finish the job himself.

Exactly what a Greek or Roman woman thought when she saw it can only be wondered at, but as Britons were merely the *other*, like slaves, it may not have been very much at all. Britannia's tragic face is certainly meant to inspire a little pathos, but the message is less about sparing the conquered, than never to be conquered oneself. It could almost be an enlistment poster: *Roma Victrix!* And to the victor the spoils!

The carving is, of course, metaphorical, showing the emperor, godlike, in a pose he had probably never struck in his life, overpowering and subduing an entire land in the form of a desirable woman ripe to be pillaged in whatever way he sees fit, and we all know exactly how he intends to do it. It is about power, and the right of the strong to dominate the weak, and in portraying the province as a helpless young woman and the Roman state as her virile rapist, it represents the potential fecundity of this new conquest with Rome as its bedfellow.

Rome's own foundation myth was, after all, based upon the rape of the captured Sabine women. Although the impregnation of *Romanitas* into Britannia is being violently forced, it is for her own good – the fruit of the union will benefit everyone, and for all the manifold horrors of empire building, the Romans really did like to think that annexation was ultimately beneficial to its provincials.[48]

Although doubtless no Roman soldier serving in Britain had seen the distant frieze, it represents the wider mindset they would have carried with them, that of a Roman warrior brutally raping a felled and helpless barbarian woman, exactly the behaviour that was expected on the ground. The Roman army was not a lawless, armed mob, but allowing the men licence to reap the spoils of war was a strong incentive in battle, and a warning to others of what awaited those who resisted or crossed Rome. The provincial Greek man or woman in Aphrodisias staring up at the scene was undoubtedly well aware of that message, too.

It is easy to overstate the terror of the first two decades of Roman rule, because Tacitus concentrates on the fate of the Silures, Trinovantes and Iceni, but other areas clearly thrived. A client ruler in the Chichester area, King Togidubnus, of uncertain tribal attribution but probably of the Atrebates, seems to have done very well indeed out of overt loyalty to Rome, and it has often been suggested that the vast glory of Fishbourne Roman Palace was his reward.[49] For the tribal leaders who accepted clientship, Roman citizenship for themselves and their immediate families would have been part of the gift.

High status native burials continued to be interred in the vicinity of Colchester, so clearly some of the native elite went unmolested.[50] The Roman army also brought huge wealth with it that would ultimately dissipate into the province. This was a mixed blessing for the Britons, allowing some to cast off their tribal subservience and become rich in their own right by dealing directly with the army, but further destabilising traditional social systems.[51]

It was a balance that provincial administrators often got right – the Romans were, after all, a very successful imperial power, and they relied upon compliant provincials to grow their crops and pay their taxes, but Britannia in the AD 50s was an object lesson in how wrong it could all go. This is the landscape of confusion, double-standards and brooding mistrust, above which we must see the storm clouds gathering, and, just perhaps, an increasing culture of isolationism on the part of the Iceni.

The seventeen years of Roman rule before Boudica's war did not leave a distinct layer of Romanisation or Roman material culture in Icenian lands for archaeologists to dig up. As in the decades before the conquest, there was no great influx of wine amphorae, no comprehensive adoption of Roman pottery forms, no widespread appearance of alien burial rites.[52] Roman coins inevitably made their way into the territory in some numbers, but many had long been melted down to make tribal ones, and independent coin production may have continued right up to AD 60,[53] later than any other tribe if so.

One hoard of valuables buried in the mid-first century at Crownthorpe in central Norfolk, consisting of a Roman-styled drinking set of bronze bowls and cups, has been taken to suggest that Roman tastes were being cultivated by some of the Icenian elite. Albeit that part of the set is locally made to distinctly British tastes, and may have been employed for drinking local beer rather than imported wine,[54] it does indeed suggest that Roman style wasn't despised for its own sake.

A hoard of Roman silver wine cups and bowls from Hockwold had been irreverently beaten and dismembered as scrap,[55] and another five silver cups were buried at Blackdyke Farm on the Fen Edge,[56] but once more, hoarding or recycling precious metal is not in itself proof of cultural purification. Occasional valuable items of Roman manufacture and style might represent war loot, traded bullion, rich native Romanophiles, or diplomatic gift exchange – they are probably all of those things, but they do not necessarily suggest widespread aspirations of *Romanitas*.

There is certainly no evidence that this was a British good, Roman bad attitude,[57] nor that Roman material culture was actively discouraged or demonised – the Iron Age settlement at Spong Hill in central Norfolk has yielded Romanised pottery, brooches and glassware from pre-AD 50 contexts[58] – but it might be argued that the Iceni were simply not very covetous of Roman fashions. They could have used their client status and injections of imperial wealth to develop Roman-style towns, villas and lifestyles, as the Atrebates and Catevellauni were doing enthusiastically at the same time, but they chose not to,[59] and it must surely have been a deliberate choice.

The brutality of the disarming and the enslavement of the Trinovantes had hardly been the best advertisement for the *Pax Romana*, and the Iceni carried on doing what they always seem to have done – they remained aloof. If accepting the authority of an absent overlord, paying taxes, and supplying an annual levy of adventurous young men for the auxiliary regiments was what it took to hold the inundation back, so be it. Whether the tribe at large, or even Prasutagus knew it or not, it was a dam that couldn't hold forever. Never before had the life of the king and the future of the tribe been so tightly bound together.

At the end of the summer of AD 59, every man, woman and child laboured to bring in the harvest. The wheat, barley, oats, peas and beans would, along with the smoked, dried and salted meat of the autumn slaughter, provide the tribe with the food it needed to survive the long moons of winter, and the seed-corn to replant in the autumn and spring; an endless, timeless cycle of planting, growth and harvest. There is some small evidence[60] to suggest that the harvest that year was not a good one, and the elderly king Prasutagus had just gazed upon that cycle for the final time.

In a society where the fertility and bounty of the land was probably seen to be inextricably linked to the health and virility of the monarch, Prasutagus may have stared into the half-empty grain stores by the light of the harvest moon and seen a long shadow fall across his path. Perhaps a growing tightness of breath or painful weight on his chest had prepared him for what was coming, or simple old age had hailed the inevitable, but either way the king had pondered his demise long enough to take the precaution of drawing up a will, in the Roman fashion, to safeguard the future of his tribe and family.

At some point between that harvest and the following spring, King Prasutagus drew his final breath, but unlike any other monarch the Iceni had ever known, that dying breath did not contain his final words; they were preserved, unnaturally, in a script that few of them could read, on a scroll that few of them would ever see. Whilst a distant, untrusted authority read and re-read those final sacred words of their king, it would seem likely, given what was to come, that the tribe naturally devolved monarchical power to their widowed queen-consort, Boudica.

Tacitus gives us an insight into those unnaturally preserved final words:

> *Prasutagus, king of the Iceni, famed for his long prosperity, had made the emperor his heir along with his two daughters, under the impression that this token of submission would put his kingdom and his house out of the reach of wrong. But the reverse was the result.*[61]

So here was no friend of the Romans, but a king in check, knowing that checkmate was only a move away unless he could entice his opponent towards another reprieve, to leave another unguarded square in which to sidestep. Such a hope is not a long-term strategy, and largely depends upon the opponent wanting to prolong the game. Had that opponent been Seutonius Paulinus, the governor of the last two years, fighting in the west with his army as governors were wont to do, Prasutagus might have got his extended game, but he was pitched against the other half of Rome's representation in the province, the procurator, Catus Decianus.

Decianus was a money man, a sort of Chancellor of the Exchequer with an expectation that he would feather his own nest in the course of his duties. It was an office that suited men greedy by nature, and with such a personality comes an inherent impatience to get what's coming to them. In short, they like to win the game, not play it. Whether what happened next was conducted entirely on his own authority or if an exchange with Rome had given the nod of Nero, we do not know, nor of the time that elapsed between the death of the king and the arrival of the Romans in Icenian territory, but Tacitus does not draw breath in his narrative:

> *His kingdom was plundered by centurions, his house by slaves, as if they were the spoils of war. First, his wife Boudicca was scourged, and his daughters outraged. All the chief men of the Iceni, as if Rome had received the whole country as a gift, were stripped of their ancestral possessions, and the king's relatives were made slaves.*[62]

It was an atrocity, even by Roman standards. The Roman army might have sacked cities and annihilated entire populations on campaign, but this was not a campaign. It may have been an overtly aggressive diplomatic mission with the heavy hand of the law behind it to justify a forced removal of property, or the declaration of full annexation, but there were no circumstances under which it could justify, legally or otherwise, the flogging of a female Roman citizen of high rank and the sexual abuse of her family, not to mention the flurry of violence and rape around the settlement that must have accompanied it.

These were not the cowed and dispossessed Trinovantes, they were the Iceni, a client tribe, a people mourning their king and wrestling with the inevitable confusion over the power vacuum developing in his absence. The widowed Boudica would have held unimaginable importance, spiritual and physical, to the Iceni. There can be no doubt that rulership held great religious significance, and every aspect of royal power, fecundity, health and bloodline was heavy with supernatural consequence. It has been suggested that Boudica was a priestess, or Druidess,[63] something we will never know for sure, but either way she and her daughters, virgins, the future of the bloodline, perhaps priestesses in waiting themselves, were surely sacred to the tribe.

We do not know how old the princesses were, except that they had yet to be married off, and were old enough to be raped by men who came from a society where girls might be married by twelve. There is little to be gained in contemplating exactly how young they could potentially have been in suffering a very public act of sexual violence deliberately intended to pollute, shame and effectively end the royal line, but the parameters would surely suggest not much younger than ten or older than eighteen. Boudica herself would therefore have been between her mid-twenties and mid forties, with a cluster of likelihood in the middle years of her thirties.

The queen had been tied up as a recalcitrant slave and beaten like one; she would have lost the flesh from her back and was probably half-killed by the ordeal. Roman centurions administered justice with their staff of office, a vine stick, a serious beating that could inflict internal injuries as well as laceration of the skin and muscle. Beaten or whipped, she would doubtless have been unconscious by the end, her tormentors little caring whether she still breathed or not.

Anyone familiar with the story of Boudica knows this scene, but in the brief retelling of the tale at school or a sentence-long recap in a bigger history, *Boudica was flogged and her daughters raped* is an outrage told and gone in a breath, the detail and horror unvisualised until someone else does it on our behalf, and then we recoil.

Although Tacitus is mercifully brief in his description, this is a scene that has inevitably been imagined and reimagined, particularly in fiction, by every writer that has gone near Boudica; not only is it an absolute gift dramatically, but also the turning point upon which the entire story hinges, the crossed line from which there can be no resolution but blood-vengeance. It is the moment in any version when the reader can make no more excuses for the

Romans, their shock and indignation no less than that of the Iceni themselves.

One of the most affecting accounts, perhaps because it was ostensibly written for children and was necessarily oblique in dealing with the worst of the affair, is to be found in Rosemary Sutcliff's *Song For a Dark Queen*. The narrator of the tale, the Queen's harper, Cadwan, is knocked unconscious during the initial fight to protect Boudica and her daughters, and half-wakes to see a 'man-beast in bronze scales' flogging a woman, her hair 'all blood-dabbled and fouled':

> And I knew that it was the Queen. The beast in bronze scales checked for a moment, and looked, grinning, towards someone I could not see. And the Procurator's voice said, 'Ten more strokes, I think. Yes, ten more should help to quench her fires.' And dead men were lying round me, and others standing with their arms bound behind them and their wounds running red; and some-where, a girl was still screaming, the terrible high screaming of a wounded hare, that went on, and on . . .[64]

We don't know where this outrage took place. Although many Icenian sites still await discovery, it is likely that the royal house-hold was centred upon one of the known settlements; Caistor St Edmund on the edge of Norwich, or Saham Toney near Watton are strong candidates, and Thetford, perhaps, the prime contender. Visiting these places now, all centred on rolling, gentle valleys with a small river meandering through, all quiet, farming landscapes, it is easy enough to visualise the clusters of conical roofs in the drift-ing woodsmoke, horses, cattle and sheep grazing the fields beyond, as they still do.

Whichever, if any, Boudica thought of as home, these were places she knew. Take away the hedgerows, pylons and telegraph lines, and those horizons are the same ones she saw; that fold there, that prominence and rise, that falling slope, were familiar to her. And it could have been in any of them that this terror descended.

Intriguingly, Dio, despite his access to Tacitus's account and his eye for ghastly detail, does not mention the flogging or rapes at all, preferring more general explanations of discontent, and it is in these details that his account is especially useful, for they complement the emotive tale of Tacitus with one of simple extortion – the Iceni were being fleeced of their riches with the backing of the Roman administration:

> An excuse for the war was found in the confiscation of the sums of money that Claudius had given to the foremost Britons; for these sums, as Decianus Catus, the procurator of the island, maintained, were to be paid back. This was one reason for the uprising; another was found in the fact that Seneca, in the hope of receiving a good rate of interest, had lent to the islanders 40,000,000 sesterces that they did not want, and had afterwards called in this loan all at once and had resorted to severe measures in exacting it.[65]

So Claudius had lavished the British rulers with gifts of gold and silver, and moneylenders had handed out more, sweeteners to ease the progress of colonisation, and now that the foothold was secure, they wanted it all back. This provides the motive for Prasutagus leaving half of his property to the emperor in the hope of putting an end to the demands for repayment, to no avail. It was against this backcloth that Boudica had presumably stood her ground, and although Dio does not mention her personal mistreatment, he is explicit that it was she alone who finally raised the standard of rebellion:

> But the person who was chiefly instrumental in rousing the natives and persuading them to fight the Romans, the person who was thought worthy to be their leader and who directed the conduct of the entire war, was Buduica, a Briton woman of the royal family and possessed of greater intelligence than often belongs to women.[66]

Catus Decianus's expedition must have included a military escort large enough to overpower local resistance and protect the procurator's staff. As would soon become of critical importance, the closest garrisons representing more than a token force were the Ninth Legion in the Midlands, and the Second Legion, probably at Exeter. A fort at Gosbecks, near Colchester, if in use at this time, may have housed a cohort of *auxilia* that Decianus could have appropriated, and his departmental staff could have included any number of soldiers seconded on detached duty for day-to-day protection and enforcement.

Either way, without a legion waiting in the wings to occupy the territory, at least temporarily, the mission had been as reckless as it was crass. The attack may even have included the beginnings of annexation – the assertion that Icenian chiefs were being *stripped of their ancestral possessions, as if Rome had received the whole country* does rather smack of colonists penetrating the southern borderlands and treating the frontier Iceni as the Trinovantes had been treated before them.

We have no calendar on which to pin these events. Tacitus gives us the year, but it is ambiguous. I have long accepted the case for AD 60,[67] but the arguments for 61 are equally convincing.[68] We do not know what time of year Prasutagus died, nor how soon after it Boudica was attacked, and we have no idea how long it was for the idea of rebellion to be conceived and put into action. Tacitus remarks that the Iceni failed to plant crops that year, intending to seize Roman supplies, presumably suggesting that the planning had taken place by the spring, but this assumption ignores the possibility of autumn-sown crops.

At the moment the rebellion started, Governor Paulinus was conducting his campaign against the Druids on Anglesey, so the army was out of winter quarters and in the field – again, spring or early summer. There is also the question of whether these events were entirely piecemeal, or if a wide net had been cast out from Anglesey to draw them all together.

There is something very likable about linking these

simultaneous explosions of resistance at opposite ends of the country,[69] and it forces us to confront exactly how much power and influence we are prepared to cede to the Druids in this story, a mysterious order rarely enough mentioned by the Romans, but clearly a very real force. It is a matter to which we will return, but it is fair to say that their presence, real or imagined, has come to haunt this story.

Tragically, we have no British voice to tell us of the call to arms, and the classical authors fail us utterly, Dio putting a speech into Boudica's mouth as ridiculous as it is unlikely that any Roman ever got to hear of her words. It is also from this passage that he gives us one of the most enduring images from ancient Britain, that of the tall, fierce, red-headed warrior queen, hair tumbling to her hips, with her gold torc and tunic of many colours, alas, long accepted as a northern barbarian archetype conjured up by Dio's fevered imagination.[70]

He does, however, give two intriguing details of her harangue that are difficult to reconcile with the remaining farce of the scene; firstly that she released a hare from the fold of her tunic, divining victory from its direction of escape, and secondly that she thanked the goddess Andraste for the auspicious sign. Much has been made of these details,[71] but it is impossible to know if this was reportage extracted and preserved after the event, perhaps from Icenian prisoners, or whether Dio simply added a few barbarian stock-images from the archives.

Tacitus merely notes that the Iceni and Trinovantes plotted in secret, *and others* rose with them. The archaeology is almost silent, except for a curious flurry of small holes suddenly appearing in the Norfolk landscape. We have seen before how the Iceni appeased their deities by burying material wealth, and they did so again now, in a rash of coin hoards dating from this time.

In a world without banks, hoards concealed in times of trouble are often seen as unclaimed savings accounts, the unfortunates who buried them overtaken by the troubles they feared. In this instance, however, numerous deposits were made where the composition of the hoards is so similar that they are unlikely to be individual accumulations of wealth, but to have come from the same centralised source.[72]

It is impossible to quantify exactly how many of these hoards were buried at the time of the rebellion, for Icenian coins are not precisely dateable; also, we can, of course, only consider the hoards that are known – many may have gone unreported and illicitly disposed of by the finder. There is also the unanswerable question of how many still await discovery. At present approximately seventeen or eighteen hoards can be ascribed to this event with some level of confidence, with many more still awaiting the sweep of a metal detector.

They occur in north-west Norfolk, the Fens, across the southern borderlands, and along the river valleys within the territory. There is a strong votive suggestion to this pattern of hoarding,[73] and I find it hugely tempting to see it as a deliberate courting of divine aid on a vast scale, supernatural threshold deposits placed at key locations along the tribal borderlands.

I don't doubt that this oversimplifies a complex phenomenon, but the composition does suggest that the hoards were being sent from a single source, be it royal or religious, to specific places, the significance of which might be lost to us but was obvious to the Iceni. There was clearly a complex relationship between Icenian hoarding and the landscape.[74] Perhaps each location was a place of power, maybe a shrine or grove, or strategic places where rivers or tracks gave access to the territory, but there is surely more to these coin-filled pots than the mere safeguarding of tribal silver.

It may be indicative of the very late date of these hoards, and that the Iceni had not been entirely resilient to all things Roman, that in addition to Roman coins in some of the caches, the surviving pottery vessels containing them are often of wheel-thrown, Romanised styles.[75]

Numismatist Dr John Talbot has identified that although the coins in these hoards appear to be significantly worn, they are in fact mostly mint and completely uncirculated, the apparent wear being due to the die stamps from which they were produced, not to the coins themselves.[76] Another intriguing element is that a coin which accounts for over 20 per cent of the assemblage,[77] known as a Late Face Horse, or Norfolk God,[78] differs from other Icenian portrait coins. Normally these images are animated, with large eyes obviously expressing life, and include the neck and shoulders; the Late Face Horse bust, however, has no neck, and the eyes are small, showing no hint of life.

Talbot believes that this represents a decapitated trophy head.[79] Some examples of this enigmatic coin may be the latest Icenian issue to be produced, right up to the eve of the war,[80] and two hoards, from Scole and Forncett St Peter, have helped to date these late hoards to the very year of the rebellion. Both included Roman coins as well as native ones, and each contained an almost mint coin of Nero dating to exactly AD 60/61.[81]

Make of them what you will, whether a cry to the gods for help, or anchor points for a web of supernatural protection, this enigmatic flurry of interring unused coins in specific proportions, some perhaps rapidly minted for the purpose, is the most overt physical evidence that exists for the war in Icenian lands. For me this is the most compelling evidence for a religious or Druidic influence in the planning of the war, but it is not in itself proof of a larger strategy encompassing Anglesey; on the contrary, as with so much to do with the Iceni, it is something peculiarly local and exclusive.

A month after visiting Stonea Camp at Beltane, I am finally able to return to the Boudica gallery at Norwich Castle, to see what detail the silent witnesses within the display cabinets could add to this story of escalating crisis.

The first cabinet I visit contains evidence for slavery: iron wrist manacles from Saham Toney; a particularly grim set of ankle shackles fished out of the river Wensum at Worthing, and a tiny bronze figurine of a slave with wrists manacled to a neck ring, found at Dersingham, by Snettisham. It is difficult to imagine artefacts that could hammer home more forcefully the potential horror of life in first-century Norfolk, and impossible not to see the bleeding wrists and ankles of real, living souls enclosed by the rings. Although Iron Age slaving items do exist, these are all interpreted in the display as being Romano-British, dating to the period of Roman rule.

Turning behind me to the coin section, I stop to inspect one of the tiny silver coins of a man we variously think of as a hero or a quisling, but rarely as a potential slave-trader – King Prasutagus. Neither the light nor my eyes are up to making out the detail of it, but it is really the only artefact in the museum that has a demonstrable connection to Boudica, by association at least. The assumption that Prasto is Prasutagus (or Prastotagus)[82] is not uncontested, but Dr Amanda Chadburn has made a compelling case for it,[83] suggesting the extraordinary coincidence of a historically recorded client king in a known place and time, called Prasutagus, and the coins of a ruler, with a Romanised design, in the same place at the same time, called Prasto.

The legend on the coins actually reads: SUB ESUPRASTO / ESICO FECIT. The last two words, on the reverse, suggest that 'Esico made it'; the first two words seem to mean 'Under Lord Prasto',[84] although Celtic names, whether or not influenced by Latin or German, had distinct meanings, and *Esuprasto* has been interpreted as Chief Protector, or Chief Priest,[85] an intriguing name for anyone seeking a Druidic connection to the Icenian ruling house.

Lying behind the chariot display are the two really martial pieces of the museum collection, a rusty iron short-sword found at Shouldham, and a much longer bronze scabbard from Congham, both within a few miles of the Wash. Having recently sat on the ramparts of Stonea Camp, where the right to own such items might have been so bitterly contested, these are emotive pieces. The sword has an anthropomorphic hilt in the shape of a spread-eagled man, a type commonly dating to the last few centuries BC,[86] but swords were not throwaway objects, and might have been treasured, and used, for generations. Like the weapons of ancient Ireland, I wonder if it had a name.

The scabbard is much longer,[87] to house a more typical long sword. The corroded bronze is chased top and bottom with the exquisite detailing of La Tène loops and curls, but it has been broken in the middle, and the bottom half is bent. What a sight it must have been, straight and polished and gleaming with, perhaps, an equally gleaming spread-eagled bronze or wooden hilt emerging from the top, strapped to the waist of an Icenian warrior.

Swords were clearly of huge importance in the British Iron Age, and were surely the weapon of choice for those who could afford them, or had the status and authority allowing them to sport one. Spears for fighting hand-to-hand, and lighter javelins for throwing, were surely the everyday weapons of most. Bizarrely, the bow and arrow is almost entirely absent from Britain in this period, replaced by the sling, a simple belt-sized loop of leather or linen, with a small pouch from which a stone or sling-bullet could be cast with huge force – a deceptively simple and effective weapon that could be made by anyone, weighed and cost nothing, and was probably used by kids from the moment they were old enough to scare birds from the newly planted fields.

The rebellion against the disarming in AD 47 is prominently covered in the Boudica gallery, with a life-size reconstruction of an armoured legionary wrestling a long sword from an Icenian's hand, before we move into the final section dealing with AD 60. Here is a hoard of several hundred silver coins ploughed up at Honingham, one of the rash of hoards buried at the time of the rebellion, in and around the remains of a small wheel-thrown pot, a little votive, supernatural sentinel, perhaps, to stand guard when the army marched to war.

Here too is the Crownthorpe hoard of native-made, Roman-style drinking items, mostly of bronze, with a beautiful, green-brown marbled verdigris patina, purported to have belonged 'to a wealthy Icenian with obvious Roman tastes'. Fair comment. Also displayed is a fragment of a bronze statue, part of a horse's leg, found at a ritual enclosure at Ashill, an artefact and story to which we will return. These final, seemingly innocent artefacts of the gallery are the sole physical echoes of the storm that was about to break.

And so, the Iceni gathered for war. The southernmost of the great tribal centres, Thetford, would be a reasonable locale for the muster, deep enough into native territory to be unobserved, hidden in the folds of the Thet and Little Ouse valleys, and auspiciously overlooked by an extraordinary ritual enclosure on the commanding high ground to the north. We must use archaeology and what we know of the Britons in general, and the Iceni in particular, to imagine the scene.

The host collecting in southern Icenia must have been one of the greatest tribal gatherings ever witnessed, tens of thousands of souls, and as many animals, to kick up the dust; horses for the vast array of chariots and cavalry, oxen for carts, and half the herds of the eastern lands as meat on the hoof. Possibly they combined the muster with one of the great annual feasts when the tribe would naturally congregate in numbers, Beltane at the beginning of May, perhaps, convincing the Romans that nothing out of the ordinary was brewing.

Despite the dark events that had led them here, it would have been a carnival atmosphere, of drumming and shrieking boar-headed *carnyx* war trumpets, war cries and bellowed promises to the gods. The cream of the warriors, the tribal champions, in torcs, helms and mail tunics, strutted with heirloom swords, hidden beneath the thatch of their great circular feasting halls since the disarming of AD 47, slung across their waists. Many more went naked but for a cloak, their muscular bodies tattooed and painted, brightly coloured shields sporting the bristle-backed boar, the running horse, and the beak-jawed Iceni wolf. The vast majority were farmers, in their checked trews and rough woollen tunics, with spears and hunting knives, slings, wood-axes and fresh-cut quarter-staves.

Archaeological evidence suggests that the Iceni may have done far more than simply limewash their hair into the white, punk-like spikes so beloved of reconstruction artists. An unusual bone assemblage excavated from the western edge of their territory was dominated by beaver and wildfowl,[88] which suggests they were hunting specifically for fur and feathers, and heads on Icenian coins show a range of extravagant headgear and hair-styles, the first sometimes resembling feathers, some of the latter suspiciously like Mohawks or even wild-boar fur hoods.[89]

There could have been feather headdresses, war bonnets, beaver caps and feather cloaks[90] complementing the war paint and tattoos, a scene more immediately reminiscent of eighteenth-century North America and *Last of the Mohicans* than our tradi-tional image of first-century Britain and first-season *Britannia*.

Families and children shouldered their own sacks of posses-sions and food or bundled them into the carts and climbed up behind. Every trackway was thick with carts, chariots, animals and people, and thousands upon thousands of spears gave the army itself that same bristled back as the shield-painted boars and wolves. As the vast host began to stream south, those left behind could have watched it for the better part of the day, and at dusk would have seen a blaze of fires and smoke across the Breckland as it made camp.

It must have been agonisingly quiet. The shepherds and herds-men tended their depleted herds, and the fires in the huts were stoked and fed, but the great round halls, places of feasting and laughter and stories, seemed dark and cold and silent. As the days passed they must have sought news hungrily. Those who remem-bered the falling star heralding the arrival of the Romans half a lifetime before may have gazed expectantly at the skies, and the empty trackways were watched day and night for travellers.

Rumours passing from shepherd to hunter to herdsman told of

the Roman Legion, the IX Hispana on the far side of the Fens, marching south with hundreds of auxiliary cavalry to fight Boudica's army, and days later of the horsemen alone returning to the fortress, where the sounds of hard labour and digging could be heard coming from within. More days still and there was talk of a great battle, a wide vale where thousands of bodies lay strewn, Briton and Roman entangled together, fed on by the crows. Some even said that from the borderlands of the tribal territory, a great glow, like a blood-red sunset, had lit the horizon for day after day beyond the southern hills.

The Ninth Legion had never returned, and Camulodunum was burning.

3

Till in Her Ashes She Lie Buried

The Fall of Camulodunum

The Romans beholding from the citadel the city filled with the enemy, and their running to and fro through all the streets, some new calamity presenting itself in every different quarter, were neither able to preserve their presence of mind, nor even to have perfect command of their ears and eyes. To whatever direction the shouts of the enemy, the cries of the women and children, the crackling of the flames, and the crash of falling houses, had called their attention, thither, terrified at every incident, they turned their thoughts, faces, and eyes, as if placed by fortune to be spectators of their falling country.

Livy on the fall of Rome to the Celts in 386 BC

When Rik Mortimer Wheeler peered owl-like through the gloom of the Vaults beneath Colchester Castle in 1919, simultaneously damning them as dungeons and proclaiming their Roman date, he was not the first to do so. However, in recognising the foundations of a Roman temple, he did not assume that the Norman castle sitting above them was the actual temple itself, which singled him out from his predecessors and the justified academic scorn that had assailed them.

On 31 October 1850, in the impressive interior of Colchester Castle, the Reverend Henry Jenkins, Rector of Stanway in Essex, read a paper before the Colchester Archaeological Society outlining his enthralling, and superficially convincing, treatise,

Colchester Castle Built by a Colony of Romans as a Temple to Their Deified Emperor, Claudius Caesar, subsequently published in 1853.[1] Jenkins argued that the upstanding castle ruins were indisputably the remains of the Temple of Claudius. The castle is indeed constructed of reused Roman building material, and the overall effect, once weathered by the centuries, looks not unlike the physical make-up of some upstanding Roman buildings.

Many of his other observations were pure fantasy, however, and having convinced himself, if few others, that the castle really was the temple itself, he painted vivid pictures to illustrate it:

> a deep gutter . . . runs along the base of its western wall. Supposing this area to have been the place where the victims were slain, before the priests offered their sacrifices, the gutter might have been the channel by which the impurities of the slaughter and the cleansings of the pavement were carried off.[2]

We should certainly refrain from sniggering at Jenkins. He was a respected antiquary, soon to be President of the Society to which he was speaking, and the contemporary Roman historian Charles Merivale described him as 'a man of genius', whilst admitting that, with regard to the castle, he could not accept his 'ingenious and eloquent arguments'.[3] If his imagining of Romans in the castle belongs to the fantasy of another age, he was quite right that the temple stood on the site, and his observations concerning the Vaults are worth repeating:

> When the curious enquirer now descends into the Castle vaults . . . and traverses their dark extent – and, by the flickering light of torches and candles, catches a faint view of their spacious width, and their height, and pebble-encrusted roofs – his mind reverts to the dreary dungeons and Udolphian mysteries of the feudal ages; and he listens with astonishment, perhaps with regret, to be told, that from the first foundation of the Castle, till the latter end of the seventeenth century – i.e., for more than

sixteen hundred years – the whole of this space was filled with sand, which was placed there solely as the means of elevating the floor above, and as the permanent centerings of the superincumbent vaulting . . .

Not only is such a plan of elevating the basement floor unknown in Saxon or Norman castles, but the very form of the arch used in these vaultings (evidently not Norman) corresponds with that of the Roman arch still existing at the Decuman-gate of the town on the Balkan-hill; and we may therefore reasonably attribute the work to a Roman architect.[4]

Quite so, Reverend. It is easy to understand the temptation to combine all of this evidence and see the Norman castle itself as the vestigial Temple of Claudius, a Norman doer-upper of a derelict Roman building. However, that same year, William Wire, a local antiquarian, wrote in private letters that, 'Revd. Jenkins is at war to prove that the castle stands on the same site as the Temple of Claudius,' and the following year that, '. . . there will be some of the most out of the way and absurd opinions that ever emanated from any man suspecting the antiquity of a place.'[5]

Jenkins' enthusiastic treatise was subjected to a scathing reply in the *Essex and West Suffolk Gazette* and a subsequent booklet by Edward Lewes Cutts, unambiguously entitled *Colchester Castle Not a Roman Temple*. Cutts prefaced his assault with a kindly appreciation of Jenkins as an antiquary, 'lest anyone should do me the injustice to think that because, in the interest of Archaeological science, I shew no mercy to the Theory, I am therefore deficient in a proper appreciation of its Author.'[6] Cutts systematically pulled apart Jenkins' theory, although he was rather stumped by the foundations. 'These vaults at Colchester were probably only intended to elevate the ground floor, and form a resistance to the attack of the battering ram, and to the approach of the miner.'[7]

In 1869 Jenkins was at it again, assisted by a local architect, George Buckler, reiterating his points in another ramblingly titled publication, *Colchester Castle Shewn to have been the Templed*

Citadel Which the Roman Colonists Built at Colonia Camulo-dunum to their Deified Emperor Claudius.[8]

Mistaken he may have been, but I doff my cap to Jenkins. Not for him the difficulty of mentally removing the castle before standing in the Temple of Claudius; Jenkins stood within the very walls of the temple every time he entered that castle, no doubts, no niggling uncertainties. Standing in the castle myself, I hold my battered Victorian originals of his books, each once held by the man himself, for they are both inscribed in his hand, and I consider that he wasn't so very wrong. Every time he entered the castle, he *did* stand within the temple, upon its foundations, within its footprint, and surrounded by its very fabric, reused in the walls. Jenkins wasn't wrong, he had the right place and many of the right materials; it was simply a matter of *form*. He died in 1874.

Jenkins' sword was belatedly taken up with gusto by his old supporter George Buckler who in 1876 published *Colchester Castle a Roman Building, and the Oldest and Noblest Monument of the Romans in Britain*,[9] a tired regurgitation that, true to the spirit of the original, failed to win converts. It had, however, all proved very confusing to the layman, who wasn't sure if he was looking at a Roman temple, a Norman castle, or some combination of the two – I have a postcard, produced by the Great Eastern Railway and posted in 1905, purporting to show *Colchester Roman Castle*. It would take Mortimer Wheeler, forty-five years after Jenkins' death, to confirm that the castle really did sit upon the foundations of the Temple of Claudius.

There is nowhere quite like Colchester for the hunter of AD 60, for it has evolved from its Roman origins in a manner that lends its ancient past a strange immediacy. Perhaps the starkest example of this is to look at the Ordnance Survey Explorer map at a scale of 1:25000. In the city centre, to the right of the big letters denoting COLCHESTER, is a ghostly rectangle of streets, like a slightly deformed playing card, about four by two centimetres. You might have to stare hard for a moment, as if it's one of those Magic Eye things, but once you spot it, the image leaps out in much the same way.

That rectangle denotes the edge of the Roman city, and, at least in part, is a ghostly outline of the legionary fortress founded upon that spot in AD 43. It is also, except for the very northern and eastern extremities, the edge of the city when the Iceni arrived to eradicate it from the earth forever. The map is a silent witness to the fact that they succeeded in the short term only.

But the survival of Camulodunum is not merely cartographic. The High Street is the direct descendant, in slightly meandering form, of the gravelled central street of both city and fortress. It might lie two metres beneath your feet, but it is still there, its vestigial footprints and wheel ruts awaiting the archaeologist's trowel. In the eastern half of the city, the castle still dominates the layout of the streets, as the underlying Temple of Claudius did before it.

For the visitor in search of Boudica's short trip to the city, there is surely very little of that first Roman settlement to be found; she did, after all, utterly destroy it. Perversely, however, the city that Boudica attacked is so beautifully preserved *because* she destroyed it so comprehensively.[10] The early colonia was mostly built of wood and daub, and crowned with thatch, all materials that simply vanish in the archaeological record without an additional preserving element – fire. The flames of Boudica's firestorm carbonised the organic portion of the town, and seared the clay-daub walls into a friable orange ceramic. With so little to salvage, the remains were left comparatively undisturbed and simply built over. In other words, it is all still down there.

There are many artefacts in museum storerooms that were direct witnesses of the Boudican revolt. They come from these destruction layers in the towns destroyed in the war, and consist of building material – burnt daub, painted wall plaster, broken roof tiles, and domestic material – heaps of pottery, oil lamps, and jewellery.

There are also the miraculous survivals that catapult us back to those hours before the storm descended, the ephemeral detail we might expect in the dry sand of Egypt or the pumice dust of Pompeii that has no place surviving in the cold, unforgiving mud of Britain – a small bag of carbonised dates imported from the Mediterranean, scorched grain ready to be ground into flour that would have been baked that evening into loaves for breakfast, and germinating barley for someone brewing beer; the ubiquitous detritus of everyday life trampled, burnt, and frozen in time.

Two small dice were still sitting in a turned-bronze dice-shaker in the wreckage of a house in Sheepen, near Colchester, ready for the next throw.[11] Blackened wooden floorboards still lie undisturbed, awaiting the familiar tread of the long-perished inhabitants. In a room in one gutted house, two carbonised mattresses emerged from the soil, the intricate detail of the diamond-twill cover as clearly visible as the day it burned. There is no doubt about the provenance of most of these items, for they lie in well-preserved contexts, sealed by, or a part of, one of the most well-recognised, dated and unambiguous archaeological deposits in Britain – 'the Boudican destruction horizon', or 'the red layer'.

A section of this destruction layer can be viewed, sometimes, in the cellar of the George Hotel on the High Street. When I popped in to ask, I was told that the cellar was out of bounds for health and safety reasons until after ongoing refurbishments, but what you can see, if you ever get to go down there, is a window a few feet tall that protects a section cut through the layers of Roman archaeology, in amongst which is the destruction deposit. There are no treasures to see, only soil layers, a typical archaeological trench section.

It could be said that you need to be a particular type of nerd to get a kick out of seeing something like that, but this is archaeology red in tooth and claw. As you look through the glass at the fragments of orange burnt daub and flecks of charcoal, you are peering directly into Boudica's firestorm. This is the city that she destroyed, and these are its embers. It really is, quite literally, a window to the past.

I stand before the Balkerne Gate on the western edge of old Colchester. Nowhere else is the juxtaposition of the ancient and modern cities quite so uncomfortable, with an upstanding piece of Roman gateway and adjacent wall, the venerable public house The Hole in the Wall built into it, and the thundering 1970s ring road in a purpose-built cutting below them, leaving wall, gate and pub all rather stranded in mid-air. The crowning incongruous detail is the metal footbridge spanning the ring road by which you approach the gate.

If we are generous, we might concede that the 1960s, 70s and 80s were simply too forward-looking to consider the sympathetic inclusion of the past into the modern cityscape – this was a brave new era, after all, of brutalism and concrete, man-made and unstuffy, but such a kindness would be grossly misplaced. As one commentator said at the time, 'The gate is set in the middle of one of the finest surviving lengths of [Roman] town wall in the country. Being a quiet and picturesque spot, the local planning department has therefore decided to run a new dual carriageway right alongside the walls destroying whatever evidence there may have been for the ditches that fronted them, and turning the walls into a fine backcloth for a race-track.'[12]

As is sometimes the way, however, it is this inept juxtaposition of the ancient and modern that reinforces the passage of time, almost like a sensation of vertigo, which is much less apparent at a romantic ruin. It feels apt that this is a place where people have literally tunnelled into the past, and to take up this story we return to the adventures of our young First World War artillery officer, Rik Mortimer Wheeler, in 1917. Stationed in Colchester with his howitzer battery, Wheeler had tunnelled beneath the Hole in the Wall pub to make sense of tunnels already begun by a previous explorer. These had uncovered the foundations of the Balkerne Gate, and Wheeler tempted volunteers to join him:

attracted less by archaeological research than by the homely noises of – and subsequent participation in – the revelry of the tap-room overhead. The excavation, if such it can be called, was conducted largely on our backs by candlelight and was anything but a model of scientific method. But we at least did not do irreparable damage, and ultimately produced a plan designed to serve until the removal of the public-house should facilitate corrections and additions.[13]

The excavations were halted when Wheeler decided that further work might do more harm than good, and feared for the stability of the public house above.[14] It is little wonder that he remembered the time with such evident affection. Quite apart from the fact that it sounds, to an archaeologist at least, like enormous fun digging in the tunnels by candlelight before retiring to sink several pints in the tap-room above, these were the good days of the Great War. Within a couple of months, Wheeler would be in the thick of the very worst it had to offer: 'In October 1917 the ridge of Passchendaele, north-east of Ypres in Flanders, was the definition of hell.'[15]

When Wheeler wrote this account in 1955, his 1921 report based on those candle-lit adventures was still the definitive record of the Balkerne Gate. Fortunately, in 1973, Philip Crummy of the Colchester Archaeological Trust was able to reinvestigate the site during the construction of the ring road that slices in front of it. He found that Wheeler had misinterpreted the archaeology, understandable given the 1917 conditions of play.

What Wheeler thought he had found – and stick with me here – was a gateway complete with two large central carriageways and smaller pedestrian walkways on each side, built as part of the city wall.[16] What Crummy found was that the central carriageways formed a very early monumental arch, later incorporated into the city wall by tacking on the walkways to either side.[17]

This monumental arch would have stood completely alone, commemorating Claudius's capture of the site. Dating to the foundation of the colonia, this arch would have been a major monument at the entrance to Camulodunum, Colonia Victricensis, in AD 60. In walking between the surviving upstanding Roman gateway and the wall of the pub, or better still entering the pub and buying a pint, you are walking through the carriage-ways of that triumphal arch, replicating something that many of Boudica's warriors, and perhaps the queen herself, must have done, staring in wonder at the monumental scale and workmanship of it – the arch was, after all, built to impress. It is also a good candidate for the location of a statue of Victory,[18] which Tacitus claims existed in the town at the time.

The monumental arch of victory, alas, is long gone, but you can still see something of its base. At the front of the Hole in the Wall pub is a concrete balcony, beneath which, in a sunken area approached by a few brick steps, is a low section of the town wall looking rather sorry for itself. The fact that some members of the public mistakenly assume this hollow to be a large litter bin and/or toilet as occasion demands is evidenced by the broken glass and empty drink tins littering the floor, as well as the occasional but unmistakable tang of stale urine, but their ignorance is certainly their loss.

Bang in the middle of this confusing, pudding-mix section of Roman wall beneath the pub, as well as several metres away to the right, are the crumbly yellow tufa blocks of the base of the remarkable triumphal arch. It isn't much to look at now, but its survival at all is a wonder of circumstance and fortune, and we should treasure it.

Lying between the two, and also to the left, are two huge beams of wood that look like railway sleepers. These, astonishingly, purport to be the timber struts used by Mortimer Wheeler in 1917 to support his tunnelling adventures and keep the pub from falling on their heads. This unimpressive, forgotten little section of wall surrounded by concrete tells the entire story of the Balkerne Gate, from the city's foundation to the labours of that young archaeologist and artillery officer killing time *en route* to Passchendaele.

The best preserved sections of the wall lie adjacent to the Balkerne Gate, where it still survives to the height of four metres or so, and the base still stands at approximately the Roman ground level.[19] Its date of construction appears to be only ten or twenty years after Boudica,[20] making it the earliest Roman city wall in Britain – most date to more than a hundred years after that. Much of the brick used in its construction is broken, so it is possible, if not likely, that the defences are built from the rubble of the public buildings destroyed in the attack,[21] 'the fruits of bitter experience', as Wheeler called them,[22] a physical manifestation of the memory of what Boudica did here.

We do not know what first alerted the inhabitants of Colonia Victricensis to the impending onslaught, but there is one surviving site in Colchester that might hold the last trace of that moment of sickening realisation. I pass through the Balkerne Gate and follow the bustling High Street, weaving my way through the crowds until a small turning called Maidenburgh Street.

If the High Street is particularly busy, turning down this unprepossessing little road can be quite a jolt, not a soul to be seen as I walk between the back of the British Heart Foundation shop and the squat, flat-roofed entrance to a concrete Methodist church. The remainder of the narrow street is residential, an incongruous mix of old and new houses, some mid-Victorian and others fairly recent.

One of these new builds, squashed between two Victorian originals, has an information board on the front proclaiming this to be the site of the Roman theatre, and if you peer through the window you can see a low section of excavated wall. Mentally follow the line of the wall to the outside of the building, and on the floor, in the red-brick paving, is a swathe of darker bricks, as if a contractor has dug a cable trench and lazily reinstated the road with a different colour. Far from it, this is the line of the theatre wall ingeniously highlighted to show where the building stood.

It is a rare privilege, that is a recurring theme in Colchester, to visit not only a place, but an exact spot, an actual surviving individual building, specifically described in a Roman text, and it is hard to emphasise how rare that is anywhere in the world outside of Rome, let alone in the far-flung tribal wilderness of mid-first century Britannia. The theatre is an appropriate place to contemplate a particularly chilling passage in Tacitus, in which he describes the building tension and anxiety in the colonia as its destruction neared:

> *without any evident cause, the statue of Victory at Camulodunum fell prostrate and turned its back to the enemy, as though it fled before them. Women excited to frenzy prophesied impending destruction; ravings in a strange tongue, it was said, were heard in their senate-house; their theatre resounded with wailings, and in the estuary of the Thames had been seen the appearance of an overthrown town; even the ocean had worn the aspect of blood, and, when the tide ebbed, there had been left the likenesses of human forms, marvels interpreted by the Britons, as hopeful, by the veterans, as alarming.*[23]

Intriguingly, this is one of the few details upon which both Tacitus and Dio tally. Whether they used the same source, or, perhaps, if Dio used Tacitus, the later writer records:

> *at night there was heard to issue from the senate-house foreign jargon mingled with laughter, and from the theatre outcries and lamentations, though no mortal man had uttered the words or the groans; houses were seen under the water in the river Thames, and the ocean between the island and Gaul once grew blood-red at flood tide.*[24]

Even if we write them off as mere artistic licence, and they feel too weirdly specific to do so easily, the fact that both authors recounted the events tells us that they would have deliciously chilled and titillated the Roman audience at home, who wouldn't have questioned their authenticity for a moment.

Excavations in the 1980s exposed the theatre's curving wall, D-shaped in plan, with an external diameter of about seventy metres, and a capacity of around 3000 people. The walls were of stone and brick, and certainly in use by the second century AD.[25] No evidence was recovered for a previous theatre, perhaps built of timber, destroyed in the first century.

If there was a theatre in AD 60, this is undoubtedly the site of it. The walls discovered may well be that building, or its replacement, but these stone and brick public buildings would be difficult to burn down, and even more difficult to demolish, so Boudica's army may have left them only superficially damaged. Hard dating evidence aside, what does suggest an early date for the building is the way it sits within the city, lying close to the temple on the early military alignment of the fortress, not on the slightly shifted alignment of the colonia.[26]

Although its plot could have been reserved for it early on and the theatre actually built much later, as happened in second-century Verulamium,[27] the defining straight wall of the theatre should still have respected the dominant alignment at the time of its actual construction, and here that hints at the AD 50s. If the short, truncated section of wall in the visitors' centre really does date to the early colonia before Boudica attacked, it is an extraordinary survival, which the accounts of Tacitus and Dio imbue with a haunting magic.

The tree-dappled peace of the old Quaker burial ground behind the adjoining St Helen's chapel pretty much occupies the position of the semi-circular orchestra, or floor, of the theatre. The surrounding buildings, roughly equating to the towering auditorium seating, lend an appropriately enclosed feel to the space, where the Roman colonists and their families watched speeches and bawdy political satires enacted on the stage that now lies directly beneath the tarmac of St Helen's Lane. Once upon a time, in the spring of AD 60, something far more sinister echoed from this space.

Whether or not anyone made the connection at the time, this was a symbolic spot for a ghostly shriek to foretell the town's doom. A stage is a psychological threshold, where the boundary between fantasy and reality is naturally blurred. This stage was also on the very edge of the early town, occupying, both actually and metaphorically, the divide between the civilised and barbarian worlds, spatially overlying the prematurely levelled protection of the legionary ramparts, the physical manifestation of favouring the *agreeable over the expedient* on which Tacitus blamed the lack of defences. As we are told that *no mortal man had uttered the words or the groans*, this has to be the site of the earliest recorded ghost story in British history.

It is reasonable to assume that the wailings, cries and lamentations were meant to have emanated from the stage itself, so standing on the exact site of that stage, in the middle of the road of St Helen's Lane, looking back across the burial ground to the imagined auditorium, especially at night, gets you about as close to that ghost story as it is possible to be. As far as precedents go, it set a high bar for others to match – not many ghost stories herald the destruction and massacre of entire cities.

Whether haunted by outlandish yells and blood-red tides or not, the colonists knew the Iceni were coming. The response of the veterans was predictable enough – they sent word to the four corners of the province and requested armed assistance.

But as Suetonius was far away, they implored aid from the procurator, Catus Decianus. All he did was to send two hundred men, and no more, without regular arms.[28]

This tells us that Decianus wasn't in Colchester, so the plea for his assistance presumably went to London, where the docking facilities of a major river and its more central location may already have been making it the hub of fiscal concerns; certainly his successor would be buried there a few years later. They also sent a rider tearing up the *Via Devana*, the most direct route to the east Midlands, to alert the Ninth Legion. Their location was probably split between two or three fortresses, the closest, and likely their headquarters, being at Longthorpe, near Peterborough.

Lying just across the tribal border in Corieltauvian lands, trouble among the Iceni was very much the Ninth's concern. At a distance of about seventy-five miles by road, the legion was a three days' emergency-speed march from the colonia. News would also have sped its way to the more distant garrisons of the Second Legion at Exeter, and the Fourteenth and Twentieth Legions with Governor Paulinus in north Wales. Apart from the Ninth, they were all too far away to relieve the town, but a rebellion in the province was everyone's business.

The two hundred men, *without regular arms* sent from Londinium sound suspiciously unprepared for action. It is unlikely that fledgling London had much of a military garrison, and the men sent by Decianus smack more of regular soldiers long seconded to the procurator and no longer fully battle-accoutred, perhaps backed up by a militia of local heavies and veterans employed to keep the peace in the rowdy boomtown. These, indeed, could have been the procurator's men, *centurions and slaves*, who had recently committed the outrages against the Icenian royal house, which would lend their arrival in doomed Camulodunum an air of poetic justice.

Tacitus gives a rather confused and contradictory account of the final days, as indeed they must have seemed at the time, an unsettling fusion of dread and arrogance. On the one hand supernatural portents are tormenting the townsfolk, who are sending for armed assistance; on the other:

Trusting to the protection of the temple, hindered too by secret accomplices in the revolt, who embarrassed their plans, they had constructed neither ditch nor rampart; nor had they removed their old men and women, leaving their youth alone to face the

*foe. Surprised, as it were, in the midst of peace, they were
surrounded by an immense host of the barbarians.*[29]

Camulodunum had no defences. The city wall was built in the
decades after Boudica, and excavations have revealed that some
buildings in AD 60 had been built *over* the flattened old fortress
defences. One of these was a public building, the theatre, and the
construction of this, the temple and other brick, stone and tile
public works cost a great deal in money and labour. The local tribes
were cowed and disarmed; why waste money on a wall? Tacitus
was suitably reprimanding, with the clarity of hindsight, of course.

*It appeared no difficult matter to destroy the colony, unde-
fended as it was by fortifications, a precaution neglected by our
generals, while they thought more of what was agreeable than of
what was expedient.*[30]

All of the old soldiers would have been familiar with the story
of the fall of Rome nearly five hundred years before, when a Celtic
army surged south and entered the city, recorded in such haunting
detail by Livy at the end of the first century BC, quoted at the
beginning of this chapter.

On that occasion the Romans held out in the Citadel, the city
being sacked around them, until the Celts were bought off and
finally destroyed by a relief force. The comparison hardly needed
drawing. What the colonists needed was a place to defend, a bristling wall of swords and spears behind a defensive barrier that the
undisciplined Britons would bypass in search of easier plunder, or
might be held for a few days until the Ninth Legion could fight its
way through. The *agreeables* so disparagingly referred to by
Tacitus provided just such a site – the Temple of Claudius.

Roman temples were not always large or ostentatious, but
neither deficiency was true of the Temple of Claudius. If the
funds that could have been better spent on defences had gone
anywhere, they were most glaring in this stronghold of the imperial cult, that even Tacitus had to admit was, *a citadel of perpet-
ual tyranny*. With a podium measuring thirty-two metres long

and nearly twenty-four metres wide, this was a monstrous edifice, and at over twenty metres in height, as tall as a five- or six-storey building – taller than the surviving castle today.[31]

Gleaming white, either faced with marble, polished stone, or plastered smooth all over and painted,[32] there was nothing provincial about the Temple of Claudius; it would have been perfectly at home in the centre of Rome. Working from our knowledge of other classical temples, and the principles of the Roman architect Vitruvius, the temple would have consisted of an inner sanctum, or *cella*, windowless and with huge bronze doors, standing on a podium four metres high with steps twenty metres wide at the front; basically a vast strongbox sitting on a very high and defensible platform. Eight huge columns dominated the front aspect, each about twelve metres tall, beneath the surmounting triangular pediment.

It is impossible to overemphasise how shockingly impressive it was – the front of the United States Supreme Court building is almost identical. The Royal Exchange, at Bank junction in the City of London, is a good size and visual match. More importantly for the veterans, however, is that it was surrounded by a huge precinct; and the precinct had a wall.

We ultimately have a very good idea of what the temple complex looked like in the later city, but as ever we must be cautious about what existed in the fledgling colony of AD 60. The temple itself must have been substantially complete and active as a religious centre, for Tacitus states, *Men chosen as priests had to squander their whole fortunes under the pretence of a religious ceremonial.*[33]

We also know that by the second century there was a magnificent colonnaded walkway surrounding the sacred precinct, or *temenos*, but we are uncertain as to whether anything surrounded the temple this early – given the status of the building within, it would seem rather remiss if some sort of boundary didn't yet surround the sacred space. An altar to Roma and Augustus, probably predating the temple, also stood within,[34] so physically defining the boundary of the temenos early on would have been entirely appropriate.

If we assume, then, that the temple precinct was surrounded by *something*, the veterans would have had a ready-made defensive compound that they could bulk-up with carts, wagons, grain sacks, timber, and anything else that came to hand, measuring 150 by 164 metres. This area, about 24,600 square metres, must have been crucial in providing a haven for the local settlers. Although Tacitus clearly states that the veterans raised no major earthworks to defend the city, there is no reason to doubt that the temenos was fortified and the temple steps barricaded – such precautions could have been thrown up in the final few hours.

Population numbers for the city and surrounding territory are impossible to calculate accurately. Philip Crummy has tentatively suggested that a core of 2000 settlers, with their families and servants, would give an overall local population of about 15,000.[35] Although many might have fled (and Tacitus suggests not), it does give some indication of the numbers seeking protection within the town. As the cella (inner sanctum) of the temple itself, Crummy surmised, might have provided cramped refuge for only about 1000,[36] this wall was crucial to providing a compound upon which the defence could be based.

This is also the one part of the town where the legionary fortress defences might still have been partially intact,[37] surrounding the temple and adjoining insulas, so it is possible that this larger perimeter was initially held, or an even more extensive one, as Philip Crummy and Adam Wightman have recently suggested.[38] They have speculated that ditches partially exposed to the west of the temple, in addition to fragments of human bone in that area, might conceivably mark the site of a larger defensive compound.

This was the Colonia Victricensis. It wasn't being abandoned to a mob of natives, beaten and disarmed, a subject people little better than slaves. The very fact that the townsfolk sent for assistance rather than simply fleeing speaks volumes, and if they weren't impressed by the sorry, rag-tag militia that Catus Decianus sent them, the combined force of small local garrisons, veterans, London heavies and resident civilians, armed to the teeth with old military weapons, butcher's knives, tools and anything else that came to hand, must have convinced them that they were a match for local malcontents. Besides, they had also sent word to the Ninth Legion. They were only a three or four days' march away. They simply had to hold out until the Ninth's trumpets sounded in the distance. Then the Britunculi would run.

When Boudica's army finally came within sight of the hated town, and the Trinovantes swarmed out of the local countryside to join them, the excitement of the advancing horde must have reached fever pitch. Their direction of attack must surely have been from the northern and western arc, some following the direct line of the Pye road across the Colne, others appearing from the north-west having skirted around the boggy margins of the Stour mouth, and along the Colne Valley, swamping the modern Castle Park, St Mary's, the Dutch Quarter and the Balkerne Hill. Some must have stopped in their tracks as the theatre or temple came into view.

Most of the Iceni were farmers, from the back-end of the Fens, the chalk pastures of north Norfolk, or the heath of the Breckland. The huge theatre, the Temple of Claudius or the monumental arch of victory would cause us to stop and draw breath today – the psychological impact of them on the rural Britons cannot be overstated – it was what they were built for. It is still impressive to stand by the river at the bottom of Castle Park today and gaze up at the squat hulk of the castle silhouetted through the trees, and the temple was taller still.

The thousands crammed into the makeshift fort of the temple precinct, on the edge of the high ground, would have had a panoramic view of the assembling host. Standing today on the mound of the northern castle bailey, directly overlying the temenos wall, and gazing back across the flower beds, bandstand and playground, beyond the Cafe in the Park to the river valley beyond, it is possible to get a sense of the disbelief and resignation that settled across the little compound behind you as the sheer vastness of the horde became apparent.

The wave of sound preceding it alone must have been like a

physical assault, tens of thousands of voices raised in shout and scream and war cry, the thunderous drum of spears and sword pommels hammered against shields, ululating carnyx battle trumpets, and the simple rumble of thousands and thousands of hooves, wheels and feet. The legionary veterans of the Welsh hills must have felt the familiar cold needle of fear prick their guts again. This was no mob of local malcontents. If the Ninth Legion weren't hard on their heels, they were done for.

Camulodunum was a surprisingly big place – all of the actual centre of Colchester overlies Boudica's red layer of daub and ash; all the main shopping streets and precincts, tourist spots and pubs lie within the bounds of the early colonia. Even though the later wall covers a slightly larger area on the north and east sides, walking its circuit[39] gives a good impression of the scale of it. From the Balkerne Lane ring-road cutting in the west, to the better part of Castle Park in the east, from St Helen's Lane and Nunn's Road in the north to Sir Isaac's Walk and Eld Lane in the south, all within was destroyed by the Iceni and Trinovantes. Everything.

Even beyond those boundaries are isolated areas of destruction; buildings outside the Balkerne Gate, where the St Mary's multi-storey car park now stands, were destroyed in the same frenzy of violence. The industrial complex at Sheepen was torched. The only places where the destruction layer is not found are spots that were uninhabited, such as allotments, or those comprehensively cleaned up afterwards, like the temple precinct. But every square foot within the old city is a suitable spot to stop and contemplate what happened that day, and what evidence of it might yet lie undiscovered beneath your feet.

From the 1960s Colchester was much redeveloped, allowing archaeologists an unprecedented doorway into that ancient past. Back along the High Street, the Lion Walk shopping area lies above one of those excavations. The archaeology here spanned the entire Roman occupation of the city, but the earliest layers exposed a substantial north–south ditch and rampart, which had already been built over by the time of Boudica's attack. At last archaeologists had located the long-hunted fortress of the Twentieth Legion spoken of by Tacitus, and with it the opportunity to explore its transition into the first colonia.

The excavations revealed that the veterans didn't flatten all the fortress buildings and start again from scratch but, being soldiers who were familiar and comfortable with military buildings, demolished some of the starkly utilitarian structures such as cramped legionary barrack blocks, but kept the more spacious and desirable centurions' quarters as houses, as well as raising new builds around them.

As already noted, they made no attempt to maintain the fortifications, not only neglecting them, but actively levelling and building over them.[40] These men who would instinctively have one eye on their security, never before having slept without watchful sentries pacing the catwalks and guarding the gates at night, clearly felt as unthreatened in this conquered territory as it was possible to feel.

There were undeniably some marvellous discoveries at Lion Walk and neighbouring Culver Street, but the houses destroyed by Boudica mostly contained very little, a theme continued across the city. Logically this grates a little; after all, this was a place destroyed in one fell swoop, like Pompeii. The buried houses should each emerge like a muddy *Marie Celeste*, with the dinner table still set, as it were, but of course the Romans knew the Iceni were coming many days in advance, and if truth be told, the people of Pompeii were hardly taken by surprise either.[41]

This lack of household items is sometimes taken to reflect the Britons comprehensively looting the place before its destruction, perhaps true of small portable goods, but certainly not of furniture and larger items. A flood of refugees fleeing with all their worldly goods is more likely, but this does not necessarily equate to an evacuation of the city, merely that the inhabitants, practical people, were dragging their most prized and useful possessions to the safety of the temple precinct. Even if the Britons bypassed the defensive compound, they would surely sack the city, and there was no point leaving anything of worth to be destroyed. In addition is the simple fact that wood and other organic items would only survive if carbonised, not if comprehensively consumed by flames and turned to ash.

One remarkable exception to these negative circumstances is the bed mentioned earlier, carbonised and preserved at Lion Walk. This survived tucked into the corner of a room in a building that had daub walls and a tiled roof. The house lay alongside an east–west street, around three sides of a gravelled yard. The interior walls were plastered and painted with a red, mock marble effect.[42]

The bed, or possibly couch, consisted of two rectangular mattresses resting on the floor, with the possible remains of a timber and rope frame. The mattresses were covered in a two-over-two diamond twill, and although after 1900 years in the soil they were less than an inch thick, prior to burning they would have been considerably plumper, and probably stuffed with wool. At least two plain-weave woollen blankets were also present.[43]

The bed was a remarkable survivor. A little more oxygen and the whole heap would have been consumed by the flames, to be represented by no more than an indecipherable smear of ash; even Pompeii has little to offer in the way of soft furnishings.[44] It is chilling to speculate that this may have been the last resting place of someone the night before the attack who didn't seek the safety of the defensive compound, choosing instead to hide in the maze of yards, alleyways and cubbyhole rooms of the abandoned town; for such a portable bedroll would surely otherwise have been carried to the temple precinct, rather than its owner spending the duration of the siege with nothing but a cloak to sleep on.

In addition to furniture and household items, the other notable deficiency of these excavations, and all other Boudican war deposits, which has long perplexed archaeologists, is the lack of associated bodies. Human remains are found incredibly rarely within these destruction layers.

The reasons for this may well be different in each location, but in Colchester I believe that it confirms a simple fact – the colonists of Camulodunum and their families were not cowering in their houses or running around panicked in the streets when the rebels arrived. They had gathered themselves in a defensive work anchored upon the Temple of Claudius, and inadvertently concentrated their corpses where they could be found and disposed of, rather than hunting them out of all those burnt and collapsed buildings, where many would inevitably have been missed.

In 1966, the city's principal excavator at the time, Rosalind Dunnett, discovered one such missed body, the charred remains of a disarticulated human skeleton off West Stockwell Street, lying beneath the destruction layer on the clay floor of a verandah fronting onto the main north–south street.[45] More recently, fragments of human bone have been recovered from along High Street, associated with the same Roman thoroughfare, as well as south of the temple site, but they amount, at most, to a few individuals preserved in scraps and fragments.

These chance finds demonstrate that others still await discovery, and many more would inevitably have been discovered and dealt with during the reconstruction of the town, but none at all have yet been found in the western or southern halves of the settlement, suggesting a concentration in the north-eastern quarter dominated by the temple.[46]

Walking through Red Lion Yard, I emerge into the Lion Walk shopping area. It is difficult to get any sense of location within the precinct and shops. The house with the carbonised bed seemingly lay off to my right, directly beneath Culver Walk, beside Clinton's Cards, with the street it fronted running below the Culver Walk end of Marks and Spencer, WH Smith and Topman, but this is one of those rare places where little of the past lingers around the concrete and red brick.

I pause (conspicuously, it feels) somewhere close to where the lone fugitive or small family group spent their final night huddled on the mattress in the corner of the little room, and I can visualise the layout of buildings and streets below me, but there is little left down there, bulldozed away and concreted over. I carry on, weaving through the maze of streets to the Culver Square shopping area, the site of another large excavation in the 1980s.

If anything, Culver Square seems even more bereft of its past than Lion Walk. The fortress buildings lay in parallel rows running directly across the square beneath Debenhams, H&M and HMV, the converted centurions' quarters of AD 60 beneath the square itself, but they too are long gone now, along with the souls who once inhabited them. I wander into a few shops, in search of a lower ground floor that would at least take me down to the physical level of the Roman city, in vain.

Large exposures of the ancient city are rare now, but smaller holes associated with the redevelopment of individual buildings are occasionally opened, and can be every bit as dramatic. Like a torch beam shining down into the gloom, each of these excavations enables a glimpse of the city that existed the day Boudica came to eradicate it.

One of those little windows, a tragic, frozen snapshot, was opened by the Colchester Archaeological Trust in 2014 during the redevelopment of the old Williams and Griffin department store on High Street as the new flagship Fenwick store. Three trenches were opened in areas where destruction of the archaeological deposits was unavoidable.[47] All revealed the Boudican destruction layer, but two contained that most elusive artefact of the war – human bone. The first pieces to emerge, a mandible and the proximal end of a tibia, both from men, were in a layer of destruction material that had been scraped from a nearby building during the reconstruction of the town.

Isotopic analysis of the mandible suggests a European origin for the individual, perhaps from eastern France or northern Germany.[48] If further proof were needed that they represent victims of Boudica, both bore damage inflicted by sharp weapons, one a stab or slash to the face, the other a heavy slash to the knee. Another trench, excavated to allow for the construction of an escalator, yielded a radius and fibula, from the lower arm and leg respectively, the first from an adult, the second, showing cut marks by a sword or spear, from a teenage kid of twelve to fourteen years.[49]

The final trench was being excavated to allow for the intrusion of an elevator shaft, uncovering the floor of a building with its wall still standing as high as sixty centimetres, of burnt daub blocks scored with a chevron pattern, with a thick layer of destruction material sealing it all.[50] Peeling away this layer of ash and collapsed daub to reveal the floor is about as close as any archaeologist can get to revisiting the day of the attack – whatever lies beneath is what existed in the building at the time.

The room so partially exposed was probably a kitchen. Up on the wall had been an oak shelf, almost three metres long, and as the room burned it ignited and fell to the floor against the wall, where it still lay. Scattered on and around it were the carbonised foodstuffs and culinary herbs that had been stored on it. Dates, peas, lentils, oats and grapes were littered with dill, coriander, caraway, mustard, fennel and fenugreek,[51] all blackened, some in the remains of a carved fruitwood platter. Pieces of charred textile represented food bags.

Glass and ceramic tableware, inkwells, and pieces of broken lamps and bronze vessels were found in the room, along with a collection of Egyptian blue pigment balls from Italy for making paint; a burnt and broken fragment of a small, six-sided bone dice; the remains of a pair of hobnailed sandals. These are the seemingly mundane everyday details of people's lives that bring home to us the tragedy of what happened – someone's kitchen; the contents of their shelf; the food they would have eaten; the new paint for redecorating; family games; the shoes by the door.

Imagine your own home incinerated and flattened in a catastrophe that wiped out your family, and then built over, and two thousand years hence someone digging a shaft down through the layers to alight on your kitchen floor, or your living room; what might they find? They could be lucky and dig straight down onto a collection of eclectic keepsakes that would tell them something about you; they'd be much more likely to hit empty floorspace and a coffee mug, the sofa, the kitchen cupboard, or the drawer where you keep the plastic carrier bags.

Two days before the end of the excavation, the floor of the house had a final secret to reveal, which would offer an unprecedented glimpse into the lives of a single family caught up in the turmoil of Boudica's war. A tiny hole barely a few inches across had been hurriedly scraped into the floor, and into it had been placed a bag, perhaps of leather. Inside the bag was a small jewellery box, or *pyxis*, a beautiful little thing originally, of wooden construction with rounded corners, encased in sheet silver and with turned ivory feet, containing two pairs of earrings and five finger-rings, all of solid gold, a bronze medallion, a silver coin, and a tiny glass intaglio. Beside the box was a small bag of coins, and the most exquisite collection of gold and silver jewellery.

The hole had been sealed by the destruction layer, and clearly represented something that had previously been conspicuous by its absence in the archaeological record – a hoard of valuables buried for safekeeping before the Britons attacked and never recovered by the ill-fated owners.[52]

The small hoard was lifted from the site as a solid block of earth for examination in the laboratory, where careful excavation and conservation could be carried out together. The pyxis, of which little wood survived, was represented by the paper-thin silver sheet that covered it, which now consisted almost entirely of corrosion and looked like a 'stiff black tissue'.[53] The gold had survived almost perfectly, as gold does, but corrosion from other items had adhered to it and needed removing. The silver items had fared much worse, having corroded terribly, but still very much identifiable.

It seems that men favoured silver jewellery in this period,[54] and the character of the items backs this up: the gold objects being particularly feminine, and the silver ones male. It is this obvious separation of the hoard into two distinct groups that begins the story, and the individual items within them that tell it.

The female set consists of five very similar finger-rings, each of gold, three set with pieces of emerald, one with its setting lost, and the other with an incised dolphin decoration. Two sets of earrings, for pierced ears, have s-shaped hooks for security, one a pair of hollow gold balls, the other of pearls on gold pendants hanging from a crosspiece. These were known as *crotalia*, or rattles, as the pearls were meant to click pleasingly together as the head moved.[55]

There were also three bracelets, all made of thick gold wire. One, with an expanding knotted clasp, would have been worn on the wrist, but the others, a matching pair, of an interwoven, open-work design of repeated figure eights, would have been worn on the upper arms. Parallels for this jewellery assemblage are well represented from Pompeii and the Vesuvius region, destroyed less than twenty years later, and all are likely to be of European or Italian manufacture.

Of the male collection, the least visually impressive is a bronze medallion, of a type known as a *bulla*, associated with a silver chain. This was a protective amulet worn by Roman boys that was taken off when coming of age at sixteen. Whoever it belonged to had a relatively humble background, as wealthier families might have *bullae* made of precious metal. Either way, it was a keepsake that a man would retain throughout his life, and might even wear again at particular ceremonies.[56]

A glass intaglio, or seal stone, had the image of a panther etched on the surface, an older piece that was presumably an heirloom or keepsake. Two chunky silver bracelets are of a type associated with military awards granted during the conquest of southern Britain, called *armillae*. A large armlet, or torc, also of silver, could have been worn on the upper arm or suspended from chest armour,[57] and was decorated with a hunting scene involving a mounted man riding down panthers and stags, and Jupiter seated between Fortuna and Victory.

Once more, the suggestion is that this was also a military award, perhaps for a specific deed, and the representation of the panthers is particularly interesting, as this animal was also present on the loose intaglio. Finds specialist Nina Crummy has speculated whether this hints at his having earned the cognomen, or nickname, *Panthera* during his military career.[58]

So what story is being told here? This was clearly the property of a man and a woman, more specifically a husband and wife. The relationship between the two is suggested by the fact that his precious amulet, military awards, and heirloom intaglio of the panther, share the intimate internal space of the precious little pyxis box with her earrings and ring collection – these most precious and personal of objects were instinctively kept together.

The man was a veteran of the army, the archetypal colonist of Colonia Victricensis in AD 60, had fought in the invasion of Britannia and been awarded for his bravery. At some point in the previous eleven years he had completed his service and been pensioned off.

He would most likely be middle-aged rather than elderly, and he had either made some money from the spoils of war, or thrived as a colonist, for he had soon married and was able to provide his wife with expensive jewellery of the latest fashions, despite the fact that his own origins were humble enough, evident in his bronze bulla, which he proudly retained. We can speculate that this simple amulet belonged to him rather than a son of his own, firstly because any son would likely be younger than sixteen and would still be wearing his, and, like his parents, might be ostentatiously sporting something fashioned of precious metal.

Having been decorated for conspicuous bravery, the veteran would have held a position of respect and unofficial authority among his peers, a status that would have survived his transition to a colonist in military-drawn settler society, perhaps accounting for his relative wealth. As such, it is difficult to believe that this was a man who would have abandoned the city and his former comrades, but was instead active in the defence to come.

There are no artefacts relating to children, although it is reasonable to assume that there may have been some, all below the age of ten, but in a small exposure of kitchen, and the hurriedly buried material wealth of the family, they remain invisible, as our own might under similar circumstances.

Wrapping the little silver box, bracelets, armlets and coins gently in a bag of soft leather, the veteran scooped a hole into the sandy clay floor and buried the precious parcel. Smoothing over the hole and making sure no trace of it survived, he pushed a large chest or trunk over the disturbance to hide it completely, attested to by a group of bronze and iron fittings found overlying the hole.[59] Abandoning his home, the old soldier shepherded his family directly along the side streets towards the theatre and temple, a route now entirely built over, to the gathering populace in the bastion of the temple temenos, where he would assist building the barricades whilst his wife and children mounted the temple steps.

They would wait on the podium with the other women and children gathering there, surrounded by amphorae and barrels of water being piled beside sacks and baskets of grain, bread and meat. All we truly know is that no one from the little family group ever returned to retrieve their keepsakes.

The circumstances of this hastily buried treasure were vividly and dramatically re-enacted for Professor Alice Roberts to tell the story in the BBC documentary series *The Celts: Blood, Iron and Sacrifice* in 2015. It shows a lone woman, the veteran's wife, frantically collecting the treasure, removing jewellery with trembling hands, and thrusting them into the hole, her executioner with firebrand and trailing sword entering the room just as she has smoothed over the evidence.

In this version, she doesn't reach the temporary sanctuary of the temple compound; she has left the evacuation of her home too late. With the scattered human bones collected from the other Fenwick trenches, either scenario is possible. Some must have taken the risk of sheltering in their homes or the alleyways – the newly discovered human bones suggest that they did, but why they chose that fate instead of the comradeship and resistance of the temple is beyond the scope of archaeology to tell us. Within the limited exposure of this veteran's house, at least, no human remains were found.

The Fenwick treasure, in all its enigmatic beauty, is on permanent display in the nearby Castle Museum. Of the site itself, nothing is now visible. If you walk into the busy retail brightness of Fenwick's department store from High Street and veer to the right side of the shop until you find the lift in the corner of Men's Formalwear, you are standing above the archaeological trench where the Fenwick hoard was found. Sadly, the lift does not go down here, at least for members of the public, and there is a small sign, both above and below the buttons within the lift, specifically to scotch the plans of the hopeful time traveller: *THIS LIFT DOES NOT GO TO LOWER GROUND.*

It should. If you could press a button marked *LG*, or even *AD 60*, you would descend directly into the house of the legionary veteran and his family, precisely on to the spot where that hole was frantically dug into the floor as the Iceni approached, perhaps the very morning of the attack, and those precious keepsakes – the embodiment of the family encapsulated in the little silver, wood and ivory box – placed inside.

Instead you must turn around and take the escalator down, where, directly below the gliding metal steps, the hacked bones of slaughtered Romans were recovered on the main north–south road of the town, which continued away ahead of you with gutted buildings to either side; on reaching the lower ground floor, to your right-front, the veteran's house lay a few metres beyond the curving wall in the Luggage department.

Finally, like the veteran and his family themselves, I must make my way along the bustling streets to the Temple of Claudius. My first stop lies just outside the gates of Castle Park on the little street of Castle Bailey, a cafe called Claudius Gateway. The view directly out of the large doors and windows, or from the tables outside, is of the castle fifty metres away, and it has within it a very special exhibit.

If you wish to take coffee first, there is a computer animation that places the coffee shop and yourself all together within the greater reconstruction of the temple complex, a truly awesome *from where you stand now* heritage picture board for the twenty-first century, and behind, in the exhibit room, is a larger version of the same with audio commentary. What lies within is the monumental arcade that fronted the temple complex, or what remains of it, preserved beneath a glass floor.

The small exhibition centre has three large, glass floor panels allowing a view through to the archaeological remains about a metre below your feet. What you can see are the bases of the wall and columns of the arcade at the very front of the temple complex.

When this section of the arcade was excavated in 2012, the excavator felt that the surviving temenos walls overlying the foundations were 'probably' constructed after Boudica,[60] as had previous investigators.[61] What we can speculate, if the interpretation of defending the entire temple precinct like a fort is correct, is that these remains in the cafe represent the exact location of the desperately contested line of defence in AD 60, whether or not they themselves existed by that time.

The perimeter of the temple compound is easy to visualise, delineated as it is now, in the vaguest possible way, by the buildings and earthworks that surround the castle. The buildings of Bailey Walk represent the southern extent in somewhat skewed form, from Museum Street to just beyond the War Memorial at the edge of the park. The western line lies beneath the concrete Methodist church and Ryegate Road. The northern line runs along the huge wooded earth bank of the castle defences, beneath which the temenos wall survives to the height of three metres,[62] and can be seen protruding from the western end of it, and likewise runs beneath the partial rampart to the east.

If my imagining of the final stand of the colonists has the faintest glimmer of truth in it, this was the Cawnpore entrenchment or Alamo of AD 60, a short, impromptu and desperate defence, where the outlook was bleak indeed unless a relief force could fight its way through.

The castle that stands before you is Norman, built by Eudo Dapifer, a baron of William the Bastard, and completed by 1100. In its original form it was considerably more impressive than it stands today, probably the earliest, and certainly the largest stone keep the Normans built in Britain, of which the present form is simply the last in a long process of evolution, decline and regeneration. The castle is built mostly of reused Roman building material, and much of it must derive from the ruins of the temple itself.

The podium of the Temple of Claudius lies entirely within the castle, encased by it, and proportionately smaller – the Roman podium lies approximately five metres inside the external base of the walls. Effectively, the ground floor of the castle is the floor of the Temple of Claudius, equating pretty much exactly in both size and height to the podium and its inner sanctum, the cella. In the sense of physical proximity, there is really nowhere else, in Colchester or the rest of Britain, where you can rub shoulders with the participants of Boudica's war quite so intimately, or with so vivid a mental reconstruction of what they went through.

Standing before the castle, the main doorway is approached by a wooden footbridge that crosses over the excavated remains of stone buildings, which are Saxon in date and do not concern us. However, the hollow in which they sit does get us a little closer to the Roman level of the town and pausing there is the best way to get a sense of where the temple podium lies in relation to the castle superstructure.

When I descend into the hollow, I am standing about a metre above the old Roman ground surface of the temple precinct, which means that if I sit with my bum on the floor, my head height will be about the same as that of a Roman standing in front of the temple steps. In front of me would have been those steps, about twenty metres wide and four metres high,[63] the speculated line of which was recorded during excavations in 1932.[64]

At some point during Boudica's attack, the barricades along the precinct edge must have been breached and Britons flooded the compound. There is no historical account of this fight, beyond Tacitus's dark observation that *the temple where the soldiers had assembled was stormed after a two day's siege,* but the stiff resistance of the temple precinct must have disintegrated into panic and massacre as combatants and non-combatants alike surged in chaos towards the safety of the temple platform, intermingled with the rush of Britons.

The natural bottleneck of the temple steps, and any makeshift barricade between the columns at the top, would have made the podium all but impregnable for a time to both fugitives and Britons alike, but the steps were the weak spot, the only access to the temple platform, which stood higher than two men as a sheer face for the other three sides.

However long the Britons had been held at the edge of the precinct, the fight for the temple steps must have been the bitterest contest. Slogging it out hand-to-hand at the barricades was brutally exhausting work, and the men would have taken it in turns to fight before retiring to recover whilst fresh men took their place, a military practice that the veterans would hardly have discarded in this moment of crisis. It is a testament to the spirit and single-mindedness of the British warriors that they persisted in the attack rather than slinking away, as the Romans had hoped, in search of plunder and easier targets, for the stairway must have been a death-trap until the barricade was finally forced, heaped with bodies, slick with blood, and with an impenetrable wall of deadly iron blades at the top.

The line of this second stand – and for all the speculative detail of this battle, it is almost inconceivable that the top of this stairway was not the line of the determined final stand – now lies within the entrance to the castle. Passing through the entrance passage, I enter a wider hallway with arches to the right contain-ing the castle well, and a caged area securing the stairs to the Vaults.

I am now standing exactly at the top of the temple steps, at the extreme left-hand corner of them, and on the same floor level as the podium. Running from left to right through the caged area is the approximate line held by those last, weary defenders between the great columns of the temple facade, continuing through the wall and the rooms behind it. From this point onwards to the reception desk, much of it now occupied by masonry, was the exposed third of the podium, the *pronaos*, effectively the temple porch, crammed with men awaiting their turn at the barricade, amidst the overflow of women and children from the cella and those that had clawed their way to safety in the running retreat.

As I approach the friendly member of staff to purchase my ticket at the reception desk, the front wall of the cella, that inner sanctum, passed straight through the desk in front of me, through the middle of the shop, and on into the Civil War siege displays. Beyond the wall of the shop, where the books are displayed, is a small room reserved for Staff Only; therein lay the lock and key to the final act of the tragedy – the huge, double doors of the cella.

Here in the shop, among the keyrings, fridge magnets and plas-tic toy legionary weapons, were the final dozen or so exhausted and bleeding men, forced from the top of the stairs, huddled in the shadow of the bolted bronze doors, gripping blunted swords and broken spears, with a handful of surviving women and kids behind them; all but silent now, those crammed inside the cella long deaf to the beseeching cries for sanctuary from without.

The Vaults beneath the castle, the hollowed-out underside of the temple foundations, are accessed by purchasing a ticket at recep-tion and joining the next available tour. Your guide will unlock the gate of the caged area at the castle entrance, and lead you

down twenty or so steps into the first chamber. There were originally four chambers in total, the underground layout now confused
by low passages hacked through the Roman concrete, and the
addition of supporting walls in more recent times, but the stairs
lead you into the left hand of the two smaller front chambers.

Above this space was the *pronaos*, the unenclosed third of the
podium; above the larger chambers was the cella. A wall with a
small, brick-lined doorway ahead is the weight-bearing foundation for the doors and front wall of the cella that lay directly above
it, now occupied by the shop.

Although this was a physical space not occupied by the Romans
– the chambers where you walk were solid sand, later dug out in
more recent centuries – this is the last, unadulterated presence of
the Temple of Claudius. Passing through into the second chamber, I press my hand against the startlingly rough mortar, the
foundation for the front cella wall, knowing that it once trembled
as the great bronze doors above it were smashed from their hinges.
That knowledge lends this simple act an extraordinary sensation
of connection with that single moment nearly two thousand years
ago; this mortar and stone actually reverberated as the doors were
felled, and it all looks as crisp and fresh as if it was laid last year.

There are rare places in this journey through Boudica's world
where the passing of time seems halting, drunk and confused, and
nowhere more so than here. If you are the sort of person who can
suspend disbelief for even a moment, it sometimes feels as if Time
itself has held its breath down here; but don't linger too long.
Once you have played through your mind exactly what happened
here, two thousand years is quite close enough.

Back in the world above, I pass through the ground floor exhibits, where the cella once stood, through the noise and chaos of a
school visit, and climb the stairs to the mezzanine gallery. I weave
through the corner of a mock Iron Age roundhouse, and past the
priceless exhibits of Celtic and Roman artefacts. I subconsciously
nod greetings to centurion Marcus Favonius Facilis and trooper
Longinus Sdapezi, whose magnificent tombstones loom over me

as I walk, both long suspected to have been toppled over by Boudica's warriors on the day of the attack. The far end of the mezzanine holds the artefacts to which I am drawn.

There are two cabinets here, each a glass cenotaph for the dead of Camulodunum – *kenos taphos* – empty tomb. We might not have the bodies of the dead, but we have their things; their memories. One cabinet contains a selection of the tragic detritus of Boudica's attack: burnt samian pottery; a section of orange daub wall, petrified by the heat of the firestorm; the crumbling fragments of a legionary helmet; melted glass; black, carbonised foodstuffs; coins; domestic items. This is a representative selection of the possessions and material culture of the colonists that was scattered, smashed and burnt in the attack.

There is nothing particularly precious here, the normal physical residue of everyday life, and the sight of it all drums home quite how long two thousand years is. The iron is brown, blistered and shedding; the copper and bronze a deep, time-worn green. The designs are pretty and classical, but grating and alien for all of that. A large bowl of fire-blackened samian pottery is of a size and shape I would unhesitatingly serve salad from at home, but the raised decoration is wrenchingly ancient.

These artefacts somehow connect us with the event at the same time as reinforcing the distance, just as the awkwardness of the modernity surrounding the Balkerne Gate inspires a sense of temporal vertigo. If each year separating me from Boudica's war was represented by a single metre, I would be standing on a cliff practically two kilometres high; I simply make the mistake of looking down. The burnt dates, plums and grain are perfect survivors, but their black, ashy surface betrays their raw antiquity. After the immediacy of the Vaults, there is something almost shocking, and certainly sobering, in the realisation that it all happened so long ago; panic that even attempting to get to the bottom of such remote events is pointless and meaningless. The antidote lies in the cabinet to my left.

With the reopening of the museum in 2014 after its extensive revamp, the Fenwick treasure, found the same year, could almost have been excavated to order as the exciting new exhibit; it is undeniably the star of the show. The tragic little hoard of the veteran and his wife is beautifully displayed. There are reminders here too of the passing of the millennia; the silver is a dusty grey, composed mostly now of corrosion, and the bronze bulla amulet is an almost unrecognisable blob of green verdigris, but the silver armband still reveals the running panthers, and it is possible to imagine the bulla hanging by its crumbling suspension loop to the silver chain.

But the gold is timeless, almost a product of yesterday, perfect and shining and modern. The earrings, apart from the degraded pearls, could sit on any dressing table. There is no woman alive who would consider the dangling pearls, the little golden orbs, the bracelet or gold wire armbands incongruous or dated. The finger rings would be every bit as desirable now as they were then. As a group, it is difficult to believe that the scent of lavender or rose-water no longer lingers around them.

Back downstairs in the shop, where the final, weary defence of the cella doors played out, another cabinet displays the Fenwick treasure, but this time the pieces are for sale. They are reproductions of the original golden pieces, constructed of gold-plated silver. I am helpless, and Clare now wears a pair of the beautiful little pearl crotalia earrings.

I make my way back to the main displays of the ground floor, within the footprint of the cella. One common interpretation of how the Britons broke into the temple is that they burnt the building to the ground, heaping wood around it, and destroying it utterly. This view seems to rest upon the fact that Tacitus tells us the temple garrison withstood the Britons for two days, and the architectural fact that the cella was relatively impregnable, but Tacitus doesn't mention fire, and however strong the bronze doors and hinges were, they certainly weren't designed to resist the repeated pounding of a battering ram. This was a temple, not a fort.

I would suggest that *the temple was stormed after a two days' siege* refers not to inside the cella, but to the temple complex as a whole, including the temenos and any upstanding wall that formed the basis of the makeshift redoubt; at the very least, it means the external podium of the temple. I reject any suggestion that the veterans simply hid in a box where they couldn't fight back and were roasted or smoked out after two days.

On the contrary, Tacitus would expect his audience to know that this was the very last, emasculating, unutterably shameful thing a group of Roman legionary veterans would do, and his reference to a two-day siege is meant to impress upon us just how determined a stand the small group of old stalwarts made. There can be little doubt that it was the non-combatants, the old, the sick, the women, the children, and those wounded early in the fighting, who found themselves utterly defenceless in the stifling black hole of the cella.

The Romans could ultimately have been smoked out of the temple by building a great fire against the doors, but I see no reason to speculate anything more imaginative or complex on the part of the Britons than battering rams, of local trees felled for the task, or constructed from the limitless building material of the town before it was fired. The cella may have been a strongbox on a fighting platform, but once the defenders of that platform were dead, and the Britons had complete access to the exterior, the obvious point of weakness was the doors. However formidable those great sheets of bronze may have looked, they surely couldn't have held the seething horde out for two days unless they made no serious attempt to get in.

However it happened, by heat and smoke, or battering the great doors from their hinges, the only place to visualise this tragedy is on the ground floor of the castle, beneath the great open space of the mezzanine galleries above.

This is not a place that you have to imagine the events happening *somewhere in the vicinity*, or metres beneath your feet. It was exactly here, on the same floor level, that the temple stood, and its physical make-up surrounds you, reused in the walls of the castle. If you could see back to that moment, the inhabitants of Camulodunum would be standing beside you; as you wander through the displays on the ground floor of the museum, of medieval pottery and a scale model of the Norman keep, you are walking among their shadows.

It was here that the many hundreds of terrified women, children, elderly and wounded crowded together in the terrible unreality of the windowless cella, barricaded behind the bronze doors, illuminated by the flickering light of a hundred guttering oil lamps, a thousand pairs of lungs heaving for the same almost unbreathable air. The owner of the Fenwick armbands and jewellery was undoubtedly in here, perhaps sheltering any children she had behind the meagre defence of her own body, frantic that her husband had never returned from the fight for the podium, which had clearly now been lost. The sole mercy was that the purgatory couldn't last. The defence was over.

Those final moments in the fetid, suffocating darkness, as the crammed hundreds waited for the bolts of the door to give way with the next reverberating blow, shaking the very foundations beneath, are beyond imagining. All hope was gone now. The pleas for assistance had gone out long days before, and for long days they had waited, and held the precinct, then the podium, and now the cella. But no help had come, and they could hold no longer, for there was no one left to man the doorway; the able-bodied men were dead, almost to the last.

Their only real hope had been the Ninth Legion, many miles north on the edge of the bleak flats of the fenland. Had the Ninth even marched? Surely they could have reached Camulodunum by now? Perhaps they had their own war to fight in the sodden marshes; perhaps they hadn't dared leave their fortress.

The Ninth never marched!

But the Ninth had.

4

Paths of Glory

The Game's Afoot

> *To the Legion of the lost ones,*
> *To the Cohort of the damned . . .*
> Rudyard Kipling, *Gentlemen Rankers*

I don't do golf. To me, it is a mysterious, tribal, almost Masonic pastime, which takes normal, respectable middle-aged people and turns them into garishly attired obsessives with their own secret language, peppering conversations with pars, double eagles, birdies, *bogeys* and *stymies*; they speak in tongues. There is something cult-like about it. But glasshouses and stones and all that, I retrace the footsteps of dead people and like nothing better than to sit down with a report detailing the stomach contents of ancient bog bodies. I'm really not in a position to criticise anyone else's hobby.

So why, oh, why, on this blustery autumn afternoon, am I standing on Thorpe Wood Golf Course on the outskirts of Peterborough with my fellow archaeologist and brother-in-law Jonny, clutching a 9 iron, a scorecard and a little luminescent ball? Well, Petilius Cerialis and his Legio IX Hispana, better known as the Ninth Legion, have something to do with it.

The Ninth is surely the most famous Roman legion of them all, due in no small part to Rosemary Sutcliff's wonderful 1954 children's novel *The Eagle of the Ninth*, based around the legion's mysterious disappearance in the savage tribal mists of Caledonia in Scotland. The tale follows the journey of Marcus Flavius Aquila, whose father was a centurion in the Ninth when it disappeared twelve years before, as he hunts for their lost eagle standard and the true fate of the legion.

My dad bought me a copy of the book when I was about ten, the 1980 Puffin paperback edition, still in remarkably good shape, considering. Because, of course, I read the book a hundred times, haunted by the fate of the missing legion, and waiting for the moment I could become an archaeologist and, like Marcus Aquila, head off in search of the Ninth myself. Except that nothing could be further from the truth. I was far, far too idle to read the book as a child, although I have done justice to Dad's kind purchase now, alas, too late to discuss it with him.

Sutcliff's book, however, is set about sixty years after Boudica's war, in the second century, and in the northernmost corner of Britain. In AD 60 the Ninth Legion, or a good portion of it, was probably here on this Cambridgeshire golf course.

Relating the tale of Colchester, Tacitus tells us: *Petilius Cerialis, commander of the ninth legion, was coming to the rescue.* Crucially, although he tells us exactly where the Ninth were marching *to*, he does not tell us where they were marching *from*. We know that the Ninth Legion garrisoned the eastern side of the country, based on associated finds and the tombstones of its soldiers. These link them securely with Lincoln (Lindum), probably in the AD 50s and 60s, which has often been suggested as the base from where they might have marched.

But another military site was occupied at this time in the Ninth's jurisdiction, much closer to the events of the south-east. It was a type of fortification known as a vexillation fortress, on the edge of the Fens a couple of miles west of Peterborough, at a place called Longthorpe. A vexillation was a detachment operating away from the remainder of its legion, often mixed with auxiliary units. We know that Cerialis marched with only a part of his legion, for in a later passage Tacitus hints that he had with him no more than two thousand legionaries – less than half the strength of a legion.[1]

Longthorpe fortress was discovered in 1961, appearing to a pilot as a crisp, unmistakable cropmark. Aerial photographs showed the double line of the defensive ditches like a draughtsman's architectural plan, so parallel and straight, the playing-card curves of the corners so perfect, that a layman might have written them off as modern, machine-dug pipe-trenches. The ditches enclosed a rectangular area of about twenty-seven acres.

Excavations were conducted between 1967 and 1973 by Professors Sheppard Frere and Kenneth St Joseph,[2] whilst a separate project uncovered an associated military works depot.[3] The fortress was founded in the AD 40s, perhaps in the aftermath of the first Iceni revolt of 47, and occupied until after the Boudican mopping-up operations, sometime in the early AD 60s. During this pivotal period, Longthorpe was a strategically important garrison. It lay hard against the bank of the navigable River Nene, and close to the junction of the major roads of Ermine Street and King Street, and the Fen Causeway, the only major route east across the military nightmare of the Fens, possibly still an island-hopping native trackway at this time.

The fortress lay bang in between the Iceni and their suspected partners in crime in AD 47, the Corieltauvi, and occupied a presumably sensitive tribal borderland between those two and the Catuvellauni. With the south-east pacified and settled, Longthorpe provided its closest major garrison, whilst still covering the east and Midlands.

The fortress would have been impressive and highly visible in that flat country, deliberately intimidating and awe-inspiring. The double ditches encompassing the ramparts were three metres wide and two metres deep, backed by a turf rampart three metres high. This formidable obstacle was topped with a timber palisade, and double-storeyed gatehouses more than seven metres tall on each wall. Numerous buildings were recorded within the fortress, including both legionary and auxiliary barrack blocks, and a granary. The unusual centurions' quarters suggested the presence of the prestigious First Cohort, perhaps a double-sized unit by this period.[4]

The excavators surmised that the garrison would not have exceeded 2800 men, perhaps consisting of up to 1760 legionaries and 1000 or so auxiliaries, at least a sizeable portion of which would have been cavalry. The artefact assemblage reflected all this superbly, with many fragments of legionary armour as well as parts of a cavalry parade helmet, shield, and horse fittings. However we juggle the numbers, it all fits seductively well with Tacitus.

The excavations opened vivid little windows on the daily life of the garrison. Fragments of imported amphorae witness the presence of wine and olive oil, but suggest supplies were limited, so lower ranks probably drank local beer. There were also vessels for *garum*, the decomposing sea-food sauce to which the Romans were addicted. In addition to rations of bread and flour, attested to by the granary, the bones of ox, sheep and pig were found in abundance, supplemented by small birds and wildfowl, red deer and hare which, in addition to several dog burials, tells us the garrison enjoyed its hunting.

Many pieces of perforated pottery represent cheese presses, which must have made a hugely welcome addition to the monotonous bread and meat. A tiny number of fish bones all came from marine species, but someone in the garrison spent their off-duty hours daydreaming on the banks of the Nene with a rod and line, as evidenced by a perfect little barbed bronze fish hook.[5]

Fortunately, with the expansion of Peterborough the fortress site was not altogether lost. It was incorporated into the Nene Park, an area of countryside, rather than being developed for housing, and now lies beneath the golf course where Jonny and I are annoying the real golfers with our painfully slow progress.

Longthorpe cannot have been a popular posting. Remote and alone, the local town of Durobrivae had yet to be built, no more than a small satellite fort and a few native huts at this time.[6] Though providing opportunities for trade, the presence of the garrison would have been a mixed blessing to the locals. It is estimated that filling the granaries would have required the entire harvest of three square miles of arable land, which must have had a significant impact locally, even if some of the need was met from elsewhere.[7] This would be acquired in part payment of tax or bought from the locals, but it would be a compulsory purchase, and the soldiers' idea of a fair price might have differed greatly to the farmers'.[8]

Tacitus specifically mentions this issue in the *Agricola*:

He lightened the exaction of corn and tribute by an equal distribution of the burden, while he got rid of those contrivances for gain which were more intolerable than the tribute itself.[9]

Such abuse was real enough – a bronze grain measure from Hadrian's Wall exceeded its stated capacity by 20 per cent in order to fleece the locals.[10] Agricola clearly knew what has recently been deduced by archaeologists, that the grain supply for the army need not have been at all onerous for native farmers to supply, so long as the burden was evenly spread.[11]

For whatever reason, it seems no native shanty grew up near the ramparts to service the needs of the men. There was precious little chance of action, and limited comforts of any kind. A few items traditionally viewed as female – an armlet, a nail-cleaner and an earring – were found in the living quarters of an officer,[12] so there may have been some female company, but the armlet and nail-cleaner are not exclusively female items, and it is hardly conclusive proof of girlfriends, unofficial wives or conjugal visits.

An officer may have had his family living with him, and forts were not necessarily all-male and all-martial – there is ample evidence from Vindolanda near Hadrian's Wall for women and children living on-site.[13] In keeping with armies throughout history, the Ninth may have marched into the Midlands with any number of prostitutes, unofficial wives and children tagging along with the baggage, who might equally unofficially have cohabited in the cramped barrack blocks in the guise of domestics, cooks and nurses. But at Longthorpe, in AD 60, with tensions simmering towards the bloodiest home-turf war in British history, it is difficult to imagine Happy Families being enacted. Local fraternisation might have been forced more than willing.

The earring, a fat little gilded bronze ring,[14] is the ray of hope here, an unusual item for a bullied local woman to drop; there could be so many reasons for its presence, but I hope it was a gift from a soldier to his girlfriend, lovingly given, joyfully received and painfully lost, not the carelessly forgotten bauble of a reluctant slave gilded for the job.

Either way, Longthorpe was a grim place. The Fen Edge might have had its consolation in the form of achingly beautiful sunsets, and sport for those with a taste for waterfowl, but I suspect that when the trumpets sounded 'Fall In' that spring day, as a sweat-soaked dispatch rider leapt from his steaming, foam-flecked mount and ran to the commander's office to deliver Camulodunum's plea for help, there would have been an eager anticipation for the game afoot. If nothing else, they might get to visit the bright lights of the big city.

Tacitus gives us the name of the Ninth's commander, Quintus Petilius Cerialis Caesius Rufus, and we are fortunate, for we know far more about his subsequent life than would normally be the case for a young legionary commander, and it was quite a life.

In AD 60, Petilius Cerialis was in his early thirties, and seemingly replaced an adoptive brother, Caesius Nasica, as legate of the Ninth. He was almost certainly married to Flavia Domitilla, the future emperor Vespasian's daughter. Long after the Boudican revolt, in the civil wars of AD 69, he led a disastrous cavalry attack on Rome, and soon after took command in the suppression of the Batavian revolt in Germany. In AD 71 Cerialis was in Britannia again, as its Governor, and held an active tenure, putting down the Brigantes. By AD 74 he was back in Rome, and we hear little of him again.[15]

Although Tacitus had little good to say about Cerialis, attributing his successes to *fortune helping him where skill had failed*,[16] he is also quick to point out his courage, coolness and leadership, however rash. During the revolt of the Batavi in AD 70, Tacitus makes an observation about Cerialis's attitude to warfare that is crucial to our understanding of the younger, perhaps more impetuous man of ten years before:

> *Eager for battle, and more ready to despise than to be on his guard against the enemy, he fired the spirit of the troops by his bold language; for he would, he said, fight without a moment's delay, as soon as it was possible to meet the foe.*[17]

Telling words indeed.

What all this gives us is an insight into Cerialis's character, as a natural risk-taker, and the disregard for potential negative consequences that is an inherent part of that psychological make-up. Tacitus describes him as reckless; he might have been, but he had no lack of personal courage and there is no suggestion that he was stupid. He was certainly lucky personally, but unlike truly great commanders, that luck did not always encompass the men under his command.

Those men have left little to inform us of their lives, but the legion's tombstones of this general era from Lincoln give us an insight into the origins and stories of some of their comrades. Quintus Cornelius, whose stone was found in 1800 but is now lost, was a trooper in the select legionary cavalry century under Cassius Martialis. He was forty years old and had served for nineteen years. Gaius Valerius, a standard bearer of the century of Hospes, had served for fourteen years and died at the age of thirty-five. His partial gravestone can be seen in Lincoln Museum. Both men hailed from Italy.

Gaius Saufeius, from the Balkans, who had served for twenty-two years, died at the age of forty; his marvellous, simple memorial is now to be seen in the British Museum. Lucius Sempronius Flavinus, of the century of Babudius Severus, was a Spaniard from Clunia who had served only seven years before he died at the age of thirty; his stone is to be seen in the British Museum. A fragmentary monument records another soldier from Italy.

Despite the brevity of the inscriptions, each of these men has the name of his hereditary voting tribe preserved alongside his name. By multiplying these scant memories of a few individuals must we reconstruct the marching files of the Ninth.[18]

Camulodunum lay sixty-eight miles away as the eagle flies, or about seventy-five as those men of the eagle marched. Three or four solid days of hard marching. Cerialis was close enough that a threat to Colchester was his business and he would have received the news and acted long before Paulinus knew of it. As the local commander he had the authority to act on his own account in an emergency without waiting for orders, and he was not of a cautious disposition. I suspect the Ninth were issued emergency rations and marched within the hour.

The route was direct and simple enough, south along Ermine Street to Godmanchester, and then fork south-east along the *Via Devana*, which led to the gates of the city. Via Devana might sound like a Roman name, and it is meant to, but it derives from an eighteenth-century scholar,[19] Dr Charles Mason, Woodwardian Professor of Geology at Trinity College, Cambridge, and later rector of the beautiful Church of St Andrew in Orwell, south Cambridgeshire, where he rests, his 1770 floor-slab tombstone proclaiming him *Profeffor of Foffils*. Mason proposed that the road ran to Chester, *Deva* (hence *Devana*), but it was then known locally as Worsted Street, Wool Street, or, my favourite, Wolves Street.

A couple of months before Jonny and I visit the site of Longthorpe fortress in the only way possible now, wielding golf clubs, I walk the section of the Nene Way that follows the north bank of the river, passing within a few yards of the western corner of the lost ramparts.

I had driven through torrential rain to reach the fortress site, but arrive during a brief lull, with warm sunshine. The muddy path winds alongside the weedy riverbank at the edge of the golf course, fairways on one side and riverboats on the other. The boat moorings come to an end at a small divergence in the river, close to where a road from the fortress must have crossed, and probably where a jetty provided moorings for Roman boats.

As I reach the spot where the western corner of the fortress would almost have touched the footpath, the riverbanks are naturally overgrown on both sides, and superficially unmarked by the hand of man. Behind me the golf course has been land-scaped in such a way that the golfers on the near fairway are not only roughly on the line of the fortress rampart, but perhaps at about the right height to rub shoulders with the sentries pacing the catwalk.

I mudlark for scraps of Roman pottery in the few patches of bare earth, physical mementoes of the Ninth, to no avail. I stand instead and think of the legionary angler, his eyes on the line, watching for the first inquisitive twitch as a fish takes hold of that little barbed bronze fishing hook found in the fortress excavation; his imagination perhaps staring away and beyond, through the dark water, dreaming of his parents, or his girlfriend, or simply sitting in a bar in Camulodunum with cheap women, warm wine, and no sentry-go at dusk.

Like me, he knew the fortress lay behind him, but also like me, staring west, he couldn't see it, and across the river, with the Ham Mere Bird Sanctuary as a backdrop, the view probably wasn't so very different then from now. The peace here is both blissful and almost absurd, considering that the sprawl of Peterborough's suburbs surround me in every direction except to the west; I could be in some remote corner of the Broads.

This is the place from which the Ninth Legion marched to relieve the colonists of Colchester, and it is this journey, following the closest route possible to theirs, that I have come here to replicate.

If the Roman road Ermine Street directly south of Longthorpe, now the A1(M), was continued northwards, it would run straight to the west of this fortress, just about where the road from the southern gate would cross the river. It is possible to attempt following the vaguest approximation of that lost route by negotiating a twisting maze of housing estates, but the main road is close, and I join the old Roman road as the pre-motorway Ermine Street that survives as a road for local traffic running alongside the A1(M). Continuing along this road to Huntingdon, and then on through the driving rain to Godmanchester, I have followed the Ninth Legion's march to reach the start of the Via Devana. Whatever else they may have called it, this was the Camulodunum Road.

The A14 – that modern testament to the logic that no matter how many sections of road you widen, the queues just get fatter, not shorter – currently follows the route of Via Devana all the way to Cambridge. The purist will need to pull off at Fenstanton and follow the High Street (where there's an excellent bakery, or I'm no judge of a custard Danish), but major road 'improvements' are shortly to bypass this section altogether. If you need to keep an eye on the maps as they change, you should have plenty of time to do so *en route*, as getting into second gear tends to be little more than stall-inducing optimism on the A14. Pulling off at Cambridge with a weary sigh of relief, the Roman route continues as Huntingdon Road.

The distance thus far for the Ninth Legion to have marched is thirty miles, not much of a drive for me, but more than a day's hard slog at emergency speed for them, in full armour and equipment. These are details we will try not to forget in the miles to come, for this is where we ditch the car, shoulder our packs and join their ranks. As I leave the car, the rain clouds erupt into a monsoon.

For the Ninth Legion Cambridge was, at best, a smudge of woodsmoke on a long road. By the modern road's junction with Marion Close, the men of the relief column slogged past a major (and probably abandoned) Iron Age earthwork, perhaps a ring fort, little enough understood today, for it was only discovered by a small excavation in 1996,[20] on which I was lucky enough to work briefly. Occupied or not, a patrol would have crossed the deep ditches to reconnoitre.

Half a mile further on, cresting the ridge of Castle Hill, the Ninth may have marched past a small Roman fort on their right, now beneath the apartments directly opposite the Sir Isaac Newton pub. The archaeological evidence for a fort here is fragmentary, of suspect date and much contested,[21] and, if it ever existed, may have been constructed in the rebellion's wake.[22] A crossroads at the same spot, heading west towards Ermine Street and east towards the Fens, may also have been a later construct.[23]

Either way, with its panoramic view south, this was a good place for the infantry to halt, to survey the land ahead whilst the cavalry horses were watered in the river below. Beneath them lay no city, no Oxbridgeian dreaming spires. Their road downhill was a little to the left of modern Castle Street, running just behind The Castle Inn. A small bridge crossed the river Cam at the foot of the hill, perhaps with a wooden causeway spanning the boggy margins,[24] and flat, open country lay ahead, the road a thin spear of gravel for three miles or so, when it kinked to crest the opposing low ridge of the Gog Magog hills.

Obscured entirely by buildings now, the best way to replicate the view the Ninth Legion had that day is to climb the mound of the long-gone Norman castle, behind the pub, which gets you above the rooftops and almost onto the line of the ancient road. The smoke of small farming settlements lay on every side. Little would have been moving in that seemingly peaceful landscape, and it was open enough to see that no vast army of hostiles occupied the plain. The hills beyond were a different matter.

Walking along Huntingdon Road and down Castle Street into town, you are unwittingly walking among the shadows of Petilius Cerialis and Legio IX Hispana as they march towards their destiny in the spring of AD 60. Inevitably the modern roads are not exactly on their Roman forebears, and the spectral army would now be crashing through the beer garden of the Castle Inn, and grunting their way through Waterstones, Marks & Spencer and

Lloyds Bank. They would also, sometimes, be below the modern ground surface, for archaeological deposits are always deeper within cities where ground levels have risen because of constant rebuilding, levelling and rubbish deposition.

At the bottom of Castle Street, a deep excavation by the Cambridge Archaeological Unit exposed a tiny section of the Via Devana in 2000, four metres below the modern tarmac.[25] The roadside ditch was exposed, but the early road itself was rather rough, with no *agger*, or camber, and only patchy gravel metalling – perhaps a typical conquest period military road. I was fortunate enough to work briefly down at that level, and well remember how high the edge of the excavation seemed in the narrow confines of a three-metre diameter hole. Conversely, around Addenbrooke's Hospital, away from the city centre, Roman remains are only a few inches beneath your feet.

The Ordnance Survey marks the line of Hills Road as the Roman route through south Cambridge, but archaeologists plot the line some twenty to forty metres to the west of it, based on old observations.[26] I have excavated several trenches across this projected line,[27] in places where some trace might have been expected, at least of the flanking ditches, and found no hint of it whatsoever, raising the possibility that it actually does lie closer to or beneath Hills Road itself.

Either way, hard up against the other side of Hills Road, at the junction with Cherry Hinton Road, where Tesco Express now stands, we also uncovered an extensive area of digging, containing no artefacts later than the first or second centuries AD, which may represent the original Roman gravel quarrying to build and maintain that section of the road, next to the site of a now lost Roman fort.[28]

I pause at the Addenbrooke's Hospital roundabout on the southern edge of Cambridge. In 2002–3, I excavated an Iron Age and

Roman settlement behind the hospital,[29] and whilst there I was always very conscious that some of Cerialis's horsemen may have broken away from the main column on Hills Road to visit the village, clattering along the minor Roman road we had uncovered there, to seek any intelligence they could gather, or to requisition food or fodder. They were marching hard and wouldn't have lingered; the entire column would have passed by within half an hour or so.

I know that my old site is built upon now, but I bear right, through the main entrance to the hospital complex, to have a quick look. This is a place I used to know well. Quite apart from my painful stay with a kidney stone, Clare worked here for six years, and we had lived only a mile away across the fields. The overgrown footpaths and bridleways that criss-crossed the land-scape beyond the hospital, especially along the old railway line to Hobson's Brook, were my daily commute to work by mountain bike. More importantly I spent about five years, on and off, excavating these fields and beneath these buildings.

The overgrown old railway is a guided busway now, whilst the bridleways and footpaths are tarmac cycle superhighways. It is all so starkly twenty-first century, this very necessary expansion, but it has lost something since I last tore across the fields, my cycle path then being the overgrown ballast of a Victorian steam-powered guided bus, a superhighway of a different kind, fringed with wildflowers, and meadow grass brushing my pedals.

The fields bordering the hospital are built on now, flyovers and tunnels replacing the old gates and railway foot crossings. There are access roads and roundabouts, remarkable architec-tural fantasies of shining glass and steel rising heavenwards in every direction. It is all unrecognisable now. I last worked here only ten years ago, but without a *now and then* map, it is almost impossible to get my bearings. I am momentarily a lost soul, a time traveller emerging from the past into the dazzling light of the future, stumbling along in my singed and smoul-dering frock coat, pocket watch in hand, grabbing a passer-by and gasping, 'My God, how far have I come? What year is it? What *century*?'

There is no comforting point of reference anymore, except for Robinson Way, a narrow ring road that used to encompass the entire hospital complex, but is now an *inner* ring road swamped by the wider development. Like the Roman road itself, it is only this fossil relic of the old landscape that enables me to place myself within the past and find my old site. I eventually reach Staff Car Park 5, which I *know* was built on the edge of my site, and I mentally try to extrapolate the Roman and Iron Age ditches, houses, pottery kilns and cemetery out from beneath the concrete, glass and steel, with limited success.

When I arrived here in the late summer of 2002 to direct the excavations, this was a timeless oasis of genteel Englishness, of cricket whites and cucumber sandwiches, the playing field of Downing College, with its groomed sward and 1920s pavilion, which served as our site office. I had even found a weathered old cricket ball with its shrunken, faded leather skin as an appropriate souvenir. The site we uncovered was a late Iron Age and Roman Conquest period village, spanning the first centuries BC and AD, including the period of Boudica's war. At the southern edge of the site we found the parallel flanking ditches of a minor Roman road, which led directly across to the Via Devana.

I search for the Cancer Research Li Ka Shing building that was developed at the edge of the site, for this at least contains one last vestige of that ancient settlement. One of the numerous early Roman pottery kilns that we excavated was painstakingly recorded and a cast copy set into the floor at the entrance of the centre as a memento of the site. I have never seen it before, which is rather remiss, given that even Her Majesty the Queen had a peek at it when she opened the building in 2007.

I find my way in, sopping wet and incongruously dripping water all over the entrance hall of that prestigious research centre, and stand above the display. A small brass plaque explains what lies beneath your feet, but it rather resembles some sort of grotesque H.R. Giger-inspired prop egg from the *Alien* movies. It was actually a baked clay kiln from roughly the time of Boudica's war, give or take a decade, and produced high quality wheel-thrown pottery. It is hardly a thing of beauty, but it gives a sense of foundation to the surrounding development, a linchpin securing the worlds above and below. Without it, there would be no trace whatsoever in the whole of the new Addenbrooke's cityscape of the myriad of souls who have walked there before us.

The view is completely obscured by buildings now, but the villagers would have seen the Ninth Legion snaking along the Via Devana that day, standards raised, hundreds of cavalrymen, and a couple of thousand footsloggers with a train of pack mules. It must have been quite a sight. Remarkably, you can still stand exactly where they might have done to watch the Ninth marching past half a mile away, in Staff Car Park 5, or on the paving in front of the Li Ka Shing building, both of which lie only a few inches above the archaeological level of the settlement.

To your right, somewhere beneath the southern end of the brand new Capella Laboratory, lay the little roadside cemetery where we found the graves of nineteen of those villagers who lived here in that era and might have witnessed the march of the Ninth. Intriguingly, of the skeletons that could be sexed, nine out of thirteen were female, suggesting a very female-heavy population. Had the men been drafted into the Roman auxilia as part of a tribal levy?[30]

As the column angled along a kink at a crossroads, now known as Worts' Causeway, and began to disappear from view, climbing up onto the chalk bluffs behind the Iron Age hillfort of Wandlebury, we can only wonder at the relative fear or confidence the legionaries had for the task ahead. They knew that a fight was in the offing, but whether it was a local belligerence that would melt away at the first sign of military authority, or something with bigger teeth, they may have been unaware. Either way, somewhere in the next thirty miles of rolling downland before them lay the site of their doom. They never reached Colchester.

The Roman road above Wandlebury Hillfort is a remarkable surviving section of the Via Devana in its original form. Because it is rather overgrown, that form is not immediately apparent, but you get to walk along the actual surface of the road, where compacted gravel caps numerous foundation layers. On each side are trees and undergrowth, almost completely blocking the wider view.

It is barely half past five in the afternoon in early August, a mile out of Cambridge. It should be bright, warm, buzzing with insects and busy with dog walkers, surrounded by the summer woodland and the hum of life. But it is dark. The rain lashes down. Not a soul can be seen or heard, no insect or bird makes a sound. It feels closer to eight o'clock, in October. I march on. My left ankle, that had started needling at Addenbrooke's, is now properly painful, and I am soaked to the skin.

For the next hour I see and hear not a living soul, human or beast. It is a relief to finally turn off the Roman road into the Wandlebury woods to make for home, but even here, I can only describe the atmosphere as oppressive. The woods are even darker than the road, and if I stand still, all I can hear is the growing wind buffeting the canopy, and a hundred-thousand leaf-drips falling on the forest floor, one of the most primeval (and strangely lonely) sounds in the world.

When I reach the ringwork of the Iron Age fort, I find my way down into the huge ditch and walk half the circuit, until a path leads into the fort itself. Climbing the ramparts, I pass the spot where an Iron Age skeleton was excavated twenty years ago by Dr Charly French and his team from the Archaeology Department.[31] The remains were those of a middle-aged man, violently treated in the months leading up to his death, with a blade wound and fracture to his chin and a broken rib, who finally met his end with his hands bound, dumped in a grain storage pit.[32] A human sacrifice? An executed prisoner of war?

He was not alone. Numerous ancient bodies suffering violent ends have emerged at Wandlebury.[33] One was a child, wrapped in a sack, minus its severed legs, and placed in a pit.[34] Alone in the unnervingly early twilight, it is probably best not to dwell on the many old stories of spirits that linger hereabouts.

I cross into the grounds of the long-demolished country house that once occupied the interior, where its magnificent stable block, almost a stately home in itself, still stands. Just as at Addenbrooke's, it is inconceivable that I am not replicating the journey of a mounted patrol, wanting to know what, if anything, remained behind the ramparts of the hillfort. Perhaps they found it as dead and empty as I do. If the stable block, now residential, is occupied this evening, no light shows at the windows.

That mounted patrol, cautiously nosing their mounts into the deserted earthworks, may have been the lucky ones of the Roman relief column. The footslogging infantry, audibly pounding along the gravel road a hundred yards away, did so beneath a less fortunate star.

According to Tacitus:

> The victorious enemy met Petilius Cerialis, commander of the ninth legion, as he was coming to the rescue, routed his troops, and destroyed all his infantry. Cerialis escaped with some cavalry . . .[35]

Routed and massacred. The Ninth had been wiped out, the location of the killing ground as lost to us as the identities of the men who perished there.

My ankle throbs. The sky is dark. I bunch my shoulders against the rain and limp back to Cambridge.

The Eagle of the Ninth

Last Stand of Legio IX Hispana

And we die, and none can tell Them where we died.
Rudyard Kipling, *Gentlemen Rankers*

To visualise the Ninth Legion as they slog through the future site of Cambridge and past the hillfort of Wandlebury, and, perhaps more importantly, to share that march with them, we need mentally to burden ourselves with their equipment and try on their boots. This was a flying column, probably unencumbered by wagons or artillery, and heavier equipment would be slung across pack mules. The column would have disappeared back into the dust haze, perhaps four or six men wide and several hundred legionary ranks long. In addition to the many hundreds of cavalrymen and auxiliaries, and a couple of hundred mules, the column may well have covered a mile or two of road.

Each legionary wore a woven woollen tunic, visible on the upper arms and legs. These may have been red, as they are often portrayed, but would be faded, leading a hard, outdoor life, bleached by rain, sun and sweat. Over this came the armour, a segmented cuirass, *lorica segmentata*, for some, and perhaps the older style mail shirt, *lorica hamata*, for others. This was a transitional period for armour, the newer segmented iron strips encircling the torso, held together by riveted straps, replacing the chainmail that had little changed since before Caesar's day, and was still the standard armour of the auxilia.

We are blessed in this particular instance with a degree of certainty, for numerous fragments of *segmentata* were found during the excavation of the Ninth's fortress at Longthorpe. Each man also wore a helmet, perhaps generally of iron in this period, of the Imperial Gallic type, with large cheek pieces (again, one was found at Longthorpe) and flaring neck protection, all trimmed in brass.

They all carried a large, curved, oblong shield, *scutum*, brightly painted, but protected on the march beneath a hide cover, a shoulder strap bearing some of the weight. A sword, *gladius*, with a blade about eighteen inches long hung on the right hip, and each carried at least one javelin, or *pilum*, possibly two, seven feet long, the upper third a slim, deadly length of pointed iron. The remainder of their equipment was slung on a crossed pole carried over the shoulder, with leather packs secured to the crosspiece, and various accoutrements dangling and clanking.

These were not the shiny, parade-ground soldiers familiar from re-enactments. They had been hammering along the road for a good day and a half by now, at twenty-five miles or more a day with full armour and kit, caked in sweat and dust, unshaven faces smeared with grime and careworn with fatigue. Their armour was dulled and grey, tinged orange in the wet. If the weather was cold, they would have pulled rough woollen cloaks over their shoulders.

The Roman legionary famously wore sandals, a rather limp word for the open-toed, iron-shod marching boots, or *caligae*, that they actually were. The pointed hobnails clustered on each sole (think five or six dozen fat cricket studs) were multi-functional, protecting the boot, providing a solid grip on most surfaces, and becoming a fearsome blunt weapon on the slick filth of a battlefield, trampling enemy wounded underfoot. The writer Juvenal specifically warned against being kicked by soldiers wearing caligae.[1]

With the openwork upper allowing the free passage of water and air, it was about the healthiest environment a hard-marching soldier's foot could hope for – contrast it with the unenviable lot of the Victorian soldier, who habitually urinated in his boots each night, to soften the leather and ward off constant fungal infections.[2]

Caligae were smart, comfortable, practical and durable. On the premise that you shouldn't judge a man until you have walked a thousand miles (or yards, at least) in his caligae, I've walked a good many miles in them, and if they don't initially feel big on comfort to the soft, pampered feet of a devout non-sandal wearer of the twenty-first century, in the ancient world, they were an enviable product. If you are tempted to try caligae, it is necessary to hunt out a good pair, for there is a world of rubbish to be found on the internet that a Roman soldier wouldn't have been seen dead in – a strangely relevant detail of vanity, as we shall see.

Most of the endless miles of military road in the province were capped with rammed gravel or locally procured equivalent: hard-wearing, free-draining, fast to build and easily maintained. Paved sections existed, and still survive, particularly where the local geology provides abundant, readily procured rock slabs, but some of these may be showing the underlying foundation, not the working surface.[3] Although roads would quickly be utilised by the civil community, they were surveyed, planned and built by and for the army, and gravel was a far better marching medium than stone. I have walked many miles in caligae on stone paths and their modern equivalents of tarmac and concrete, but they are hard on both feet and footwear without something for the hobnails to sink into.

In 1921, a mature Cambridge student called Cyril Fox, who was starting what would become an illustrious career in archaeology, excavated sections across the Via Devana on the Gog Magog hills above Cambridge. His section drawings beautifully illustrate its construction, of layers of rammed chalk rubble overlain by thick gravel metalling, giving a total road width of about ten metres, but an actual working surface of three metres.[4] A public footpath follows this remarkable eleven-mile stretch of preserved Roman road as far as Haverhill in Suffolk, the very road that the Ninth Legion sweated along that early summer day, which then simply ends. Like a full stop. The remaining twenty miles of road, along which, surely, this vexillation of the Ninth was all but wiped from the face of the Earth, has disappeared entirely.

Where did the Via Devana go? Roman roads did not always run spear-straight across the landscape with a cheerful disregard for topography. They kink, gently turn, and follow no rules – for every hilltop avoided, another was crested almost as an act of defiance. Studying the Ordnance Survey 1:25000 Explorer series of the route, despair and bafflement initially descend. There is nothing to point the way, no old hedge-lines or Parish boundaries, farm tracks or footpaths that continue the line of the road as a ghost of its former presence.

> They shut the road through the woods,
> Seventy years ago.
> Weather and rain have undone it again,
> And now you would never know
> There was once a road through the woods
> Before they planted the trees.
> It is underneath the coppice and heath,
> And the thin anemones.
> Only the keeper sees
> That, where the ring-dove broods,
> And the badgers roll at ease,
> There was once a road through the woods.[5]

Kipling knew.

But as your eyes adjust to the contours and detail of the map, much as they adjust to the fall of evening, clarity emerges from the gloom. Even for the most blinkered Roman jobsworth with a surveying staff and a plumb bob (and looking at the map of Roman Britain, there was surely no shortage of them), pegging out a straight line from Haverhill to Colchester afforded no advantage when, by a slight deviation from that route and a couple of gentle kinks, the topography provided a ready-made highway straight to the gates of the city. Through Haverhill to clip the valley of the Stour, over the ridge of Ridgewell, and into the gentle mouth of the Colne Valley by Halstead, where a natural corridor runs effortlessly to Camulodunum.

This route is not without its supporting evidence. Charles Cardale Babington, a professor of botany, who was once given first refusal in the purchase of some beetle specimens that resulted in a jealous Charles Darwin threatening to kick the specimen dealer down the stairs as a 'damned rascal',[6] was also a keen Roman road hunter. In 1883, he published the second edition of his *Ancient Cambridgeshire: Or an Attempt to Trace Roman and other Ancient Roads that passed through the County of Cambridge*.

In this he gives a detailed account of the Via Devana in its Cambridgeshire manifestation. Unfortunately, being outside of Cambridgeshire, and annoyingly faithful to the remit of his carefully worded title, he says merely of this missing section that it 'entered Suffolk near Withersfield . . . Its course from thence to Colchester, by Haverhill and Halstead, it is unnecessary to notice.'[7]

In February 1910, the Reverend F.G. Walker addressed the Cambridge Antiquarian Society with a paper entitled *Roman Roads into Cambridge*. Using numerous old sources, and the evidence of visible sections of the road that were, even as he spoke, disappearing from the landscape, Walker tracked the route of the Via Devana from its north-west approach to Cambridge, and south-east all the way to Colchester, proposing this same Colne Valley route. He leaves us with tantalising gems, such as, near Haverhill, 'In the years 1800–1 the continuation of this road was distinctly traceable a little to the south of the modern road,' and north of Birdbrook, in the eighteenth century, '. . . here the embankment of the road was then quite marked.'[8]

He was also acutely aware of the ephemeral nature of land-scape features, not just physically, but in local memory:

> When I made enquiries during 1909 about village mazes in England it was repeatedly and plainly proved that an object, well-known and well-marked for centuries, could disappear in 60 years not only from sight, but from the memories of almost all the villagers and educated people who had lived in such a locality all their lives.[9]

Not for Walker the romantic notion of the folklorist, that such detail is subtly but indelibly etched in perpetuity in the local subconscious.

> Yet, if you enter the woods
> Of a summer evening late,
> When the night-air cools on the trout-ringed pools
> Where the otter whistles his mate,
> (They fear not men in the woods,
> Because they see so few.)
> You will hear the beat of a horse's feet,
> And the swish of a skirt in the dew,
> Steadily cantering through
> The misty solitudes,
> As though they perfectly knew
> The old lost road through the woods.
> But there is no road through the woods.

The study of Roman roads was gathering pace even before Walker presented his paper. The earliest attempt at a comprehensive survey of the road system was by the elderly Victorian road engineer Thomas Codrington, who published his landmark study *Roman Roads in Britain* in 1903. Inevitably dated now, this awesome synthesis is still worth dipping into as a first port of call, but in our quest he is all but silent, merely mentioning that from Haverhill the road 'was formerly traceable five miles further in the direction of Colchester', and that in 1790 remains 'were very visible on the west of Ridgewell'.[10]

And then came Margary.

If film buffs have Leslie Halliwell, Roman road buffs have Ivan Donald Margary. Born in 1896, he served as an infantry officer in the Great War with the Royal Sussex Regiment, seeing his fair share of action, and was dangerously wounded in August 1917. A chemist by training, with a keen interest in meteorology and botany, it was his joining of the Sussex Archaeological Society in 1927 that led to his most remarkable legacy – the study of Roman roads. His monumental *Roman Roads in Britain*, which paid homage to Codrington's earlier work of the same name, was first published in 1955, and revised until 1973.

It is to the ancient road enthusiast what *Gray's Anatomy* was to generations of medical students, or *Wisden* to cricket. He individually numbered each and every known road and then described them in detail, area by area. It was hugely gratifying to find the Addenbrooke's Roman road, for despite no one having proved its existence before, its presence was strongly enough suspected that it already had its own Margary number: *Margary 241*.[11]

Of course, this is the point where Margary takes us by the hand and leads us along the lost section of the Via Devana (aka *Margary 24*); he doesn't, for he could not trace what is no longer to be seen any more than Walker or Codrington, but he added the detail his masterful intuition divined, and he certainly had few doubts about the route. He traced the road directly along Haverhill High Street, alongside the road to Sturmer, and to the west of Ridgewell. From Great Yeldham the main road itself 'runs in notably straight lengths from point to point, designed to follow the Colne Valley conveniently, and may reasonably be regarded as the continuation.'[12]

The remainder of the route is gone, but clearly followed the line of the valley, and probably a prehistoric trackway. He also reminds us that a section of Roman road was uncovered outside Colchester, at Lexden Heath, heading north-west – directly along the Colne Valley towards our speculated road coming in the opposite direction. Margary was hardly infallible, but he entirely supported the assertions of Babington, Walker and Codrington, not to mention my own humble map-gazing: west of Ridgewell, and into the Colne Valley, by Sible Hedingham and Halstead, and then simply follow your nose.

Now, I do own the reproduction kit of a Roman legionary of this era, which I have slowly put together for research and display, and I won't pretend that I haven't considered yomping the final half of the Ninth Legion's route in full legionary marching order, but I am not a re-enactor, and I am not the sort of person who welcomes incredulous stares and boisterous, if friendly, shouts of 'Hail Caesar', or, 'Romans go home'.

Likewise, I don't want to walk in thirty kilograms of arms and armour, or caligae, especially as much of the route will take me on tarmac and the narrow verges of dangerously busy roads, and, unlike the Ninth, I haven't trained to carry that weight. I do feel, however, that wearing marching sandals along the preserved portion of the Roman road, across the Gog Magog downs to Haverhill is an appropriate gesture.

If I personally shudder at the thought of men in sandals, let alone sandals with socks, the Romans had no such qualms. A pair of thick woollen walking socks quickly eases any discomfort and, I have to say, transforms a potentially painful experience into a sublime one, from preventing rubbing and blisters, to keeping gravel out of the holes.

Caligae with thick socks are more comfortable than either my high-tech walking boots or running shoes. I have worn them on walks purely for the pleasure of wearing them, and the simple, innocent joy of embarrassing my family, and I have even been for a pain-free cross-country jog. I have trekked over the mountains of both Spain and Switzerland in them, with and without socks, on almost every type of surface, including several all-day Alpine treks from the summer snowline at 3200 metres above sea level all the way down along rocky paths and scrambles to the lush valley bottom 1700 metres below.

After these experiences, I declare caligae capable of almost anything required of a modern walking boot, and sometimes a good deal better – they grip icy snow like crampons. They lack a heel, which tells on long, steep climbs, and the poor purchase of the hobnails on smooth stone is legendary. During the siege of Jerusalem in AD 70, Josephus tells us that a centurion called Julianus, suddenly running onto the smooth stone of a temple floor, slipped arse-over-head because of his hobnails, and was promptly slain by the Jews he had been chasing.

Generally, though, pointed hobnails provide an infinitely better feel for the ground you are walking than rubber, from the pleasing crunch of gravel, the click and spark of flint, and the silent yield-ing of soil, turf and chalk. In Spain, our friends' son made the observation that my caligae wrapped themselves around the rocks as if I was barefoot, with the hobnails gripping like pliers. Suffice to say, of all the falls, stumbles and blisters on these holidays, none of them were mine.

There is good evidence for sock use with caligae, from depic-tions in carvings, to archaeological discoveries. The first of the Vindolanda tablets to be found – small wooden postcards from the late-first-century fort close to Hadrian's Wall, preserved in the boggy local conditions – famously told the soldier recipient, *I have sent you . . . pairs of socks, from Sattua two pairs of sandals and two pairs of underpants.*[13] Surely a sort of ancient M&S voucher, and as if to prove the point, the excavation then turned up a preserved sock in addition to the largest collection of Roman sandals and shoes in the world. No underpants yet though.

Interestingly, the exact form of the word for underpants, *subli-gariorum*, that occurred in this letter stumped scholars until the same form was found, predictably enough, in the steamy poems of the ever-randy Catullus,[14] a pretty good place to start if you're searching for references to Roman underwear and, in particular, its frantic removal.

Three days after my monsoon walk, I am back at Wandlebury bright and early with Clare, Tristan, and Jojo the black Labrador. Accompanying us is Clare's sister, Emma, another archaeologist, who still works in Cambridge and is married to Jonny, my Longthorpe golfing partner. Emerging from the car wearing caligae with thick socks and joining the Roman road exactly where I had left it a few days before, nothing could have been more different. It was a warm and bright summer morning with my family and dog, not cold, dark, lonely and sodden. The juxtaposition made me realise how miserable and wet the end of the last walk had been. Even my *subligariorum* had been dripping. Nice.

The Roman road is a glorious walk. Leaving Wandlebury, the path soon loses the arching roof of branches, although the trees and hedges along the sides never really disappear, and the wider landscape, rolling and beautiful beyond, is rarely seen in more than fleeting glimpses; a restriction of observation that the Roman army would never have allowed. The surface of the path is mostly grass and wildflowers, but here and there it has worn away to allow my caligae to crunch on the original gravel of the Roman road.

A distant beefy growl makes us look to the sky, and a Spitfire passes straight over us at a few hundred feet, quite the most beautiful single thing to emerge from the twentieth century, followed a few minutes later by the biplane silhouette of a 1930s Tiger Moth – the glory of walking near the Imperial War Museum Duxford. The Moth, seeming to have nowhere to go, performs a little aerobatic display of our very own.

The sky is heavily marbled with cloud, with columnar sunlight bursting through like searchlight beams, pure Paul Nash, and the day is increasingly warm; I could half believe that we've momentarily slipped back to August 1940. Such illusions are quickly dispelled by crossing the thundering A11 by the bridge at Worsted Lodge, the old junction with the Icknield Way, after which the Via Devana becomes less pronounced, and the route a little less straight.

We stop for lunch at the Old Red Lion at Horseheath. Everyone chats. I am now concerned about my ankle, which had been wincingly painful by the end of the last walk, and is becoming so again. I reluctantly remove my caligae and pull my walking boots from my rucksack. Apparently, Clare tells me, when I first met her over twenty years ago, I unaccountably informed her that I would never, ever wear sandals, unless I could get hold of a decent pair of Roman army marching boots. I have no recollection of this at all, but it sounds far too much like the lame sort of thing I would say to someone I fancied to doubt its authenticity. It seems I've always had a thing about caligae, even before I knew I had.

Of all the human remains I have excavated, the one I remember most vividly, which penetrated the professional detachment of the task, was a skeleton I exposed as a site assistant during the excavation of a Roman settlement in west Cambridge in early 2000. It was less than a mile off the Via Devana, part of a small cemetery that lay beneath what is now the Centre for Advanced Photonics and Electronics off Madingley Road.[15] The cemetery, dating to the third or fourth century AD, included the skeleton of a young man, whom I had the privilege to excavate. He lay on his back in a north–south aligned grave with his head to the south.

There was no hint as to why he died preserved on his bones, shattered by centuries of the clay swelling and contracting with the seasons, but his left hand was broken around the time of death.[16] He had a distinctive jawline, but didn't have great teeth. Small iron nails attested to his having been buried in a coffin. There was nothing accompanying the body, except that his feet disappeared into a cluster of rusty hobnails, almost a hundred to each foot, which were later interpreted as the remains of military caligae;[17] buried in his best marching boots, so this anonymous soul could trek to the otherworld, the footslogger's version of paying the ferryman.[18]

In all, seven of the thirty individuals in this cemetery seemed to be wearing shoes, based on the recovery of hobnails, both men and women,[19] and it is possible that others wore shoes without nails, which have left no trace. In contrast to so many burial practices that seem to bind the dead to the grave to prevent them wandering, here the dead were actively encouraged to walk.

H. Lang Jones, the young archaeologist-poet, put these words into the mouth of a dying soldier of the Fourteenth Legion:

Oh! lay me close beside the Road, that so
My spirit, liking not this place, may go
By easy journey on the way to Rome,
And by my fathers' Shades be welcomed home.[20]

Whenever anyone asks the stock meeting-an-archaeologist question, 'So, what's the best thing you've ever dug up?' I always say *him*; those feet, those boots. It seems a bit disappointing, to the enquirer, at least, that I haven't found a gold torc or a Viking sword. 'Hobnails?' Yes, it was the hobnailed feet of that skeleton, and the thought of his shadow-walk along a ghost road that led to wherever it was that the dead were meant to go, which was a real enough place back then simply because it was real to the people buried in that cemetery, in their world, and imaginations; in their prayers, dreams and nightmares.

I lace up my walking shoes. They feel tight, airless, modern and charmless, a wrenching return to the present day, as is the tarmac and traffic with which I will now share the walk – my family (hell, even the dog,) are abandoning me for this next slog with the lost Ninth Legion.

I'll go with you then, since you must play this game of ghosts. But who will? It seems only the Ninth are game.

The remainder of the known section of road is hardly

recognisable as such except on the map. From Horseheath it is a normal footpath, followed by farm tracks, and forges across fields of crops, easily missed as a seeming tyre track. It emerges, with a sense of finality, onto a tarmac road running at a right angle to it about a mile before Haverhill.

I almost immediately join the main road, the A1307, a rude awakening that will dog me for the remainder of the walk, negotiating the overgrown, nettle-thick verges inches away from thundering traffic. Jumping on and off these a few times, and finding all those fascinating tendon-wrenching holes that hide in the undergrowth, finally does for my ankle, and I helplessly limp on, each step a wincing pain. When I stagger into the centre of Haverhill after a seeming eternity, each step is a jaw-clenching stab.

Over lunch, Clare had told me that I had a 'shin splint', a strain or tear at the base of the *tibialis anterior*, and recommended, in an authoritatively medical way, that I call it a day. I had made the derisive throat-clearing noise that such a defeatest suggestion warranted, and now feel like a six-inch nail is being driven into my lower shin with each step. Slogging on out of Haverhill, through Sturmer and into the countryside, I finally leave the stress and verge-hopping of the main road to climb up onto the Birdbrook hills.

At last I have a view worthy of the name. Just by the OS spot height of ninety-two metres, I sit by a hedge in the afternoon sun, swallow painkillers, and rest for the first time since lunch. It is half past five. Directly north the wide, gentle Stour Valley runs east to west less than a mile away. Directly behind me, the gentlest of valleys contains the dual trickling sources of the River Colne. Ridgewell, as its name suggests, lies on the high ground between the two.

The road and paths I am taking to Ridgewell's southern edge must roughly follow the line of the Via Devana mentioned in the old accounts. We have no idea if the Ninth would have been in time to save Camulodunum, or whether it was already destroyed when the Britons hunted them out, but it would probably have been from here that the smoke of the burning city would first have been visible to them darkening the horizon. This was a spot of either hope or despair, depending on the view.

I declare that the hedgerows between Birdbrook and Ridgewell produce the most delicious and refreshing blackberries on God's earth and I gorge on them, spurred on by the combined rush of sugar, analgesics and a pretty view. At Ridgewell I rejoin the main road, the A1017, and slog on much less joyously to Great Yeldham. Here my resolve falters.

I momentarily stop to admire the monstrous stump of the Yeldham Oak, the crumbling remains of a tree of huge antiquity. It wouldn't have been here when the Ninth marched through, but its parent or grandparent might have been. It is seven o'clock and my almost natural high has been boosted by chocolate and a second wind that has appeared from nowhere, when I see the Waggon and Horses, a free house pub advertising hot food and traditional ales. My leg really hurts. The thought of a pint and a pie is like a siren song. I limp on. I'll get to Sible Hedingham. Just another two or three miles. There will be a pub there to put this to shame. And then I pass the White Hart's award winning restaurant and bar. *No.* I'll get to Sible Hedingham. It will be even better there.

I reach Sible Hedingham at a quarter to eight, limping like a comedy peg-legged pirate. I find a pub at each end of the village, the Sugar Loaves at the near end, and the Swan at the far end. Both are long closed, with black windows and firmly bolted doors. The Swan looks like the archetype of an abandoned pub, a ready-made film set. It only needs the sign to swing in the windless night and the rotting door to creak open at my approach. To be honest, I'd be tempted. I walk the length of the village twice, and then try the width. A third old pub, devoid of its sign, is now a luxury residence. At half past eight I stumble into the White Lion in the old quarter, suitably packed for the only pub left in town on a Saturday night, and slump in the beer garden with a pint.

It is almost dark when Clare picks me up. I describe how I have spent most of the day hopping on and off nettle-infested verges avoiding speeding nutters. Then, a few miles west of Sible Hedingham, a hare runs into the road.

I like hares. Many years ago I saw David Attenborough's haunting documentary *The Shadow Of the Hare*,[21] with music by Maddy Prior, fusing the natural history and mythology of these remarkable creatures, impossible to understand the one without the other. Since then, the hare has assumed an obsessive, almost mythic status for me, a reverence that both the Celts and the Saxons would have fully understood; I fear to eat hare, and I cannot condone their persecution in any form. Their absolute protection should be enshrined in law. They represent an echo of the ancient landscape, a whisper of 'a wildness that no longer exists', encapsulated in their traditional names: the friendless one, the cat of the wood, the cat that lurks in the broom, the purblind one, the furze cat, the starer with wide eyes, the dew-flirt, the faith-breaker, the ill-met.

Often said to have been introduced by the Romans, hares actually occur in prehistoric contexts, seemingly pre-dating the Romans by millennia. Julius Caesar tells of the Britons considering hares unlawful to eat in 55 BC, a curious taboo if they had yet to be introduced, and Boudica herself is claimed by Dio to have released a hare from the folds of her tunic to prophesy victory. When we lifted those Bronze Age cremation urns in the rain, as I related in the Preface, dodging fat raindrops and ancient curses alike, an enigmatic satellite cremation contained no identifiable fragments of bone, except those of a hare,[22] a revelation that still prickles the back of my neck.

Clare sees the hare as it bursts onto the road and safely comes to a rapid standstill. It is a beauty, a youngster about two-thirds grown, all inexperience, daring and long-limbs, strong, quick and clumsy. It crossed from the left, stumbled and rolled, and now sits dazed in the middle of the other side of the road, staring at our lights. Clare reaches for the door handle to encourage it onto the verge, when a car speeds around the corner on the other side, with plenty of room to stop. The driver spots the hare, flashes their lights, and begins to slow; then they simply accelerate again, and our bright-eyed spirit of the ancient fields lies twitching and flattened on the tarmac.

I return to Sible Hedingham with my bicycle. Limping through the town at dusk three weeks before in desperate search of beer, I had noticed something the map had previously hinted at – a slight change in the fall and rise of the landscape. It was here, between Sible Hedingham and Halstead that I was spending the afternoon, following the many footpaths and roads between the two.

I start by walking the main road, the valley bottom route, to Halstead, as near as damn it on the Roman road, presumably. I am walking my bike, which will be useful for exploring later, but for now I am still marching. I decide to leave the road to follow a footpath along the River Colne. Somewhere along this stretch of river is the approximate location of an important crossroads in Roman times, where the Via Devana and the Peddars Way crossed. From here the Peddars Way ran northeast into the Iceni heartlands, and south-west to Chelmsford and the London road.

Like many Roman roads, it might have had a prehistoric precursor, but it is questionable whether the Roman form existed just yet in this north-east section. It would, after all, have been heading directly into nominally independent tribal lands until now, although military access roads into Icenia could have been a condition of peace and continued independence after the rising of AD 47.

The walk between Sible Hedingham and Halstead is remarkable, not for its prettiness, which it has in abundance, but because there is so little sense of being in a valley. The valley side to the west is nearby and little more than a gentle rise; that to the east seems distant. They are both illusions, and very dangerous ones for a soldier leading an army along it.

With the best will in the world, this is not a dramatic landscape, but it has clusters of closely spaced contour lines that represent the relatively shallow Colne Valley, with many smaller defiles running off where tributary streams once ran, and some still do, draining the downs to either side. The ground never plunges, but it rolls, rises and dips again. Once upon a time, it may well have been heavily forested, but even now I don't doubt that tens of thousands of people could conceal themselves in the folds and hollows without any difficulty at all.

None of this is apparent as you enter Halstead and walk uphill along the main street. You need to get on your bike, my equivalent of morphing into one of Cerialis's cavalry scouts, and follow the roads that cross the top of the eastern scarp. Not only does the vulnerability of anyone moving an army along the valley suddenly become apparent, but also the sheer quantity of hidden defiles that funnel down towards the Colne, and another valley just beyond the heights, running parallel but completely hidden. Its tributary stream carves a funnel to the Colne a mile north-west of Halstead.

Every time there is a break in the big hedges and tree cover, I dump my bike and wander through to get the view, and each shows the same commanding height and concealing rolls, with glimpses of the valley below. In one timeless hidden fold two roe deer graze unconcernedly, a doe and half-grown fawn, those evocative denizens of the wildwood that instantly transport you to a remoter, more ancient landscape.

Further along, almost back at the Hedinghams, is another creature enjoying its natural habitat, a metal detectorist inching his way across a ploughed field with a methodical swing. He is too far away to trek over for a chat and, as with the deer, I watch in silence before moving on, reminded of my late teenage years engrossed in the same hobby. Many archaeologists don't 'get' metal detecting, but I do, that strangely obsessive world so gently and affectionately brought to life in Mackenzie Crook's beautifully observed BBC comedy series *Detectorists*. I cycle back down to Castle Hedingham and recross the river.

The western side of the valley looks less promising, from an ambush point of view, until you get up there. Again, shallow valley after shallow valley, all hidden, create hundreds of acres of dead ground that ultimately funnel down towards that Roman road.

Of all the landscape that I have walked through since leaving Cambridge, fairly or unfairly, I couldn't help but feel that walking into an ambush would have been an act of gross incompetence pretty much anywhere along the route, prevented simply by adequate cavalry screens. But not here. There is no single stretch of commanding high ground where scouts could have seen all they needed to see. Unexpected miniature valleys and deceptive dead ground lie out of sight in every direction, a landscape that could simply absorb an army, and the road must have run straight through it. For my money, it was marching along the Colne Valley, somewhere in the few miles between Sible Hedingham and Halstead, that Cerialis first smelled a rat.

If I'm right, and if the danger of the Colne Valley seems so glaringly obvious to me, why did Cerialis not see it until it was too late? Well, he undoubtedly did, but the dice were weighted against him. Cerialis may well have travelled this road before and barely given the valley a second glance. Why would he? It looked completely innocuous from within, and had been in the settled portion of the province since the army had built it a generation before.

Now, in a time of war, he would have taken the basic military precautions of sending cavalry pickets onto the high ground and proceeding with caution, but he had no Ordnance Survey map to consult, something we often forget as we stare at ours, and it is unlikely that any of his men knew this country much better than he did. He simply wouldn't have known that dead ground surrounded him beyond the valley heights, nor of the numerous defiles that could funnel attacks towards him, and even if his scouts had reported it, he had little option but to proceed and send the scouts out further.

We are watching the Ninth descend into the folds of the Colne Valley *knowing* that disaster loomed; Cerialis had not the slightest idea that he was facing oblivion. He was probably fairly confident that a minor rebellion by farmers long since disarmed and pacified would be easy meat for the Ninth. If he saved Camulodunum, or slaughtered the bastards in the shadow of its ruins, he would be the hero of the hour. He was marching hard, now within twelve miles of his glory, perhaps spurred on by a thick column of smoke in the direction of the city, and undoubtedly knew that he was making one of those reasoned gambles any commander has to make. He was not a cautious man by nature, and like any risk-taker, he was not overly preoccupied by thoughts of disaster.

Perhaps a troop of cavalry failed to return from beyond one of the rises. Or a band of Britons suddenly blocked the road ahead, and while all attention was focused on them, a flood of warriors poured down the wooded defiles, punching through the thin line of march, splitting the column into two or three groups. Maybe it was the harsh, mournful banshee cry of a hundred carnyx war trumpets that heralded a storm of missiles to shield the first chariot charge. However it happened, strung out over a mile or two of road, with no chance to form more than relatively small defensive groups of back-to-back shield walls, the Ninth were done for, and they must have known it. There was nothing left for them but to sell their lives as dearly as possible.

The ferocious, nightmarish savagery of such a fight can hardly be imagined today. As fighting erupted along the battle line, it would have been marked by a smog of dust and blood spray, a boiling haze of keening metal and gobbets of flesh, severed hands, arms and heads flung back at the enemy, brains spilling from cleaved skulls, and the wounded collapsing into pools of steaming blood and viscera. As the fight pushed across the field, heaps of half-dismembered carcasses and struggling wounded lay entangled in its wake, men clutching their opened abdomens to prevent their guts spilling over their knees.

Cerialis and the bulk of the horsemen must have looked back along the road in horror. Almost as far as the eye could see, that painfully thin line of legionaries was being overwhelmed, or forced into struggling groups increasingly separated from one another as the tide of Britons swamped them. It had all happened so quickly, and what little order remained was fast being overwhelmed. No matter what he did now, the two thousand infantrymen of the Ninth Legion and foot auxiliaries were doomed.

The centurions were instinctively attempting to rally their men to effect a fighting withdrawal back the way they had come, but it was a forlorn hope, too predictable and long anticipated by the Britons who had plugged the gap behind them. Cerialis might have marched the Ninth into that valley, but he would never march them out of it.

The horsemen were the only cohesive body of troops left on the field, and they had a single, fleeting chance to cut their way out. Drawing their long *spatha* swords, for good or ill, they took it, and carved an escape through the slaughter.

My imagination. Nothing more, nothing less. But get your caligae on and walk this route. This is the spot that leaps out, and this is the story it tells. Referring to the chaos of another close-run battle ten years hence, Tacitus tells us that Cerialis was *undismayed by the confusion*,[23] praise indeed from Tacitus, so I doubt he lost his wits now. Abandoning his doomed infantry cannot have been an easy choice, but the sacrifice of many hundreds of cavalrymen could only increase the tragedy, not prevent it.

It was undoubtedly a mercy that most of the legionaries would have been too involved with their own struggle to see their legate and cavalry flee the field. If the eagle standard had marched with them,[24] it must have been near enough for Cerialis to spirit it away, for Tacitus would certainly have mentioned its loss, even if it was later recovered.

There are other stretches of the Colne Valley with tributary defiles and dead ground, but nowhere else does such a perfect storm of topography and opportunity play into the hands of the Britons. There is, of course, not a thing to hint at any of this now. The towns and roads, hedges and woods all help to obscure the story. The Colne, a diminutive stream in this section, is much as it would have been, but I picture it being more reedy, its margins less cropped. It is a spot that our daydreaming angler, on another day, alone and without his armour, would have rather enjoyed, but it is all too possible that he died here. Forgotten men in a forgotten battle on a forgotten field.

I don't believe that a single man of that relief column passed the present-day site of Halstead.

I return the next day, park in Halstead and mount my bike. My journey with the Ninth is over, for now. It is time to complete the pilgrimage. I simply need to follow the road to Colchester, for my own sense of completion. I could, I suppose, do it in the car, but that feels wrong now, having come so far under my own steam. It's about twelve more miles.

The A1124 is a beautiful road, but it seems to have been planned by a frustrated rollercoaster designer, or someone who adored the Colne Valley so much that they couldn't decide which side of it they loved the most. At Halstead the valley kinks to run almost east to west, and the road then follows the top of the northern edge, plunges down to cross the river and slowly climbs the southern side. I cycle along the southern edge, descend and climb out of a tributary valley, and then at Earls Colne fly down to cross the river again and climb back up onto the northern side, which I follow whilst gaining and losing height with alternate pedals.

Predictably enough, at Fordstreet, I simply can't resist how nice the southern side of the valley must be, and plunge down again, cross the river and – long climb this time – agonisingly regain the height I have so often lost but will now mostly maintain to wheeze my way into Colchester. If there is one thing we can say for sure, the Romans would never have been so bloody silly and whatever route their own road followed, it wasn't this; a revelation pressed home by the knowledge that I shortly have to pedal the journey in reverse.

Although the Via Devana doesn't survive in Colchester, long built over, it joined the surviving Roman Stane Street, now London Road, at the junction with King Coel Road, and headed diagonally off beneath the houses on the western side. I pause at this mundane and historic spot. From here to its end point at Godmanchester, I have followed its whole route. I now follow Stane Street and cycle on through Lexden where, in what is now a private garden, a British king was buried fifty years before the legions camped here, in one of the richest burials yet uncovered in Britain, with his weapons and chainmail shirt, amphorae of wine and silver medallion of the distant emperor Augustus, whose dynasty would cast such a shadow across this land. I pedal on and park my bike at the edge of the Roman town itself.

I walk between the remains of the Balkerne Gate and The Hole in the Wall pub, as that was the exact location of the monumental arch the Ninth would have marched through had they relieved the city. I then turn and walk through the ruins of the Balkerne Gate itself. Camulodunum. *Colonia Claudia Victricensis*. The Ninth never got here, but I have. I lay my hand on the cold stone and brick of the arch. It is not enough. I must return to the Temple of Claudius, and pay my respects to the poor souls who prayed so hard for the Ninth to complete what has taken me little more than an hour. A morning's march. Twelve miles. To the huddled fugitives in the gloom of the cella, it might as well have been a thousand.

The Ninth never marched!

Oh, but the Ninth had.

I wander the ground floor of the castle, and then simply sit inside the physical space occupied by the cella. I feel suddenly deflated. The enormity of what happened here, on this spot, in this very space, has begun to sink in. Every time I have come here there is no doubt that I have viewed this massacre from the Britons' perspective, that the bloody Romans had it coming. It is still not a feeling I can fully shake off, and it follows me on this journey around the country, wherever I may go. But not today. Rather than a Briton looking in, all torn with righteous bloodlust and pitiless fury, I am looking out: a Roman, and a helpless one.

I can't help but think of the men whose company, at least in my mind, I have shared, from the outskirts of Peterborough all the way to Halstead in Essex, who were so longed and prayed for by these people; good men to have on your side, but diamonds in the rough. I wonder if I have transgressed something by coming here, by completing their journey for them, but just as helpless to change events.

I walk around the recently revamped, brightly lit displays, of the scale model of the Norman castle, artefacts of medieval craft-work, carved wood and green-glazed pots, with kids and families running round; amongst the tightly huddled groups of crying and praying women, the groaning wounded and mewling children in the stinking darkness all around me.

The Ninth marched. They did try to get here.

All the artefacts of this massacre, the melted glass and broken pots and frenziedly buried jewellery are on the mezzanine above, not down here among the people to whom they belonged. The only artefacts within the actual site of the cella remotely appropriate for this scene of its history are a garish mock-up of the Waterloo Bridge helmet and a brightly polished, comedy pressed-brass bra for a pantomime warrior queen. They were worn by a Mrs Evelyn Gibson in 1909 at the Colchester Pageant.

She played the part of Boadicea.

Twelve miles north-west of the temple, in the undulating Colne Valley, Cerialis and the cavalry had swung their swords and hacked their way through the Britons, back along the Via Devana. About two miles west of Peterborough, Jonny and I are swinging golf clubs. For on that terrible day in the spring or early summer of AD 60, when he extricated his cavalry from the slaughter of the ambush, leaving the last stands of his doomed infantry to their fate, Cerialis finally reached this spot, the site of his fortress, exhausted and bloody, and bolted the gates behind him.

Standing about a quarter of the way along the thirteenth hole, I estimate I'm standing somewhere near the spot where those gates closed behind the cavalry that bleak day. For Cerialis they were the same gates that only a few days previously had seen the Ninth Legion march from their fortress, in neatly spaced ranks and standards raised, to relieve Camulodunum. Barely a man of that legion had returned. For us it is a narrow piece of fairway near the tee, wooded to either side, where both of us have just lost balls.

Cerialis was in an unenviable situation. He had escaped with his life and his cavalry, but had managed to leave his entire infantry contingent, perhaps as much as half the fighting strength of a legion, dead on the field – a monumental catastrophe. He was in a fortress, but it was sandwiched between the borders of the Iceni and the Corieltauvi, considered firm favourites to have fought with the Iceni in the AD 47 uprising. Were the Corieltauvi hostile now? Had they already risen in revolt? And if not, would they?

Cerialis had no insight into Boudica's plans. As the only organised military force anywhere close to the rebels, would they now seek him out to destroy him? His fortress may have been a logical place for him to fall back, but it was now far too large for his remaining troops to defend. He needed a smaller, more compact compound where he could concentrate his force. His weary troopers dismounted, but the day's work was not yet over.

The flight back to Longthorpe is based on Tacitus, of course, who states that he *escaped with some cavalry into the camp, and was saved by its fortifications.*[25] At least one writer recently has taken this to mean that Cerialis sheltered in a fort local to

Colchester,[26] but it is unclear exactly which fort they are implying. Obviously the old legionary fortress no longer existed, occupied by the colonia, and its defences long gone.

There was a fort locally at Gosbecks whose garrison, *if* it was in use at this time, would have fallen defending the city. But whether one of these or another, unless there was a fort with not only the space but the tons of fodder and food required daily by five hundred or even a thousand men and horses, not to mention the hundreds of gallons of water, Cerialis would have lasted about forty-eight hours before being starved out and making a limp for it on famished mounts. He couldn't allow his horses to graze and his men to go foraging whilst in actual and serious contact with an overwhelming force of the enemy, and even if a well-stocked fort miraculously appeared in the vicinity, he wouldn't choose to hole up his force in an instant siege.

I believe Cerialis would have made it back to where he knew a well-stocked fortress awaited him a decent distance from this horde that he had no chance of beating unassisted. What we need is some archaeological evidence, or at least a hint, that we are heading in the right direction. Perhaps, incredibly, it exists.

The fortress at Longthorpe was composed of those deep double ditches and towering ramparts, encompassing an area of twenty-seven acres, but there was another ditch, inside the ramparts, that enclosed just eleven acres. It was almost square, and shared the original south-western rampart, but it was clearly built as a separate entity.

There can be no certainties here, but could this not be a hurriedly constructed defence built by Cerialis?[27] Escaping *to the camp*, he would have found the original defences far too long for his residual cavalry force to hold, and constructed the smaller fort to house them. The new compound encompassed many of the older buildings, providing shelter, food and forage for both man and beast. Cerialis could hold the walls of the original fortress for now – the scale of the place alone would deter a half-hearted attack by marauding locals. But if Boudica's force appeared, or the Corieltauvi looked like they meant business, they could quickly fall back to the smaller fortlet within.

As with so many of the sites in this book, thousands of people come here without ever giving Boudica or Cerialis a second thought. Why would they? There is nothing to tell you that a Roman fortress once stood here, glowering over the Fens, with its ramparts and ditches, barracks, stables and granaries, of the thousands of men from all over the empire who knew this place; that the famous Ninth Legion was garrisoned here, nor of the haunted survivors who expected to die here as they hacked a miniature fortress out of the bigger one to make their final stand in AD 60. And as with all those other sites, if you visit it with these events in mind, you can begin to imagine some of that grim endeavour going on around you. You can visualise that high earth and timber rampart crossing the fairway ahead of you, and the unshaven sentry intently watching the southern horizon: Are they coming? Will they come?

But Boudica's army never came. Cerialis never got his second chance to be surrounded by the rebels, nor gave the order to fall back on his new fortlet as the enemy flooded over the main ramparts. They sat out at least a part of the war in this bleak fortress of the Fen Edge, waiting; cut off.

For a couple of reasons, our golfing trip to this remarkable spot had the potential to be an introspective day for Jonny and me. It was good for us to spend a few hours in the fresh air, with little to concentrate our minds but the determination to knock a small ball into a tiny hole on the other side of the landscape by thrashing it repeatedly with a stick seemingly designed to make the job as difficult as possible.

Jonny and Emma had just learnt that her breast cancer, absent for six years, had hailed its unwelcome return, and the new round of scans and biopsies was in progress, but they were strong and optimistic and their positivity effortlessly buoyed-up those around them.[28] My own weight, in addition to that, was a more expected progression of life's cycle. My mum had died three weeks before.

I had last seen her a fortnight after her ninetieth birthday, the day after my limping slog from Cambridge to Sible Hedingham, and the return to Longthorpe felt like the completion of so many journeys and stories. The same back-lit Paul Nash sky that had smiled on us on the Wandlebury Roman road shone down on me again, but it lacked something; my mum was no longer beneath it.

I had driven up to Bingham, near Nottingham, the day before the funeral, to see Mum at rest, for the final time, and say my silent farewells. I had a drink with my sisters, and then took a solitary stroll through a familiar, familial landscape, past the old family home, and pubs and shops and schools, each a cinematograph projecting its memories; but there was somewhere in particular I had to pause before making the long journey home, to clear my head and get some caffeine and sugar in my veins. It was somewhere I needed to go, this day of all other days, an unlikely destination on the face of it – Costa Coffee in Bingham market square.

Costa Coffee now occupies the site of the demolished house where my grandma and her brothers had lived in the 1900s, and where my mum was born and lived until she was about five. Her childhood memories of birthdays and Christmases, toys and family games must have swirled invisibly round the place, although I don't ever remember her having any interest in it, an utterly charmless 1970s red-brick development that replaced the old building.

Grandma's nineteen-year-old kid brother, Sydney, left this house to follow his older brothers to war early in 1916, first to Ireland, and then to France and Belgium. He never came home, but it was upstairs, where I go to sit among the few people sipping their lattes, where his mum, my great gran, had woken in the middle of the night to see him standing by her bed, telling her not to worry for him, the day he was posted missing in action.

Whatever the origin of the story, whether she dreamed it,

imagined it, or really did see her boy reaching out to her in his final moments from the unimaginable hell of Passchendaele, it was an image I had often conjured in my mind when I was growing up; a shadowed khaki figure standing forlornly by the bed of his mother.

A soldier from a lost legion come marching home.

It was important to come here today, of all days, to remember my mum as a little girl playing in this space, after seeing her, so very old and finally at peace, the day before her funeral, but also to remember Sydney and his mum, meeting here in the twilight. The strange coincidence that had brought me on my painful act of farewell, and thence to this spot, was that it was one hundred years to the exact day that Sydney's battalion, the 2/8 Sherwood Foresters, had left their trenches at dawn and assaulted the German positions at Toronto Farm near Zonnebeke on 26 September 1917, and then held them during a vicious counter-attack.

Sydney's body was never recovered. It was a hundred years before, to within a few hours, that my great gran saw her kid for the final time through the comforting haze of half-sleep, and it was somewhere here, in the almost deserted upstairs of Costa, that she saw him.

At the end of our golf match, Jonny and I sit on a wooden bench at the beginning of the sixteenth hole, which lies pretty much dead in the centre of both the large fortress and its smaller fortlet. Here around us lay the legionary headquarters building and legate's accommodation, as well as the building where the earring was found. This is probably the very spot where the breathless dispatch rider sprinted into Cerialis's office clutching Camulodunum's plea for help.

I take out my carefully wrapped copy of *The Eagle of the Ninth*. I can still hear Dad, nearly forty years ago, having told me something of the story, searching in vain for his own volume, saying,

'We'll get you a copy this afternoon when we go into town.' I flick through the amber-tinged pages, looking for a quote I told myself I'd read here, a quote I hadn't been able to shake from my head in the coffee shop a fortnight before, imagining my great uncle Sydney standing beside his mother's bed in the twilight.

It was a passage that Sutcliff had written about York, Roman *Eboracum*, the future garrison town of the Ninth Legion, but it could have been written for Longthorpe, as well as for that lost generation that Sydney had the honour and misfortune to be a part of. Rosemary Sutcliff had a wonderful feel for the lingering memory of place. She has a Roman legate explain to Marcus Aquila:

> Eboracum is still – how shall I put it? – still more than a little ghost-ridden by the Ninth Legion. Oh, I do not mean that their spirits have wandered back from the fields of Ra, but the place is haunted, none the less. By the altars to Spanish gods that they set up and worshipped at; by their names and numbers idly scratched on walls; by British women whom they loved and children with Spanish faces whom they fathered. All this lying, as it were, like a sediment under the new wine of another Legion. Also they linger strongly, almost terrifyingly, in the minds of the people.

As I gaze around at the bunkers and fairways, thinking of the real sediment the Ninth left behind here – the floor plan of their barracks, the detritus of the hunt, scraps of armour, the earring of a girlfriend, and the little bronze fish hook of the daydreaming angler, it is the Legate's final words that lend a chill to the air, as he makes a small gesture with his open hand:

> It sounds little enough, put into words, and yet it can create an atmosphere which is unpleasantly strong. I am not an imaginative man, but I tell you that there have been times, when the mist comes down from the high moors, when I have more than half expected to see the lost Legion come marching home.[29]

My game ended 86-over-par (whatever that means). It was time for my 25-yearly affirmation that I'm not cut out for golf, and to head on back down to join Boudica. Her army was streaming back from the battlefield, laden down with swords, javelins, armour, helmets, shields and severed heads; perhaps scalps and more gruesome trophies were carried away, and bound captives marked for sacrifice. These farmers-turned-warriors may have been shocked at the ferocity with which they had attacked and overwhelmed the Romans, appalled or exulted at their first taste of war. And now, like them, we should turn towards distant Londinium lying helpless to the south-west.

Camulodunum is a smoking ruin, the pavements greasy with human fat,[30] the bodies of the veterans strewn around the Temple precinct, their wives and children heaped in the bloody ruin of the temple cella. The Ninth Legion lies scattered across the Essex countryside, stiffening and swelling in the spring sunshine. The crows have more than they can eat, and a black cloud of bloated flies will follow.

But I am not turning towards London; not yet. I must switch my focus to a man and an army many miles away, for this wasn't just Boudica's war. It takes two sides to make a battle, and that other side was about as far north as a Roman army could go in AD 60, on the North-West Frontier of the Roman Empire. I need to find General Gaius Suetonius Paulinus, Governor of Britannia, and his grim-faced legionaries as they stare across the straits of the dreaded Isle of Mona.

I'm headed for Anglesey.

6

Enemy Coast Ahead

The Storming of Ynys Mon

The endless ground under us.
The water is shining among the trees.
The lake is a window into the earth.
Tomas Tranströmer, *The Half-Finished Heaven*

The Roman offensives against the hill tribes of Wales had been long and bloody. The people were tough and unyielding, and the landscape a tangled nightmare of forest, intercutting valleys, bogs and mountain fastnesses. When the Romans had first landed in southern Britain, those distant tribes, and their brooding, cloud-hung hills, were no more than a darkness beyond the horizon. But as the army marched and consolidated the lowlands, punctuating the landscape with their forts and roads, bribing, slaughtering and bullying their progression north and west, that interlinking pattern of road and fort seemed to align itself towards one objective. The legions knew it, and so did the hill tribes.

The storm had broken in the autumn or winter of AD 47, when those tribes had launched pre-emptive strikes into Roman allied territories, sparking more than a decade of murderous guerilla warfare. The main players were the Silures of south and central Wales, and the Ordovices in northern Wales, initially led by the errant prince of the Catuvellauni, Caratacus. He was finally brought to bay in AD 51 by Governor Publius Ostorius Scapula, and made his stand on a hill overlooking a difficult river crossing, defended by stone ramparts and steep crags, perhaps along the Severn valley.

It was a disaster. Scapula, potentially fielding an army of over 20,000 men,[1] led the attack and the British position was stormed. Caratacus escaped, but his wife, daughter and brother were taken captive. Hoping to upset the fragile balance of power in Brigantia, he fled to the north, where Queen Cartimandua promptly seized him. Prince Caratacus, scion of the royal house of the Catuvellauni, son of King Cunobelin, and arguably the greatest British war leader of the entire conquest period, joined his family in a slave cage on the long road to Rome.

If Scapula hoped that his crushing victory would rupture the spirit of the hill tribes, he must have been bitterly disappointed as the war intensified. What Tacitus then describes gives us a taste of the misery that ensued for soldier and warrior alike, that for want of a better analogy, reads like nothing short of a Roman Vietnam:

> *Now began a series of skirmishes, for the most part like raids, in woods and morasses, with encounters due to chance or to courage, to mere heedlessness or to calculation, to fury or to lust of plunder, under directions from the officers, or sometimes even without their knowledge. Conspicuous above all in stubborn resistance were the Silures, whose rage was fired by words rumoured to have been spoken by the Roman general, to the effect, that . . . the name of the Silures ought to be blotted out. Accordingly they cut off two of our auxiliary cohorts, the rapacity of whose officers let them make incautious forays; and by liberal gifts of spoils and prisoners to the other tribes, they were luring them too into revolt.*[2]

This passage, perhaps more than anything else Tacitus wrote, brings home the terrible nature of war on the British frontier, of hatred between enemies and an actual policy of genocide, of search-and-destroy patrols bent on nothing but murder and plunder, spurred on by the command of the governor himself to exterminate the tribe. For the Roman soldiers there were no non-combatants in those soaking, hostile hills. The only good Briton was a dead Briton, and the Silures were paying them back in kind.

The hardships of the constant fighting were too much for Scapula, who died in office. Before a replacement could be sent, the Silures overpowered a legion, either the Twentieth or Fourteenth. The extent of this disaster is unknown, but they must have been forced from the field with heavy loss, and the tribesmen raided far and wide in its wake. Such was the unenviable situation inherited by the new governor, the aged Aulus Didius Gallus, who consolidated rather than attacked, and then Quintus Veranius, the first British governor appointed by the new emperor, Nero, who raided the Silures, but died after only a year.

The next governor, Gaius Suetonius Paulinus, needs no introduction. Taking control of the British garrison in AD 58, Tacitus does not record the first part of his tenure beyond telling us that he *enjoyed success for two years; he subdued several tribes and strengthened our military posts*,[3] but his impact on south and central Wales must have been devastating. The Silures, the tribe that had pinned the imperial Roman army to the foothills and Marches for the better part of a decade, were a threat no longer and Paulinus was able to march north. Whatever desolation, hostage-taking or genocide had forced their passivity, the testament to their downfall is the simple fact that they were spoken of no more. It would be seventeen years before they were even mentioned again in the surviving histories.

This pacification did not bring Wales within the province, but neutralised the threat by force and occupation. Many fugitives had fled north, where the spirit of continued resistance was still to be found, inspired by the religious caste of the Druids, who had a holy centre, or final citadel, on the Isle of Anglesey. This remarkable island, *Mona*, or *Ynys Mon*, lying off the most northerly point of the Welsh mainland in the Irish Sea, not only gave refuge to those able to flee there, but could provide supplies, warriors, religious fervour and martial orchestration to the beleaguered hill folk of the valleys, *a place from which the rebels drew reinforcements*, as Tacitus described it in the *Agricola*.

With the Druids and resistance leaders able to act with impunity from the island fortress, the Welsh tribes could never be truly pacified. However many fires of resistance the hobnailed caligae stamped out, the wind from Mona would fan them back to life. The final objective for Paulinus was clear enough. Early in AD 60, with a vast fleet of flat-bottomed landing craft being churned out of purpose-built shipyards in the Dee estuary,[4] Paulinus marched Legio XIV Gemina and perhaps some cohorts of the XX Valeria north with a similar number of auxiliaries to make camp on the southern shore of the Menai Strait.

As if symbolic of its impending fall, the Roman soldiers watched the sun sinking over the island at the end of each day, and arise bright each morning from the peaceful, settled province behind them.

If driving from the east of England to north Wales rewards you with anything, it is an appreciation of the sheer distance between the two, an investment of five or six hours cruising along at a mile-a-minute or more in the leather-seated luxury of a VW Passat, but a huge distance to march or ride. Admittedly, the soldiers assembling on the southern shore of the Menai Strait had not just marched there from the south-east, but from campaign bases scattered across Wales and the Marches, and perhaps Chester, at the mouth of the Dee, where early military activity predates the later fortress.[5]

Some of them might not have visited the south-eastern half of the province for years, but it was the only place this side of *Oceanus* with anything approaching the description of a town. The thought of it must have occupied many a bored sentry, of marching south-east to the Via Devana and visiting Camulodunum, or of retiring there like their older comrades, with pensions, land, wives, and slaves to fulfil their every need.

I leave home dark and early on a brisk January morning, and reach Bangor before lunch. The drive along the north Welsh coast is exhilarating, and then finally my first sight of Anglesey – the thin black harpoon-tip of Penmon Point reaching towards the motionless whale-back of Puffin Island. So here is Ynys Mon at last, Mona. The Isle of the Druids, if Tacitus is to be believed. Well, sacred island or no, in AD 60 Governor Paulinus brought the Fourteenth and Twentieth here to smash the final resistance of the Welsh tribes, in addition to auxiliaries and a naval complement to supervise the vast armada of flat-bottomed landing craft moored up in the Strait. The enemy coast ahead measured eighteen miles in length.

This traditional view might be overstated – Paulinus couldn't leave newly conquered Wales ungarrisoned, and Tacitus doesn't give us the numbers, or legions, involved in this assault. Perhaps, therefore, only the Fourteenth attacked Anglesey, matched by a similar number of auxiliaries, whilst the Twentieth secured a stranglehold on the Silures and Ordovices. Either way, one legion or two, the little island was living on borrowed time. Every Druid and priestess could raise their voices in ululating curse, and every hill warrior bring a sword or spear to the beach. No matter. With several thousand legionaries boarding landing craft that would launch them onto those very same beaches, Ynys Mon was doomed.

Parking up in Bangor near Garth Pier and climbing the roads uphill, I follow the heights all the way to the Menai Bridge. For much of the walk, the opposite shore looks particularly forbidding, steep cliffs and wooded scrambles, although the jutting promontory of Menai Bridge itself would have made a superb strongpoint to seize and fortify at the narrowest crossing point. Carrying on to the west, through the Botanic Gardens and onwards to the Britannia Bridge, the Anglesey shoreline is more inviting, with gently sloping beaches for landing and fighting inland.

If Roman military purists will forgive me, there is no better way to imagine the scene around you as you walk from the Menai Bridge through the woods to the Britannia Bridge, or simply sit in the Antelope Inn with a pint, than to watch the first few minutes of *Gladiator*. As Russell Crowe walks through his army assembling to fight the barbarian hordes in Germania, if you substitute the muddy valley bottom for a stretch of water, with landing craft on the near shore waiting to load the soldiers, then the scene is pretty much set for you to project onto the Strait.

The broad visual canvas it provides, of a campaigning Roman army prepping itself for action in the ubiquitous drifting smoke of a military camp, deploying into assembly areas denoted by the raised standards of the various units, is superbly drawn, whatever the niggling inaccuracies of Hollywood. The miles south-west of the Menai Bridge and Antelope Inn would have been a series of identical assembly areas, of churned ground and splintered tree stumps, with thousands of troops, begrimed, unshaven and grim, waiting to board the boats or swim their horses.

Tacitus gives a vivid account of the attack across the Strait, which he could reasonably have disposed of in a sentence had he chosen. It is one of those rare descriptions that really smacks of first-hand testimony, precious flickering film footage that once played through someone's memory – perhaps Agricola's – and the specific mention of flat-bottomed boats and shifting shallows lends his account the air of solid authenticity. To appreciate this story you really need to read Tacitus standing on this shore, gazing across to Mona, knowing that this is not some untouchable ancient epic from a long-lost field half a world away, but that it happened here; where you stand, south-west of Pont Britannia, another soul once stood, staring across the water at those same bluffs:

He built flat-bottomed vessels to cope with the shallows, and uncertain depths of the sea. Thus the infantry crossed, while the cavalry followed by fording, or, where the water was deep, swam by the side of their horses. On the shore stood the oppos-ing army with its dense array of armed warriors, while between the ranks dashed women, in black attire like the Furies, with hair dishevelled, waving firebrands. All around, the Druids lift-ing up their hands to heaven, poured forth dreadful imprecations.[6]

Unlike me, and many of you, Tacitus hadn't seen the Menai Strait, but his description fits very well with the landscape, of what was really a glorified (albeit technically difficult) river crossing rather than a naval assault.

Of course, the Menai Strait is not a river, although the Welsh name, Afon Menai, lyrically denotes it as such. It is actually the sea running through a glacial striation along a geological fault line. The notorious Swellies, lying in the narrowest neck where the bridges now stand and a few hundred metres wide, have jutting outcrops of rock, some permanently submerged or exposed, others appearing and disappearing with the tide, caus-ing tidal rapids and whirlpools. To either side lie broader sections, increasingly wide as they approach the ends, all with shallow sections concealing deep, narrow channels within.

All of this is combined with a staggered double tide, first from the west, and then an hour or so later reaching the eastern entrance and running completely in reverse whilst continuing to rise. With a fast flow and a tidal range as much as seven metres, it is little wonder that Thomas Telford's Menai suspension bridge, opened in 1826, and Robert Stephenson's Britannia Bridge in 1850, were considered such godsends.

The Strait has a bad reputation, with good reason, but crossing in purpose-built vessels should not have been hazardous in itself, nor the auxiliary cavalry swimming their horses. In the 1800s, farmers had been swimming their cattle across the water at Ynys-y-Moch, the narrowest point where the Menai Bridge now stands, for hundreds of years with rarely a loss,[7] and at low-water-slack little of the channel would have been impassable. The risk, particularly in this narrower section, was the current once the tide started moving.

Unless one lies preserved beneath the silt, we can only speculate upon the design of the boats used in the assault, but Tacitus uses the word *navis* – ship, not *ratis* – raft.[8] They were surely smaller than standard, ocean-going troop transports, which held between 80 to 120 men,[9] but large, flat-bottomed river patrol boats with a draft of only eighteen inches have been recovered from the Rhine.[10] Simple flat-bottomed barges, likewise found on the Rhine, would also have sufficed.

It is questionable whether Paulinus, facing a seriously opposed crossing, would simply hurl his troops like a sledgehammer against one beach. Unlike naval landings on a larger scale, forces beaching almost anywhere along the Strait would require only limited gains before becoming mutually supporting, whereas fragmentation into smaller groups would weaken the Britons, lacking the professional organisational structure enabling dispersed units to act in concert.

This scenario is supported by known Roman military doctrine. Dio's all too brief coverage of the AD 43 invasion states that Aulus Plautius divided his armada in three, *in order that they should not be hindered in landing, as might happen to a single force*.[11] He then describes the opposed river crossings where the Batavian auxiliaries, swimming across in armour, took the Britons by surprise and caused havoc amongst the chariot and cavalry horses before the main assault began. The Roman general Julius Frontinus, governor only a decade after Paulinus, noted approvingly in his book of military stratagems, examples of attacking across rivers by deceiving the enemy with more than one crossing point.[12]

The Roman assembly areas on the mainland would have been starkly visible from Mona, and Paulinus could have established decoy camps along the entire length of the Strait to keep the enemy dispersed. Alternatively, in the tried and tested tactics of AD 43, the main assault could have taken place to the south-west, whilst the amphibious Batavians crossed at the opposite end, north of Bangor, where the water opens up to over three miles wide, but the mudflats are walkable at low tide. This foot crossing of the Lavan Sands has been used for many centuries, aided by a boat at the far end.

In about 1460, Welsh poet Rhys Goch penned a couplet concerning this very spot:

> To Mona's shores 'spite Menai's flow,
> The sands are crossed when tide is low.[13]

Assembling in silence and without torches overnight, the auxiliaries could have crossed whilst all attention was on the armada splashing across miles to the south, leaving only a narrow channel to swim across to Beaumaris where the craggy coast gives way once more to gentle slopes. From there it was less than six miles to the first good landing beaches south of the Swellies, where the legionaries might have been fighting their way ashore. The Batavians, in their now classic manoeuvre, could have outflanked the defenders.

Of course, the Britons knew better than Paulinus that the Lavan Sands could be crossed, but it was hardly a place that any Roman general would send heavily laden troops and, anyhow, the final channel was impassable without boats. Such was the value of the Batavians; they didn't need boats. Not for nothing have they become known as 'Rome's Navy Seals'.[14]

Swimming in armour is no mean feat. Modern reconstructions of *lorica hamata* mail tunics regularly weigh in at twelve kilograms, the equivalent of trying to swim carrying five bricks in a rucksack, in addition to a sword, bronze helmet, and hobnailed caligae. We know that they must have left the rest of their equipment behind, because swimming with much more would have been physically impossible. If the armada of landing craft and squadrons of swimming cavalrymen were not enough to daunt the watching Britons, the sight of these mud-smeared amphibians rising from the water in full armour would have appalled them. Were they sea creatures or devils? They could hardly be men.

The battle on the beach and the struggle for the bluffs must have dominated the day's action. Frances Lynch in her classic *Prehistoric Anglesey* suggested that the defenders could have retired to Llangefni to hold the pass across the marsh that bisects the island only four or five miles inland;[15] it was a forlorn hope. Every Druid and every warrior must have known what Paulinus and each of his professional soldiers knew – the battle for Ynys Mon would be won or lost on the beach. Once the Romans had established a secure beachhead, no matter how many Britons were left or whatever they had planned, the island was lost. Denying them that foothold by sword, spear, sling and magical curse, was probably the only real strategy.

And, for a time, it worked:

Scared our soldiers [were] by the unfamiliar sight, so that, as if their limbs were paralysed, they stood motionless, and exposed to wounds. Then urged by their general's appeals and mutual encouragements not to quail before a troop of frenzied women, they bore the standards onwards, smote down all resistance, and wrapped the foe in the flames of his own firebrands.[16]

The auxiliaries may have been the first on the beach as skirmishers, to secure enough of the shore for the legionaries to land behind them and form into line before going into action. It has to be wondered if the Druidic curses haunted these men even more than they did the legionaries. They might not have understood the language, but they would have appreciated the intent and power of the scene, many coming from lands that may have fielded similar cursing priests in battle, including, perhaps, even Druids – many auxiliaries would have hailed from Celtic lands.

The ancient Irish texts, committed to writing in the Middle Ages just a few miles across the water to the west, tell of Druids in war, encircling the battlefield, standing on one leg, one eye closed and one arm outstretched, hurling their curses in a ritual posture known as *corrguinecht*, because it imitates the posture of a crane, or *corr*.[17] In an episode of the *Book of Invasions of Ireland*, the god Lugh asks the Druids what power they will bring to a battle, and they reply: 'Not hard to say. We will bring showers of fire on the faces of the [enemy], so that they cannot look up, and the warriors contending with them can use their force to kill them.'[18]

If we accept that the Druids on Mona could not bring forth showers of fire, the fact that both sides believed their curses to be effective seems to have had exactly the same result. Either way the troops faltered. Perhaps some refused to disembark, and those with their feet in the water made a shield line where they stood, warding off spears and spells alike. Even such a momentary weakness must have spurred the priests on to redouble their efforts and volume as they hopped one-legged, one-armed and one-eyed, and the warriors to surge on with the zeal of fanatics who can see the power of their gods halting their foes in their tracks.

For the Romans it was do or die, for a fate far worse than a Druid's curse awaited them from their general if they didn't press on. The stiff bark of a senior officer, that no trained soldier can resist, and the blood-stirring blast of the trumpets, carried the men forward. The discipline and tactics of the Romans must have told as the bodies piled up and the slick silt of low tide became slicker still with blood and entrails; the gladius, punched under-arm into the stomach or abdomen, naturally eviscerated many of its victims. It was here that simple innovations such as hobnailed caligae could make the difference between success and failure, as the sure-footed legionaries slogged on and the British warriors slipped in the mud and gore.

Tacitus does not tell us how long the battle raged, but by the end of the day Paulinus had his beachhead. Sensing defeat, and probably exhausted beyond further resistance, the British attacks must have slackened and the legionaries pushed forward. The moment the soldiers had recovered their wits from the showering spells and curses, the outcome had never really been in doubt.

Even well-disciplined, professional armies can disintegrate and rout in the moment of defeat, and in a less organised force it is almost a certainty. This was the moment for the auxiliary infantrymen and fleet-footed cavalry to do their work, with their long-bladed swords, lances and spears. In Victorian colonial campaigns, far better documented than ancient ones, the greatest slaughter was often inflicted in the cavalry pursuit that followed the infantry battle, riding down the exhausted fugitives with sword and lance, blotting out the last knots of resistance, and it is a basic function of the cavalry alluded to in classical texts.

Moving inland, the legions were confronted by an island about fifteen miles wide and twenty miles long, with a ragged coastline, some 276 square miles all told. Unlike Snowdonia visible behind them, this was a hospitable landscape of rolling ridges running parallel to the Strait, but little that could even be called hills in this part of the world. It was not a landscape that could conceal protracted guerrilla resistance, and it was easy meat for an army that had fought its way across the mountains and valleys of Wales:

> *A force was next set over the conquered, and their groves, devoted to inhuman superstitions, were destroyed. They deemed it indeed a duty to cover their altars with the blood of captives and to consult their deities through human entrails.*[19]

Exactly what constituted a sacred grove on Anglesey in AD 60 is really anyone's guess. A clump of trees, large or small, certainly, but as to exactly what it was that the Romans hacked down and burnt, or how many or where, is not something we can ever know. The most vivid and remarkable description of a sacred grove of the Celts is described by Lucan in his *Pharsalia*, a mid-first-century source completely contemporary with the storming of Mona, although describing events relating to Caesar a hundred years earlier in Gaul, and not a history, alas, but an epic poem.

If we cannot rely on it to describe accurately a Druidic grove on

Ynys Mon, we can certainly get an idea of what the Roman troops were expecting to find:

> There stood a grove which from the earliest time no hand of man had dared to violate; hidden from the sun its chill recesses; matted boughs entwined prisoned the air within . . . but savage rites and barbarous worship, altars horrible on massive stones upreared; sacred with blood of men was every tree. If faith be given to ancient myth, no fowl has ever dared to rest upon those branches, and no beast has made his lair beneath: no tempest falls, nor lightnings flash upon it from the cloud. Stagnant the air unmoving, yet the leaves filled with mysterious trembling; dripped the streams from coal-black fountains; effigies of gods rude, scarcely fashioned from some fallen trunk held the mid space: and, pallid with decay, their rotting shapes struck terror . . .[20]

Whether this really was the backcloth to the slaughter of the Druids, or if the groves were simple, natural places of quiet contemplation, it represents a visual archetype that many a soldier must have had in mind as he cut down the fleeing priests and priestesses with sword and spear.

If Ynys Mon really was the headquarters of the priesthood, an offshore inner sanctum that the holy men and women were prepared to die *en masse* for, rather than a corner into which the fighting men and priests alike had merely been driven, then the far-reaching import of the cataclysm is not something we can ever truly comprehend, or detect in the soil, any more than the massacre itself. The curses are silent, the groves are gone and the blood has long washed away. Within the limits of archaeological inference, not a single fragment of charcoal or sliver of bone has been found to remind us of the fall of Ynys Mon.

I arrive at Hotel Cymyran about an hour before dusk. It is an imposing, rather incongruous modern building tucked away in the remote western corner of Anglesey close to Holy Island, whose exterior belies the warm and welcoming comfort within. I dump my bag and am out again within minutes. I have come here to visit a site a mere 300 metres from the hotel, but I am almost out of time to explore it, having lingered too long imagining Paulinus's D-Day landings at Menai. I grab my coat and head off along the narrow country lanes.

After a few confusing moments, angrily convincing myself that the site is inaccessible behind an impenetrable barbed-wire fence, before finding it on the other side of the road, perfectly accessible, and with information boards, I gaze out across the still water of a small lake. A rough path leads to the lake's edge, which is otherwise enclosed behind a dense barrier of reed, six or seven feet high. Looking behind me, I am only a few metres away from the fence of an RAF airfield, and workmen with a JCB are trundling around within. But gazing out across the water, the sun falling behind me, the cold breeze rustling the reeds, I feel the contentment and thrill of an old ambition finally realised.

I read so much about this place at university, the cornerstone for my project on British Iron Age chariots. It had a significant place in the first archaeology book I read as a teenager, as well as being in one of my favourite novels. It is a place of immense importance in the study of the Iron Age in Britain, of insular La Tène artwork, and of the Druids, and although it is questionable exactly how far it relates to the events in hand, the story of AD 60 and the fall of Ynys Mon simply cannot be told without recounting the story of *The Lake of Little Stones*: Llyn Cerrig Bach.

Britain's longest year, 1940, was drawing to a close. The bedraggled British Expeditionary Force had washed ashore half-drowned from Dunkirk, the Royal Air Force had seen off the worst the Luftwaffe could throw at it, and the great armada of field-grey landing craft had never braved the Channel. Hitler increasingly looked elsewhere for his adventures, and Churchill could rest assured that no jackbooted feet would be warming themselves in front of a British fire this winter.

Two days before Christmas, a solitary German aircraft flew a lonely mission over the Irish Sea. Flying at high altitude, it traversed the western coast of Anglesey hunting for targets, but the plane carried no bombs. Its weapon was a long-focal-length camera. At twenty-five minutes to two in the afternoon, the crew were flying west-north-west towards Holy Island. The pilot could see a site of great interest to the Luftwaffe, a new airfield, not yet operational and still under construction, the junction of the dark, intersecting runways on the white sand of the bulldozed coastal dunes like a great, black X on a treasure map.

It was a hugely strategic location, close to the port of Liverpool, the industrial heartlands of the Midlands, and the crucial Atlantic shipping lanes. The crew noted the time and location, worked the camera and were soon flying home along the Irish coast.[21]

RAF Rhosneigr, part of No. 9 Group, Fighter Command, opened in February 1941, soon changing its name to RAF Valley. Throughout 1941 and 1942 various fighter and air/sea rescue squadrons flew from the base, but with America's entry into the war at the end of 1941, the site became increasingly important as a base for receiving aircraft coming from the United States, especially B-17 Flying Fortress bombers.

It is the arrival of the B-17s that weaves RAF Valley into our story. These enormous aircraft needed longer runways than those that had been built for the Hurricanes and Spitfires, and work to extend them exacerbated a long-standing problem, unwittingly exposed in the 1940 German photograph – sand. RAF Valley was created by levelling part of the Tywyn Trewan dune system. Coastal dunes are relatively stable because of the surface vegetation that knits them together. With this removed, windblown sand drifted across the runways, upsetting the grip of landing aircraft, and potentially getting inside the engines.

A greenkeeper from the neighbouring Anglesey Golf Club, William Owen Roberts, had been employed as head groundsman on the station. He suggested that peat could be dredged from the old lake margins on the northern edge of the airfield, spread over the sand and then seeded with grass. The dredging began in October 1942.

What happened next has deservedly become part of archaeological folklore. A scoop pulled between two cable engines was used to harvest the bog. The peat was then loaded onto lorries, dumped adjacent to the runways, and spread by tractor-pulled harrows. One day in the early summer of 1943, a tractor driver removed an iron chain that had caught on the teeth of his harrow, and threw it aside. Later in the day one of the lorries stuck fast in the mud, and the driver broke two wire tow ropes trying to drag it out.

Roberts remembered seeing the old chain by the edge of the field, linked it up to the tractor, and the lorry was quickly pulled free. The chain did good service for the rest of the day. Before leaving the site, Roberts took a closer look at the chain, thought it of interest, draped it over the handlebars of his bicycle, and walked it for over a mile to the office of Mr J.A. Jones, the site engineer. Jones agreed that the chain was of unusual construction, and sent a drawing of it to the National Museum of Wales in Cardiff.[22] Fortuitously, it landed on the desk of the director, the eminent archaeologist Sir Cyril Fox, whom we last met in the previous chapter, as a student in Cambridge in 1921, excavating sections across the Via Devana.

The chain was some two thousand years old, dating to the late Iron Age, but most striking was its obvious function. This was no chain for hanging a cauldron over a fire or dragging a plough. It was a slave chain, punctuated by five large, neck-sized loops that opened and locked shut, for the archetypal chain gang. Incredibly, even after lying for two thousand years in the peat, the chain had not only survived the gruelling work that had snapped two wire tow ropes, but had suffered little obvious damage in doing so beyond the straightening of some of the half-rings.

Roberts, Jones and the workmen continued to collect what they found, and about 170[23] metal objects were eventually recovered, as well as thousands of bones, most of which were discarded. The richness and variety of the deposit was extraordinary. Another, shorter slave chain was found, and many items of both martial and perhaps ceremonial use – numerous swords, spears, and part of a shield; the iron tyres, nave hoops, linchpins and decorative fittings from chariots; pieces of horse harness, sword-shaped lengths of iron known as currency bars; cauldrons, a sickle, a trumpet, decorative bronze panels, and two pairs of blacksmith's tongs. All of the material had been dredged from one tiny area of bog on the margins of a little lake, Llyn Cerrig Bach, and it was in the spreading and harrowing of this peat that all of the artefacts were recovered.

This was no Snettisham treasure, of priceless gold, silver and electrum, but the real wealth, a snapshot of the beating heart of Celtic society in microcosm – slaving, charioteering, farming, fighting, blacksmithing and feasting. There was something almost mundane about some of the items, but it is impossible not to feel that this sacrifice was more deeply representative of what made Iron Age society tick than any quantity of precious metals.

Sadly, Fox interpreted the assemblage as being 'predominantly masculine, a bracelet being probably the only thing which might have belonged to a woman',[24] an observation that tells us significantly more about the 1940s than it does about the Iron Age. Fox also believed that the items had come from the four corners of the British Isles[25] rather than being crafted locally, and although this theory has since been criticised,[26] the assemblage was probably not entirely local.[27] And the question remains: were the slave chains complete with slaves when they sank into the cold water of the bog?

On the first page of his site report, Fox tells us that the site engineer, Mr Jones, had recorded the presence of animal bones alongside the metalwork in July 1943. However, the original letter from Jones, now held by the National Museum of Wales, records that *human* bones had been found.[28] Despite plausible modern suggestions that sacrificial human bones might have been hushed-up as bad wartime propaganda,[29] the discrepancy may be as simple as Fox inspecting the 'human' bones and identifying them as animal – it wouldn't be the first time that fragments of pig bone had been reverently bagged as 'human' by an inexperienced excavator, and I proudly raise my own hand in guilt.

Very little of the bone was collected during the dredging of Llyn Cerrig Bach, but the sample retained contained ox, horse, pig, sheep and dog, with little evidence of butchery, hinting at a sacrificial context rather than the detritus of feasting, which tends to leave cut marks on the surface of the bone.[30] I remain unconvinced that Fox hushed-up human remains, but that is not to suggest that unrecognised human bones were not present at Llyn Cerrig Bach – they may well have been, and would not be at all out of place in such a context.

The presence of the airfield, the great blue sign proclaiming *Llu Awyr Brenhinol Y Fali* – Royal Air Force Valley – the roar of aircraft, and the trundling of the JCB, could all conspire to ruin the experience of visiting Llyn Cerrig Bach, but the base is simply too much a part of the story to be intrusive. The little lake is the hole left during the wartime peat extraction, without which there would be no knowledge of the hoard, and which unwittingly recreated the environment of two thousand years ago.

Just beyond the airfield sign is an entrance gate. The artefacts were found scattered within the airfield, but their place of origin lay just between the entrance gate and the rising scrub a few metres to the right. This part of the peat extraction site was refilled to create the road that circuits the base, but miraculously, you can stand on the very spot where the priests or devotees stood to cast their tribute to the gods.

The eastern edge of the lake is formed of a long bedrock ridge, which continues to the edge of the road. Two thousand years ago it would have formed an elongated island in the bog. There is no right of way onto the ledge, and it is so beautifully overgrown with reeds reaching above head height that to go crashing through would be an act of vandalism, and there is no need. Stopping at the edge of the road, you are standing on the promontory of that old island, and the ridge of scrub ahead, within the fence of the airfield, is another original feature of the site, a bedrock platform.

Researchers who carried out a comprehensive survey of the site in 2005[31] speculated that, in the character of other votive wetland sites, a short wooden causeway might have linked the rock platform to the island, passing over the very spot where the huge haul of metalwork and bones was dredged up. It was from there, or the edge of either promontory, that they must have been thrown.[32]

The chill of the January evening begins to penetrate my jacket, and I sit by the little lake with my boots touching the surface of the water. Behind me is a truly beautiful sunset, of low, dark cumulus cloud illuminated pale yellow by the glow, below a cold and clear winter's sky; the sort of pale blue you never really notice until you're trying to describe it. Before me the lake is a darker, greyer reflection of that blue, with an unbroken, meandering line of reeds beyond, marking the lake's far edge.

The reeds on the right side of the lake denote the edge of the elongated Iron Age island. As such, this is a timeless view, the modern reeded bank reflected in the dark waters being the same one that offerings were thrown from; a sacred island, a place of once monumental supernatural importance, however lost to us that significance is now.

In the gathering gloom, with darkness and silence settling around me, and nothing at all in the direction I am looking to fix this viewpoint in the present, it is all too easy to let the imagination run, to populate the reeds with dark figures, to hear shouts of exultation, petition, or fear. You can fill that silent darkness with anything you like, for we have not the slightest clue as to what rituals were conducted here. Drunken revelry? Cruel blood sacrifice? Frenzied sexual rites? The mundane daily round and common task of the resident priest or priestess?

The great unanswered question is whether this was a single desperate sacrifice to ward off the falling sky of the Roman attack in AD 60, or a slow accumulation over many, perhaps hundreds, of years. The idea that this could have been the result of a single petition, tangible evidence of the mounting terror as Paulinus's storm gathered, is undeniably a dramatic and seductive one, and some very respectable names have favoured the interpretation, perhaps the greatest chronicler of Roman Britain, Sheppard Frere, among them.[33] But all in all the evidence is not as simple as that, and increasingly hints that this was an accumulation, not a dump.

Stylistically, the Llyn Cerrig Bach metalwork would seem to form two chronological groups. Firstly, an assemblage of military items, horse harness and chariot fittings potentially dates between the fourth century BC through to the mid-first century AD, and secondly a group of non-military items dates from the mid-first century AD and perhaps into the second century.[34] This would suggest that at least two offerings were made, but many items were clearly not new, and older pieces may still have been valued enough to be used as tribute or sacrifice.

In short, the metalwork might not all be of the same date, but could have been collected together at the same time, or collected over a longer period but finally dumped together. And that crossover period is the one that concerns us, the mid-first century AD. More troublesome is the radiocarbon dating of the bone assemblage, which dates mostly to the last few centuries BC.[35] Whilst it therefore seems unlikely that Llyn Cerrig Bach represents a major single offering made in the spring of AD 60, it is possible that part of it does, and our desire to pin down the exact year of deposition reflects the danger of having a tempting historical pigeon-hole in which to place it.

It is almost entirely dark. The sunset seemed to never end, and then I was almost plunged into darkness. In truth, I have no desire to leave, but I am cold, and have to walk along meandering, unlit lanes to get back to the hotel, so close, but out of sight beyond the rolling outcrops. The walk wakes me up a little; snaps me back to the present. I cover the last hundred yards with my torch.

Hotel Cymyran is brightly lit and warm, with the promise of a hot bath, hearty food and strong drink to revive the frozen time traveller stumbling in fresh back from AD 60. As the doors close behind me, I leave the lingering spirits of Llyn Cerrig Bach in the darkness beyond.

In the morning, I drive back along the A55, the modern dual carriageway that slices across Anglesey from Pont Britannia to Holyhead, which runs parallel to, and replaces, Thomas Telford's original London to Holyhead road, the old A5, completed in 1825.

Constructing this new road necessitated a scheme of archaeological investigation, providing the most extensive exposure of archaeology on the island in recent times. The title of the project publication, *A Corridor Through Time*,[36] really sums up the unique opportunity afforded by the work, a twenty-mile archaeological transect across the centre of the western half of the island.

Significant areas of settlement were excavated, spanning the later prehistoric and Roman periods, some clearly encompassing the mid-first century, exposing hut circles, ditches, pits and the detritus of daily life. What they did not find was evidence of destruction and murder; no obvious burning of buildings, and no abandonment or hiatus of occupation in AD 60; on the contrary, the settlements seemed to thrive well into the Roman period.

Paulinus's army left no trace of its violent passage across the island, and although the voyeuristic archaeologist, peering through the debris of other people's lives, would have it otherwise, perhaps it is better this way. They came, they saw, they conquered, and then they were gone again, at least for eighteen years, when Agricola reoccupied the island, for Tacitus tells us that their stay in AD 60 was brief. They hacked down the groves, he says, and then, *Suetonius while thus occupied received tidings of the sudden revolt of the province.*[37]

And with that unwelcome intelligence, Boudica entered the story.

The flat-bottomed landing craft pulled back and forth between the mainland and the isle, ferrying rations, fodder and the endless piles of accoutrements and stores across to Mona, and returning with the wounded. One or two vessels drifted slowly along parallel to the coast, gathering the half-submerged dead and dragging them to the shore for burial before the next tide flushed the channel clean.

Somewhere in all the comings and goings, a tired and filthy messenger boarded a supply punt and curtly bade the ferryman to be quick casting off lest he face the general for his tardiness. The black look of the sailor was lost on the weary dispatch rider, who struggled to keep his eyes open as the boat rocked beneath him. He had little enough desire to face the general himself.

The man had taken possession of the dispatch satchel many hours before, and ridden hell for leather for the general's forward base camp. He certainly hadn't opened the satchel himself, but as each exhausted rider passed the precious bag to the next, fort by fort, the news it contained would have been breathlessly shouted for all to hear. The Iceni had risen in the east, the province was aflame, and the rebels marched on Camulodunum.

I cannot leave Anglesey without pausing on the ridge that looks out towards the Strait and the mainland. I park the car at the side of the short stretch of the A5025 that runs along the high ground between the Menai and Britannia crossings. It is a beautiful morning, the sun hanging low and painfully bright over the cloud-wreathed peaks of Snowdonia.

It is a peaceful view over stunning countryside, but everywhere are reminders of the present. Telegraph poles and hanging cables, the glint from countless windows; the top of the Menai suspension bridge. But they are mere details. The outline silhouette of the hills, folds and contours remains ever unchanged. When I close my eyes against the blinding sunlight, and momentarily see the strange negative image of that silhouette replayed across my eyelids, it is the same one I would have seen two thousand years ago.

Paulinus must have stood somewhere on this very same ridge and glowered towards the south-east. He might not have said as much, out of superstitious respect, but there's no doubt what was going through his mind. The Fates had just pissed on his boots. His moment of triumph was shattered, his thunder stolen and silenced by a peasant mob led by *a woman*.

Well, his triumph could wait a little longer. He growled at an orderly who sprinted to give the order to evacuate Mona as the last screams still echoed and the pillars of smoke rose behind him. The huddled groups of brutalised captives, ready to be dragged south as slaves, were undoubtedly put to the sword. The island must have seemed impossibly remote right then, the very edge of the world, and a bloody long march to get back to towns and baths and anything half-civilised.

And those towns might be burning.

7

London Calling

The Race for Londinium

The gale, it plies the saplings double,
It blows so hard, 'twill soon be gone;
To-day the Roman and his trouble,
Are ashes under Uricon.

A.E. Housman, *A Shropshire Lad*

Gaius Suetonius Paulinus was a seasoned commander. Now in late middle-age, he had been celebrated in the AD 40s for putting down the North African Mauretanian uprising, and being the first Roman general to cross the Atlas mountains. His governorship of Britain opened with a challenge – the previous, deceased, governor, Quintus Veranius, boasted in his will to the emperor that he could have conquered the whole province in another two years. His tenure thus far, therefore, had been brutal and hugely successful, the Silures trodden underfoot, and the last flames of resistance on the holy citadel of Mona snuffed out. Gazing out from the southern shore of that island, Camulodunum's request for assistance clutched in his hands, he must have reflected that it *had* all been going so well.

His nature was the polar opposite of his rash young subordinate Petilius Cerialis, who was, perhaps at that very moment, hacking his way clear of the Ninth's Last Stand. In the civil war nearly a decade later, Tacitus recorded that Paulinus had a reputation *such that no one was looked upon as a more skilful soldier,*[1] and was *naturally tardy in action, and one who preferred a cautious and scientific plan of operations to any success which was the result of accident.*[2] However, campaigns are not won by caution alone, and by the civil war Paulinus would have been elderly, perhaps seventy years old.[3] It is the rightful lot of old men to be dilatory, but to have achieved what he had in Britannia in two campaigning seasons, his middle years must have been a good deal more vigorous. For the next few days, it is his eyes that I must look through.

I have returned to Mona, back to that same rising ground where I stared south towards distant Londinium, just as Paulinus must have done. The seasons have turned, and it is summer now, a scorching, dry July day. I am lower down the ridge, on the A5, where there is a classic view of the Menai Strait, framed by the bridges left and right, iconic features that symbolically enclose the mile of channel that has come to define the spirit of the Strait. From this spot, directly ahead there is almost nothing to place you in the present day, with the pasture falling away to the near bank, the heavily wooded shore across the water, and the dark peaks of Snowdonia beyond. It is surely a view that would still be familiar to the great general himself.

Paulinus must have had limited intelligence. The first report to reach him would presumably have come from Camulodunum, dispatched in the days before Boudica's attack. This may have been addended by Petilius Cerialis when that first messenger reached the Ninth Legion's fortress at Longthorpe, stating his intention to march immediately to the city's aid. Carried by a succession of messengers on fresh mounts, that report would have reached Paulinus the next or even the same day, and perhaps a similar report from the procurator, Catus Decianus, presumably in Londinium, half a day later. As the situation in the south-east rapidly deteriorated, it is sobering to consider that these may have been the first and last accurate reports he would receive from the theatre of the rebellion.

His initial priority would be to extricate his army from Mona, and to send orders far and wide to his further garrisons either to assemble and march to rendezvous points, or to await firm instructions whilst readying themselves to move. We know from Tacitus that Paulinus would ultimately march on London, but not whether that was his instant resolve. His initial intelligence will have been concerned with the threat to Camulodunum, by far the most prestigious settlement in the province, but rebellions can spread quickly, and for now a drive towards the south-east in general would suffice.

Suetonius Paulinus's march on London is covered in one very terse sentence in Tacitus: *Suetonius, however, with wonderful resolution, marched amidst a hostile population to Londinium.*[4] There is really nothing very ambiguous about the statement, but the assumption has long been that Paulinus rushed to London with a force of cavalry, leaving his legionaries to slog out their twenty-five miles or so a day, and thus quickly reached the settlement with a relatively small force to assess the situation. Another assumption, partly based on Dio – *on learning of the disaster in Britain he at once set sail thither from Mona*[5] – goes even further, and might suppose that he sailed part of the way.[6]

On the face of it, neither of these assumptions is unreasonable, but Tacitus and Dio do not actually tell us as much. There is now an increasing groundswell of scepticism that Paulinus would have dashed to London ahead of his infantry, although it has often been stated as fact in the past without any qualification.

Donald Dudley and Graham Webster popularised the 'cavalry dash' theory in 1962 in their *Rebellion of Boudicca*, but it long predated them – hell, even my beloved *Ladybird Book of Roman Britain* from 1959 states it as fact. The earliest proposal of the theory I have noticed is in the November 1914 issue of the magazine *The Antiquary*,[7] in which the eminent Roman scholar Francis Haverfield has Paulinus 'moving – very naturally – faster than his main body and reached London with practically no troops.' An exam-cribbers' version of Tacitus from 1882 uses the tantalisingly ambiguous phrase, *Paulinus hurried to Londinium . . .*[8] You can interpret that, and Tacitus, any way you like, but it seems we have long been willing Paulinus down Watling Street as quickly as possible to make the story fit the available space-time continuum.

The non-archaeologist might reasonably ask what all the fuss is about, but there are crucial issues of timing. Ships and cavalry can potentially travel much faster than infantry, upsetting attempts at reconstructing a time-line of events relative to each other – how long did it take Boudica to march from Colchester to London? How did Paulinus get there before her?

Perhaps most crucially, it has implications far beyond its superficial importance when it comes to hunting for the final great showdown of the war. There is all the difference in the world between Paulinus arriving in London with a small force of cavalry on the one hand, and his marching in with his entire army intact on the other. In 1986, in the prestigious journal *Britannia*, Herbert W. Benario of Emory University even published a note entitled 'Legionary Speed of March before the Battle with Boudicca.'[9] This stuff matters.

An old colleague from our work at Cambridge University, and fellow Boudica enthusiast, Grahame Appleby, attempted to reconstruct the chronology of the war in a paper published in 2009, 'The Boudican Revolt: Countdown to Defeat',[10] an important study to which we will return, and others have made less detailed attempts in the past.[11] Grahame's study is an essential piece of work, but the inherent problems of producing a timetable for the war are, to my mind, insuperable.

We have no certain place of origin for Boudica beyond mid-East Anglia, and only a guess as to how quickly she might have travelled. The weather alone could have had a dramatic impact, heavy rain almost entirely disabling a vast host too large to be restricted to the hard-standing of a Roman road. The impact of tens of thousands of feet, hooves and wheels on bare ground in wet weather would have seen the rear half of the army struggling through conditions we would associate with the Somme, and the swelling of rivers, flooding of fords and liquefying of extensive river margins, would have halted any hope of advance. Did Paulinus beat Boudica to London simply because of the weather?

Having destroyed Camulodunum, how long would Boudica have stayed there? After winning such an unimaginably rich prize, how long must we apportion her army to loot, drink, torture and sacrifice the hundreds or thousands of unfortunates taken alive? How long to rest and treat the wounded, to collect, lay out and honour the dead, and to carry out post-battle purification rituals and celebratory feasting? A day? A week? A fortnight? Boudica might have had no immediate plan to advance on London, until, overwhelmed by her astonishing success, her warlords and Druids urged her to do it all over again, and onwards to London they surged.

It is reasonable to assume that Paulinus and his personal staff were shipped along the coast from Anglesey to *Deva*, Chester, which Dio's *set(ting) sail thither from Mona* could be hinting at, whilst his infantry evacuated Mona and the cavalry clattered along the campaign roads to rendezvous with him, leaving the infantry far behind. From this hub of the local communication network, he would receive any further intelligence as it arrived and consider his options whilst knocking a good sixty miles off his land journey.

There is also a historical hint that Paulinus advanced on London with his cavalry alone. Once in London, Tacitus mentions his *scanty force of soldiers.*[12] Good evidence here for a small force, surely? With or without his legions, Paulinus was the numerical inferior of Boudica, but I still believe that the greater weakness is inferred.

The 270 miles by road from Anglesey to London might have taken the infantry, each carrying thirty kilograms or more of arms, armour and accoutrements, nine days to march at a punishing thirty miles per day, or eleven days at a more sustainable (but still punishing) twenty-five miles a day. And that was after evacuating the entire Mona expeditionary force and its equipment off the island on suitable tides, and striking base camp, hardly less than a day or two's hard work.

With his main cavalry strength (and assuming that he could not swap tired horses for fresh ones as a lone dispatch rider may have done), depending how hard he was willing to push his horses, Paulinus could have halved that time to perhaps five or six days – one writer has suggested three,[13] but was this really crucial to having beaten Boudica to the town? Could the legions have marched all that way and still got there ahead of her?

Such is the confusion behind the traditional assumption that Paulinus dashed to London with his cavalry. Some modern writers have dismissed this reconnaissance-in-strength scenario as 'unprofessional',[14] 'a gambler's dash', 'a grave tactical error',[15] and 'militarily improbable, and improper'.[16] I do not believe that it was any of those things, and we must not be too dogmatic – we will never know for sure. Accepting that Paulinus still had no clear idea of the scale of the threat he was facing, a thousand (or even a few hundred) horsemen was no mean force for a band of local marauders to stand up against.

He might genuinely have hoped to save Londinium, or Camulodunum initially, which put him at the head of the primary fighting force of the moment, exactly the place for a Roman commander, just as Cerialis, as the senior officer present, had quite properly accompanied his vexillation of the Ninth to save Camulodunum. This attempt to save London has been burdened by the idea of a cavalry dash, a vainglorious charge out of kilter with the known caution of Paulinus, but giving it the title of a Relief Column presumes something less reckless.

Paulinus's route from Anglesey is the journey I have come back to North Wales to replicate. As with the Ninth's march along the Via Devana, in times of crisis, when speed is of the essence, we must assume our ancient commanders to have taken the most direct route to their objective. The military road system was there to mainline troops directly to trouble spots at speeds that would bewilder the natives. As such, Paulinus marched along Watling Street, which ran directly from Chester to London, and mostly still does, predominantly as the A5, from Shrewsbury southwards. If I personally imagine Paulinus cantering along with a column of auxiliary cavalry, those who would prefer to visualise him walking his horse with his legionaries may do so, for it makes no difference to the route.

The campaign roads across north Wales, if they were the same as the later established routes, can be followed on the map with a copy of Margary's *Roman Roads in Britain* to hand; for my purposes the modern road system encompassing the North Wales Expressway will suffice to get me to Chester, just as a ship probably transported Paulinus whilst his troops evacuated Mona, levelled their camps and formed up into marching order. At seventy miles an hour I leave the footsloggers behind me as their general did, and race for the nearest campaign base at *Deva*, Chester.

The Dee estuary, which then came ten miles further inland, right to the site of modern Chester, was seized by Ostorius Scapula in his frontier fighting of AD 47/48, but exactly what existed here in AD 60 is uncertain. Donald Dudley, Graham Webster and Sheppard Frere all assumed it to have been the site of Paulinus's shipyard for the construction of the Anglesey invasion boats,[17] which might infer the presence of a significant campaign logistics base.

There is none of this to see in Chester now. The known legionary fortress dates to the AD 70s, and the impressive Roman remains that the city is famous for are mostly later still, but the strange incongruity of the marvellously presented amphitheatre surrounded by red-brick modernity is a good spot to eat my lunch.

Just under half of the oval amphitheatre has been exposed, the remainder mostly unexcavated and partially built over. You can stand on the floor of the arena, as many a doomed soul did before you, and a cleverly painted wall delineating the unexcavated portion gives the view you would have seen across to the other side.

We all know about gladiators, but the reputation of the Roman arena deserves to be a whole lot grimmer than it is, a spectacle of not only equally matched, highly trained fighters, but of execution, torture, and simple murder for the sole purpose of entertainment, lending the lie to any suggestion, ancient or modern, that Roman moral sensibilities were genuinely offended by barbarian human sacrifice in times of desperation.

If the Roman gods did not need appeasing with human blood, the Roman people did, in a downward spiral of addiction that resulted in men, women and children, as well as half the fauna of the known world, being hacked, burned, gored and roasted to death for the same casual, fleeting entertainment we expect from a football match. The surface of the arena, normally of sand, was there specifically to soak up the blood.

Indeed, our word 'arena' derives from *harena*, the Latin for sand.[18] A thick layer excavated here was comprised of fine yellow sand, clearly imported from elsewhere, interpreted as scrapings from the arena floor; the blood and gobbets of flesh too small to be easily separated out had long since rotted away, but it contained a stray human tooth.[19]

The early third-century author Tertullian knew it as *that dreadful place . . . temple of all demons . . . There are as many unclean spirits gathered there as it can seat men.*[20] I wonder how many Icenian warriors, women and kids ended their lives in places like this across Gaul and Italy in the months after the war, beneath baying crowds made all the more pitiless by the tales of British atrocities to Roman citizens in Camulodunum.

I walk through Chester's beautiful city centre, within the walls of the stone Roman fortress, and doubtless the ramparts of earlier incarnations, on the high ground overlooking the old estuary. Reaching the city walls at Watergate, I swing left to follow their line along Nuns Road, now defining the edge of Britain's oldest racecourse, the Roodee. This expanse of flat land was once the mouth of the Dee, allowing Roman ocean-going vessels almost to the walls of the fortress. About two-thirds of the way along the racetrack, I stop at one of the pedestrian access gates, which has an information panel about the Roman port, and the promise of something rather more exciting.

Before me is what appears to be a pair of normal pay-to-view seaside promenade binoculars, but which claim instead to show the viewer what the Roodee looked like two thousand years ago, as a Roman port. It instantly reminds me of *A View From a Hill*, an M.R. James short story in which a Victorian antiquary creates time-travel binoculars by boiling down old human bones and incorporating the disgusting residue into the optics, able to pan across the landscape and see it 'through dead men's eyes'.

I fumble for a pound coin, push it through the slot, lift the heavy metal glasses, and see a flashing exclamation mark and the words: *No signal*. Gutted, I press the coin reject button, and discover that the No Refunds notice applies equally to those the machine has just robbed as to those who change their minds half-way through.

I stroll over Grosvenor Bridge, to stand above the river and gaze across the racecourse. It is strange to consider that this field of close-cropped grass a good ten miles inland was once a major port, and it was somewhere here that a small forest of timber was split and sawn, nailed and adzed into the armada of flat-bottomed landing craft that ploughed through the swirling currents and Druidic curses of Menai; here too that Paulinus and his staff may have disembarked to make hurried plans for their ride south, still reeling from the news of rebellion. This is as close as I'm going to get to AD 60 in Chester, and, like Paulinus, I must press on with my journey.

The original Watling Street that Paulinus rode is still remark-ably well-preserved in the modern road network, except for this northernmost stretch. Its route can be plotted, and sometimes observed – Ivan Margary gives a good account of it, but it cannot be followed by car.

The A41–A49 to Shrewsbury is the closest sensible route, which I follow on its long, winding way south. I had intended visiting the next site on my itinerary, Wroxeter Roman City, this same afternoon, but the manifold traffic problems of the day have conspired to coincide my arrival with its closure, so I make for my hotel a couple of miles away on the banks of the Severn. In keeping with the unchanging high pressure of the previous many weeks, the day is very hot, and remains so into the evening as I take the welcome breeze on Atcham Bridge, overlooked by the distant black hulk of the Wrekin.

There is no great hurry in the morning as Wroxeter doesn't open until ten o'clock, but I am there early to drive and wander around. The small car park lies close to the north-west corner of an early fortress dating to the period of Boudica's war, and the main modern road, the B4380, bisects it from corner to corner, with two minor roads running off along the lines of the south and west ramparts. The later Roman city completely swallowed the earlier earthworks, although the eastern edge of both lay on approximately the same line. I wander about clutching maps with an increasingly furrowed brow, and seeing me pacing around, a nice young woman opens the gate ten minutes early.

Wroxeter Roman City, once *Viroconium*, or A.E. Housman's *Uricon* in his haunting section of *A Shropshire Lad* devoted to Wenlock Edge, was the legionary fortress of Legio XIV Gemina in AD 60.[21] Only a housekeeping force would have been present when Paulinus wheeled in with his cavalry, as the Fourteenth had formed the backbone of his Anglesey expeditionary force and had probably yet to reach Chester, but there would have been preparations afoot to house the legion for a night, and stockpile supplies for their use and onward progress. Like Chester, this would have been a local nerve centre for incoming intelligence that Paulinus and his staff officers would have quickly sifted through and woven into their plans. It may even have been here that news of Colchester's loss reached them.

Entering the site through a shop and small museum, the

impressive remains of Wroxeter spread across the grass before me, with the great ruin of the baths basilica wall looming ahead, the so-called 'Old Work', seven metres high and riddled with holes left by the scaffolding of its original construction. Swallows fly in and out of the holes from hidden nests. It is mostly the baths complex that lies excavated above ground today, all much later than the phase of earth and timber military occupation, and I must mentally bulldoze all those walls and hypocausts, and swallows, out of the way and return the site to its frontier setting, with the ominous boar-back of the Wrekin hillfort under *his forest fleece* glowering down on it.

This is a place of association with many great names. Mortimer Wheeler cut his teeth here in his student days, and Wilfred Owen's attachment to the place was intimate. Graham Webster, the archaeologist who, perhaps more than any other, has come to be associated with the story of Boudica's war, excavated here for thirty years.

The Roman name of *Viroconium Cornoviorum* is traditionally taken to be derived from 'The settlement of Virico of the Cornovii tribe',[22] but more recently the translation of the Celtic name *Virico*, or *Uirocu* has begun appearing on the internet, which apparently draws on a French dictionary of Celtic place names. If true, it now boasts the coolest place name in Roman Britain, for the dictionary claims that *Uirocu* can be translated as 'man-wolf', meaning that *Uiroconium* would roughly equate to 'The City of the Werewolf'.[23]

Exactly how the place might have earned this remarkable name is, tragically, lost to the mists of time, but it surpasses even Camulodunum's magnificent 'Fortress of Camulos (the War God)' derivation, and puts *Venta Icenorum*'s 'Market Place of the Iceni' to shame. Standing in the City of the Werewolf, it is difficult not to be reminded of Norfolk Wolf gold coins and the Iceni Fenriswolf, Black Shuck dogs on the Norfolk coast, and their terrifying, more local Welsh cousin, the Gwyllgi. Dio's Boudica likens the Romans to *hares and foxes trying to rule over dogs and wolves.* The City of the Werewolf is a fitting place to remember the quote.

I drive on to another military site a comfortable day's ride to the east in peaceful times, but merely a watering stop on a hell-for-leather dash – Wall, Roman *Letocetum*, near Lichfield. Beyond Telford, Watling Street is easy enough to follow, and deposits you directly at the site. Like Wroxeter, the visible remains are later – the early fortresses were on the high ground beyond the church, and I am careful to approach from that direction on foot, to have traversed the underlying ramparts of the military sites.

The origins of Wall are hazy. Certainly there were numerous military establishments here from the earliest advance into the area in the AD 40s,[24] followed by a fortress of perhaps thirty acres, which may have been constructed in response to the events of AD 60. What survives today are the low walls and floors of an inn and bathhouse from the second century, a posting station where travellers could find a bed and meal, change their horses, and slough the ingrained dust from their aching bodies.

From this point on, no one would attempt to drive Watling Street for fun. It is bad enough if you intend to stick to the A5, with its frequent bypasses, following the route to the nearest few miles. If you wish to travel the actual Roman road and not some vague approximation inspired by its general direction, you need determination, patience, and a good working knowledge of expletives. It must be followed along narrow, slow roads, a thousand roundabouts, and occasionally lost at complex interchanges, with countless traffic lights and yet more roundabouts at every town and village *en route*. What makes it tolerable, on this trip at least, are the sites of interest that would have concerned Paulinus.

Just beyond Atherstone, about fifteen miles on from Wall, the village of Mancetter lies nestled between the River Anker and the Coventry Canal beneath a long wooded ridge. Mancetter, or

Manduessedum, was the site of a twenty-eight acre half-legionary or vexillation fortress, presumably a major base of the Fourteenth Legion that may have been largely redundant by AD 60. At this moment, as a major military site, occupied or not, Paulinus would have paused at least to water his horses and collate intelligence.

Another ten miles and a slight kink in a rolling section of road demarcates a spot of little enough importance today that was the strategic epicentre of the province, *Venonae*, High Cross, the spot where Watling Street and the Fosse Way met, a gigantic X linking the south-east to the north-west, and the north-east to the south-west. It is an insignificant junction now, the southern continuation of the Fosse being a minor road, and the northern section missing for a couple of miles at the old crossing point.

In AD 60 it was the natural link between all the legions, the Fourteenth and perhaps some of the Twentieth at the northern end of Watling Street, the Second and remnants of the Ninth at either end of the Fosse, with Watling Street ready to mainline all directly into the fray. Not only was High Cross the natural assembly point for the dispersed garrisons of the northern frontier zone, any force there was central to the considerable military supply and support network that lay behind it.

Just off the main road is an eighteenth-century monument proclaiming it, somewhat illegibly now, to be the 'Centre of Roman Britain', and it was, almost exactly equidistant between the Welsh and Norfolk coasts, as well as between Chester and London. Its significance to Paulinus would have been immense, but at this moment it must have seemed a long way indeed from London, Colchester and the south-east – it still does today.

One comment in Tacitus suggests that the rebellion had spread fast, and was infecting the tribal territories that Paulinus now rode through, for he mentions the, *hostile population*.[25] Whether this is meant to apply to a particular section of the journey, or was an off-the-cuff assumption, there seems to have been no general uprising across the province. The great Midlands confederation of the Corieltauvi are possible suspects, and this section of Watling Street, from Wall to south of High Cross, ran through their lands.

It is another sixty-five miles to St Albans, some of it along sections of road that are strictly for local usage now, punctuated by so many roundabouts and traffic lights, especially near Milton Keynes, that I struggle to get out of second gear for about eight miles. Before four in the afternoon, however, I am approaching St Albans, and just on the right, behind the hedge, beside the gentle River Ver, lay the original line of Watling Street, and the burgeoning Roman town of Verulamium.

Our knowledge of early Verulamium is hazy compared to our reconstruction of Camulodunum, but there is one obvious distinction in its modern setting – St Albans does not lie over the Roman town, but beside it. This was originally the heart of Catuvellaunian lands, and remained an important centre even when the seat of their kings seems to have shifted to Colchester. Unlike the forced Romanisation of the latter place, however, what little evidence there is suggests that here the local elites bought into the New Order after defeat, and Verlamion as was became Roman Verulamium, seemingly already favoured by its new overlords with the status of a *municipium*, a chartered town.

Verulamium had yet to reach a great size, smaller than contemporary London or Colchester, still very much a work in progress, perhaps with a few prestigious buildings, even of stone – rare at this early date – though many of the houses and workshops were timber with thatched roofs. Paulinus and his men would have stopped here, the first non-military, properly 'Roman' settlement, to seek intelligence and gauge the local atmosphere, still unaware of how far the canker of revolt had spread.

Perhaps the inhabitants were concerned by events to their east, but not yet panicked by them. Londinium still stood, and now here was the general at the vanguard of the returning army. Both the Iceni and Trinovantes might have harboured a deep-seated tribal hatred of the Catuvellauni of Verulamium, but it was still a distant war, and the rebels would clearly be no match for Paulinus.

The high-water mark of the rebellion had surely been reached, and would now begin ebbing away.

I drive along the road at the edge of Verulamium Park, momentarily passing through the centre of the old settlement that Paulinus would have known, but like him I am not going to linger on my way south. Londinium is not much more than twenty miles away and Paulinus would be pushing on with all haste.

I had intended parking at Elstree, about eleven miles north of central London, soon after lunch time, but it is well after four, rush hour has begun, and there is no parking to be had anywhere that doesn't seem to risk instantaneous fines or clamping. Finally, at five o'clock, I find a good old-fashioned, no-nonsense pay and display in Borehamwood, heave the bike out of the back of the car and attach the front wheel. Despite the time it is still incredibly hot – Britain is basking in its long 2018 heatwave.

My bike, with a stiff back wheel that won't spin a whole turn without stopping, feels like it weighs about the same as me, with fat, knobbly off-road tyres designed for scree slopes, the bicycle equivalent of caligae, that run like glue sticks on hot tarmac, and I have thirteen miles to cycle to Marble Arch before even thinking of turning back. I have come all the way from Anglesey. I might not make the City or London Bridge this evening, but I am going to make Marble Arch if it kills me.

Outside Elstree is a long, freewheeling run downhill, which is never a good thing on a return trip, for it won't be downhill on the way back, and at the bottom is a roundabout that spits me onto the climb up Brockley Hill, significant enough that heavy vehicles are advised to find an alternative route, hardly a sign that cheers me up as I sweat sheets and drink the last of my water. Finally, though, I am on my way, and it is only now, with the wind in my face, travelling under my own steam at a similar pace to Paulinus's horsemen, that the connection with another time and another journey along this same route begins to sink in.

They were thirsty. *They* were tired. *They* were rushing to get there and knew they might soon be retracing their steps, and in the woods of Brockley Hill it is easy to convince myself that the visual scene has little changed as well. The actual Roman road has been excavated at the top of the hill here, and ran just on the western verge of the modern road.[26]

The great consolation of the ride is that it is dead straight, all eleven miles from the last curve on Brockley Hill to Marble Arch, as straight as ever a road was, the condensed spirit of the Roman road in its modern setting. After Brockley Hill and Stonegrove, it is the Edgware Road ever after, despite confusing parentheses such as Maida Vale, Kilburn High Road, Shoot-Up Hill and Shooter's Hill.

Whatever else happens, I am not going to lose my way, and can simply put my head down and ride, after a fashion – this is the London rush hour; it cannot be described as quiet, weaving in and out behind taxis and stationary red buses, my only concern being the time it is taking to do so. Ever since leaving home at five the previous morning, time has been determinedly against me.

At half past six this sweltering evening, dripping with sweat, I dismount beneath Marble Arch, this ancient crossroads where Paulinus and his men swung to the left to gallop on to Londinium, three miles hence, no pall of smoke or cloud of carrion crows yet to be seen. They had beaten the rebels; by how much, they had yet to find out. For my own part there are only three thoughts swimming through my head: Toilet, Drink, and It's getting a bit late. I take a photo of Marble Arch, text it to Clare, and appropriate the toilets at MacDonald's.

I check my watch. It is a quarter to seven. If I find a drink, fight my way along Oxford Street, the modern line of the Roman road, to the Monument and London Bridge – the site of AD 60 Londinium – spend long enough there to appreciate the moment, and then cycle back here, it will be ten o'clock before I even begin the thirteen miles back to Borehamwood, in the dark, without lights, necessitating several long sections of walking. I won't be back at the car until well after midnight, or Norwich before dawn. I press pause on my mental footage of Paulinus and his men wheeling onto Oxford Street, and begin the long ride back north with two bottles of ice-cold Coke in easy reach on the side of my rucksack.

I return to London two days later and catch the tube to Marble Arch. I had reached Anglesey late on Monday morning. It is now Friday morning, a full four days later, and I am still completing the journey perhaps two or three days ahead of Paulinus, whilst his infantry would have done well to be much south of Chester by now. It is sobering to remember how far these distances were in a world of footslogging and horses.

It is another beautiful, hot day. No bike today, just shorts, trainers and bandy walking legs. I wave Paulinus and his men on ahead of me, and follow the road they themselves had taken. Marble Arch, well outside Londinium, was an important road junction and Paulinus headed east from here, now along the line of the A40 – Oxford Street, Holborn, Newgate Street, Cheapside, to the vicinity of the Bank of England. This road system had certainly been laid out by then, and may indeed have predated the settlement.[27]

I like walking through London. As a family, we go walking in the Alps every summer, which we all love, but if one year Clare suggested a walking holiday in London, I would be almost as pleased. Walking along Oxford Street on this beautiful summer's day is perhaps too enjoyable for the dark task I am replicating. No doubt the tired troopers were glad to be approaching the town as well, with its promise of fleeting rest, food, wine and women – almost unimaginable luxuries to a soldier fresh from the fighting on the northern front and seven days in the saddle, but they knew their arrival heralded the doom of the town in one form or another. Whether they tried to make a stand there or abandoned it to the natives, it would likely soon be burning.

The exact extent of Boudican London cannot be plotted definitively. It was centred on the Walbrook Stream, which ran almost below its namesake street beside Bank junction at the heart of the modern City, and we can imagine entering the edge of the settlement close to the line of the later town walls beyond the eastern end of Holborn Viaduct. It straddled two low hills either side of the stream, Ludgate and Cornhill, barely perceivable now, with a bridge across the Thames at London Bridge.

I pause at Bank, and take in the view of the Royal Exchange, its classical portico a dead ringer for the Temple of Claudius, as well as being a similar size. Nothing this grand yet graced the streets of Londinium, often described in this period as resembling a frontier town of the Old Wild West. What we are less certain of is exactly where in the sprawl of buildings and streets Paulinus headed for. The early forum, a large, open, gravelled area at the junction of this main road with the London Bridge road, now partly beneath Marks & Spencer on the northern side of Fenchurch Street, would have been the obvious place to dismount his cavalry, with large buildings either side to accommodate the men.

If they were staying more than a day, however, a fortified temporary camp on unoccupied ground, perhaps north of the forum, would have been more appropriate. Paulinus himself undoubtedly made for the abandoned residence of Procurator Catus Decianus, which he would have appropriated for his own use. Exactly where that building lay is anyone's guess – the site of Winchester Palace in Southwark has been proposed[28] – and it might barely have survived the explosion of the Governor's fury upon learning that the oily palmed Catus had sparked this catastrophe, and then boarded a ship to Gaul in terror of its consequences. We know nothing more of his fate. He is never heard of again.

In his awesome journey through this story in the documentary *In Search of Boadicea* from 1980, Michael Wood suggests that on reaching London, Paulinus undoubtedly 'took a stiff wine in the procurator's office'.[29] I heartily concur and am determined to replicate the act but, being an evening alcoholic rather than a daytime one, I slip through to Pret A Manger on Lombard Street and take a stiff flat white. Here in the heart of the early settlement, it may well have been several metres directly below me that Paulinus necked his large cup of Falernian in fury and despair. I raise my coffee.

Here's to you, general. *Propino tibi salutem!*

I wander with my coffee onto London Bridge. The original timber Roman bridge started out both left and below of where I stand, crossing from the bottom of Fish Street Hill, straight through the people eating their lunch in the sunshine beside the Thames Path, making landfall on the southern bank practically where it does now, just on its left, eastern edge, but closer to the level of the water. Halfway across the bridge I stop in the burning heat of the sun.

Propping up the steel and marble balustrade, watching the Thames glide beneath me, I think back to the waters of the Menai Strait and the Dee from only a few days before, and what a journey Paulinus made. It is extraordinary that except for a few short stretches of road, where I had to travel to within a few miles of him, I have been able to follow the same gravelled surface, in his actual hoof prints, so to speak, still preserved in the modern road system, visiting his significant stopping points *en route*.

That wild landscape of frontier forts, military trackways and fledgling provincial settlements lies fossilised in our roads and streets and place names, and I had travelled it, *absent-minded, as you say, jumping back for a moment*, seeing in my mind's eye the earth and timber legionary fortresses of the Welsh Marches, the thatched roofs and woodsmoke of sleepy Verulamium, and twilight settling over that first London from the crossroads of distant Marble Arch. Finally I have entered that settlement, passed along the streets of daub and wooden buildings in my imagination, and taken my rest.

The strange little prickle of upstanding hairs, which I remember from clutching a portable DVD player at the Somme, brushes the back of my neck once more. I have, as far as it is possible to do at such a distance of time, glanced momentarily through dead men's eyes.

8

Apocalypse Now

Smoke from Boudica's Time

*Imagine him here – the very end of the world, a sea the colour
of lead, a sky the colour of smoke, a kind of ship about as
rigid as a concertina – and going up this river with stores, or
orders, or what you like. Sandbanks, marshes, forests, savages,
– precious little to eat fit for a civilised man, nothing but
Thames water to drink. No Falernian wine here, no going
ashore. Here and there a military camp lost in a wilderness, like
a needle in a bundle of hay – cold, fog, tempests, disease, exile,
and death, – death skulking in the air, in the water, in the bush.
They must have been dying like flies here.*

Joseph Conrad, *Heart of Darkness*

The settlers of Londinium were bewildered. Camulodunum
had fallen? To the tribes on the eastern coast? The Iceni
might have had claws once, but they were a lapdog tribe now,
shepherds, horse breeders, salt panners and marsh dwellers; the
Trinovantes were little better than slaves. The veterans were
dead? They knew the procurator's men, reluctant and cursing,
had marched there days ago to keep the peace, but the city
destroyed? And the rebels were coming *here*? All this way? It
wasn't possible. What had happened to the Ninth Legion? And
yet all the white-faced riders and the stream of pathetic refugees
were telling that same story, and the terror in their eyes was real
enough.

The merchants went about their business with one eye on their stock and the other on the ships and boats in the wharves. They were safe until the moorings started to empty. Some were convincing themselves that the vaguest smudge on the horizon to the north-east was smoke, and the increasing flood of fugitives confirmed it. Camulodunum had fallen, and the head-hunting rebels were coming.

It is difficult to imagine the relief and joy that must have fallen across the frantic settlement when Governor Paulinus arrived with his mounted men. The legions might have been left far behind, but the presence of the governor and at least some soldiers must have seemed like salvation. Paulinus was a soldier if ever a governor was, a man who inspired confidence. The people of Londinium must have hailed his arrival like the coming of a god. Paulinus had won the race – Londinium was his.

But Paulinus had been to Londinium before. He knew the town had no defensive wall, no earthworks or garrison. The exhausted old soldier knew that this sprawling mercantile boomtown was indefensible from any serious threat long before he got there. What he had come for was information. Week-old reports from unknown junior officers were of no use to him; he needed detailed intelligence provided by his own staff officers. He must have known that Camulodunum had fallen, or he would have been heading there, but what about the Ninth Legion?

In the fog of war, and on the move for the previous week, the news might still have eluded him. Had any other units marched on their own authority? The Second Legion? Where were the rebels now? What was their composition and strength? Which tribes had risen, which others were wavering and why the hell had they rebelled? Could he contain the trouble in the south-east, or had it spread? Most pressingly, might the presence of his cavalry be enough to deflect the rebels from London?

A small but threatening delegation would have sped south-west to the kingdom of Togidubnus to remind the wealthy client ruler exactly where his loyalties lay, and the terrible price he would pay for letting them drift. Dispatch riders and patrols galloped along every road out of the settlement, some as messengers, others as scouts and fighting patrols that would observe the rebels and be expected to engage small groups, securing prisoners to torture for information. As the first reports of the sheer scale of what was coming began to arrive, however, Paulinus must have wearily given up any hope of intimidating the rebels by his presence. This was a relief column no longer; it was a reconnaissance in strength.

The truth must have dampened the jubilation of the Londoners. Paulinus would have made no pretence of making a defence if the rebel army was even a fraction of the numbers now being reported, and if they were truly heading towards the town he would abandon it without a blink. Anyone capable of riding with the column could join him, when the time came, but he couldn't squander his men protecting refugees.

His advice would have been simple and stark enough – leave the town and head south of the Thames where there was the least risk of running into hostile groups, where the reaffirmed loyalty of King Togidubnus could be relied upon, or north to Verulamium; board one of the many boats and ships on the river, or find a horse and join him. Those disinclined or unable to follow that advice would be left to their fate.

Paulinus and his staff may have requisitioned the most prestigious building as their headquarters, perhaps Decianus's abandoned procuratorial offices, and set to work collating the intelligence coming in from the patrols, discussing options, and formulating a plan of campaign. They may not have had much time – a day, perhaps two or three, but the atmosphere would have been cool and workmanlike. The young staff officers, perhaps including Julius Agricola, future father-in-law to Tacitus, might have felt a good deal less calm than they behaved, but Paulinus wouldn't have tolerated a single bead of sweat on their unfurrowed young brows – if a man had time to be worried then he clearly had too little work to do, and there was more than enough of that to go round.

The London that Paulinus was preparing to abandon was quite unlike Colchester. Its origins have always been obscure, some assuming a military foundation, guarding this vital river crossing, others seeing a natural draw to the spot by merchants and settlers. A military supply base and entrepôt succeeding an invasion-period temporary camp now seems most likely, naturally evolving as the years passed.[1] Our sole literary source is Tacitus: *Though undistinguished by the name of a colony, [Londinium] was much frequented by merchants and trading vessels.*[2]

Whilst not entirely contradicted by the archaeology, this description has been seen as an exaggerated version of the later town, circa AD 100, in a recent study by Dr Lacey Wallace;[3] and in the 1980s, Gustav Milne of the Museum of London pointed out that modern archaeologists have seen more of Londinium than Tacitus ever did, and more phases of it than Agricola.[4] Despite this, that embryonic London, in the first ten years of its life, remains a shadowy place for archaeologists, incomplete from later disturbance, ephemeral compared to its stone and brick successors, and inaccessible, deeply buried many metres beneath the heart of the City, its two-thousand-year darkness occasionally illuminated by a brief small window through the tarmac, before destruction or reburial.

Over the decades, these small beams of light have lit up the early town many times, to the point where Wallace, in 2014, was able to speculate that the roads in the settlement of AD 60 provided approximately nine kilometres of street frontage. Extrapolating the data collected from excavated portions, this would suggest that around 715 buildings stood in the town, of which an impressive 12.5 per cent have already been excavated to some extent.[5] Given the enormous depth and complexity of London's archaeology, this is an extraordinary exposure of the earliest settlement, but it does still mean that nearly 90 per cent of it remains unseen.

Any estimation of the population in AD 60 must be tentative in the extreme – previous attempts have ranged from the low thousands to several tens of thousands. Using the same data as above,

The Iceni wolf gold stater, c. 50 BC. Did this beak-jawed fen-wolf guard the Snettisham Treasure?

Beneath the Lexden Crown pub? After his triumphal entry with war elephants, Emperor Claudius receives the submission of the British kings at Camulodunon in AD 43.

A sky that might come crashing down: the still lonely, windswept isle of the dead at Stonea Camp.

Sandals and socks, the new old-fashioned way: the author's Roman army *caligae* in their natural habitat: a gravelly stone road.

Ambush country: looking down a defile into the Colne Valley. The Ninth Legion had to march directly through this landscape in their attempt to save Colchester.

D-Day, AD 60-style: the view across the Menai Strait from Anglesey to the Welsh mainland. Gently sloping bluffs like these made perfect landing beaches for the Roman army.

'Their groves, devoted to inhuman superstitions, were destroyed . . .'
The last stand of the Druids on Anglesey.

'The lake is a window into the earth . . .' Slave-chains and Spitfires: the bewitching twilight presence of Llyn Cerrig Bach, Anglesey.

Ashes under Uricon: the brutalist ruins of Wroxeter overlying the earth-and-timber fortress of the Fourteenth Legion.

Telescope Man: Boadicea's ubiquitous early-twentieth-century companion.

Regions Caesar never knew . . . Boadicea (holding bucket) scrubbed up
for the Coronation of George VI in 1937.

A natural suffragette:
the Boadicea brooch
produced by the
Women's Social and
Political Union, 1908.

I, Claudius . . . or Nero. This decapitated head is widely believed to be Boudican loot from the Temple of Claudius.

'The army of Britons, with its masses of infantry and cavalry, was confidently exulting . . .' Like grainy CCTV footage – the last known sighting of Boudica at Verulanium.

'Rush'd to battle, fought and died.' A mundane enough spot now, the line of this dual carriageway might mark the beginning of Boudica's last charge.

'Close up the ranks, discharge your javelins . . .' The location of the legionary front line? The Britons would have attacked directly from the left.

Wallace favours a figure of around 4000 souls,[6] and another convincing modern study has calculated around 10,000 inhabitants,[7] not to mention the many thousands working the agricultural hinterland. The townsfolk were a diverse cultural mix reflected in their building traditions, artefact types and burial rites.

The burgeoning town effectively had three zones, one to either side of the Walbrook, and across the Thames in Southwark. The core zone was on Cornhill, east of the Walbrook, most closely representing the establishment of a planned settlement with a large, gravelled market place or embryonic forum with big, probably public, buildings fronting onto it, clearly the civic centre attracting the wealthier settlers. This was surely the zone in which citizens lived, even to the deliberate exclusion of non-citizens. Veterans from the army were undoubtedly amongst them,[8] but also incomers from Gaul and further afield.

The evidence from Cornhill suggests a cosmopolitan, literate population, using writing sets, ceramic oil lamps and imported pottery, food preparation wares such as mortaria mixing bowls, and glass vessels – types of artefact less common, at least initially, from much of Ludgate and Southwark.[9] The apsidal end of what might have been an early bathhouse has been found near London Bridge.[10]

There was a mix of indigenous and continental building styles, also partly reflected by their respective areas, from small timber shacks and native roundhouses to major structures with masonry foundations, as well as both thatch and ceramic tiled roofs.[11] Internal floors were a mixture of hard clay scattered with rushes or rammed with gravel, and wooden boards. Cooking fires were in open hearths within the buildings, and although there is comparatively little evidence of decoration, a number of more ostentatious properties did have painted walls.

Remarkably, although many seem to have settled for wattle or barrel-lined wells in the back yard, there is also some evidence for a piped water supply. Timber-lined drains criss-crossed the site to channel water and sewage, so some attempt was clearly being made to prevent the squalor into which such a settlement could descend, especially in foul weather.[12]

West of the Walbrook, on Ludgate Hill, now the area of Cheapside and St Paul's, the settlement was clearly less desirable, initially dominated by the dumping of rubbish from the main town, and with building traditions suggesting a significant native element in the population. There are hints in the archaeology that the inhabitants were scavenging through the rubbish from the richer part of town, from which they may have been deliberately excluded,[13] and development along the street frontages by AD 60 was rapid.

Across the Thames, where the bridge made landfall onto an island surrounded by creeks and reedbeds, now Southwark, another community existed, more industrial, clearly a part of the larger settlement, but naturally separate. A range of occupations are represented in the archaeology – including the possible residence of the procurator, but also an indigenous native copper worker,[14] a butcher, a grain merchant, a baker, a dairy farmer, and a blacksmith, who managed to burn his own workshop to the ground and saved Boudica the job.[15]

At that moment, however, the settled population would have been swamped with refugees, perhaps to many times their own number, from Camulodunum, Caesaromagus, and a hundred smaller settlements and farms in Boudica's path. What appears to be absent on both sides of the river is anything more than a token military presence.

Tacitus is perhaps being generous when he suggests that Paulinus was *uncertain whether he should choose it as a seat of war*, before considering his own weakness, but the result was the same. The town was indefensible. He would have to consolidate his forces and look for another site at which to hold the rebels and *resolved to save the province at the cost of a single town*.[16]

And so the exodus began. London Bridge must have been choked with carts, wagons, pack mules, oxen and thousands of people all vying for space, a great impatient, panicked mess spilling across the north bank in the area where the bridge made landfall, around modern Fish Street Hill – the early Roman river bank was a hundred metres inland of the modern one. Beneath where American Golf and the Monument public house now stand must have been where the refugees flooded back from the bottleneck, fighting and jostling to gain a foothold on that precious road to safety. Paulinus may have posted some troopers there to keep order and filter the crowd through, and perhaps provided a welcome mounted escort for the first few miles south.

The bridge, crossing to Southwark, landed almost where the present one does, just on its eastern side, around Queen's Walk and the end of Tooley Street, spitting the fugitives out along Borough High Street. Here the road network kicked in, with a route along Stane Street south-west directly to the kingdom of Togidubnus, or south-east along Watling Street to the ports of *Rutupiae* at Richborough and *Dubris* at Dover.

Others on the north bank saddled their horses and loaded on what personal items or family members they could. They would ride north with the cavalry, taking up the general's offer to accompany him, won over by the calm professionalism of the soldiers and the glinting protection of their long spatha swords. I also wonder if this was the one town destroyed where some of the inhabitants who witnessed the destruction lived to tell the tale, by the simple precaution of boarding boats.

The great draw of Londinium for the merchants that Tacitus says flocked there was the Thames, fully accessible from the sea, navigable for smaller ocean-going vessels, and with long routes inland for river craft.

It was an international port, however embryonic, and as such would have been crammed with vessels of all sizes and types, with the small, shallow-hulled sailing ships, river boats, hide-stretched coracles and dugout canoes of the natives rubbing hulls with biremes and merchant ships from across the known world, moored up at the wharves, wattle revetments, and rammed-gravel landing beaches of the first river frontage. Larger ships moored in the estuary or one of the established ports, to be serviced by lighters and barges that did the toing and froing, and those making it as far as Londinium dropped anchor midstream in the deepest water.[17]

The one thing that Boudica's army did not have was boats, so the waiting vessels provided instant safety. Many a ship or barge owner who had just emptied his cargo onto the wharves would have made a fortune reloading with terrified passengers only too eager to pay well for a square foot of deck space, and off they sailed in the last few days. Many boats, however, must have been owned by merchants whose livelihoods and fortunes lay in the warehouses along the waterfront.

Why should they sail away? The town would be undefended and largely deserted when the natives arrived – they might simply loot and burn a few buildings before moving on elsewhere, with at least a chance that businesses and much stock could be salvaged afterwards. A merchant with a warehouse full of roof tiles, samian pottery, or some other non-perishable, non-flammable product unlikely to be carried off by plundering Britons, might reasonably expect a good proportion of his stock to survive the attack, but not the looting of the townsfolk who were first to arrive back afterwards.

Mooring their ships midstream in the Thames, probably at the eastern end of town in case they were forced to up anchor and flee, somewhere in the modern vicinity of Tower Bridge, the merchants and townsfolk crammed aboard were safe enough from attack, and towards the limit of any effective range of sling-shots. Once the Britons moved on, the inhabitants who had held their nerve would be first ashore to scour the wreckage and save what they could of their property. It is something to contemplate that many hundreds could have sat it out on the Thames, watching their homes, livelihoods and businesses destroyed in relative safety from the marauding Iceni.

Finally the screen of Paulinus's cavalry pickets east of the town fell back to make their final reports ahead of the dark haze of smoke and dust that rose behind them. The Britons were within half a day's march, and advanced war parties were spreading out to encircle the town, with bands of horsemen searching the river for suitable places to swim their horses across.

It was time to leave.

Paulinus and the last of his staff mounted their waiting horses at the head of the massed squadrons of cavalry formed up on the gravelled expanse of the marketplace, beneath where Marks & Spencer now stands on Fenchurch Street, where patches of the original gravel have been excavated.[18] The impatient civilians with their overloaded mounts would follow behind, and the huge column clattered westwards in retreat, along the road on the line of Newgate Street and Holborn:

> Nor did the tears and weeping of the people, as they implored his aid, deter him from giving the signal of departure and receiving into his army all who could go with him. Those who were chained to the spot by the weakness of their sex, or the infirmity of age, or the attractions of the place, were cut off by the enemy . . .[19]

In a large town of many thousands, additionally flooded with refugees, there were inevitably those who could not travel without dedicated family members or slaves to help – the elderly, sick, disabled and drunks. There would be fugitives hurrying in who had outpaced the Iceni for days, and were simply too exhausted to carry on going.

Many in the town would have been reluctant to leave their homes and property – without which they were destitute and had no means to survive anyway – and waited in the hope that the rebels would pass them by. Others, Britons, some perhaps expats from the eastern tribes themselves, might have reasoned that as they were neither soldier nor foreign incomer, they had little to fear from the rebels, for whom they might even have felt some sympathy. Traditional native roundhouses and pottery, particularly on the Ludgate side of the Walbrook, attest to just such a native population.

Other people would have kept calm and carried on, assuming that when the time came they could board one of the many ships and boats moored along the jetties, only to find the gangplanks raised and the packed, overburdened vessels dangerously low in the water by the time the dust haze rose in the east.

Mobs of panicked Londoners with nowhere to run were left standing on the wharves, as mounted warriors, who had swum their horses across the river downstream, suddenly appeared on the southern end of the bridge. Warehouses full of grain may already have been burning, fired by the leaving soldiers to deny their contents to the enemy, wreathing the town in a flame-lit smog.

Such was the nightmarish scene the troopers and mounted civilians of the retreating column left behind as they passed through the housing, workshops and taverns either side of the Walbrook, and then out of the town and over the River Fleet, now beneath Farringdon Street, crossing by a wooden bridge where the Holborn Viaduct now stands, pushing through the crowds of frantic refugees heading west. We have no eyewitness account of this moment, but it called to my mind the words of a young British sergeant as he and his men abandoned Antwerp to the Germans in October 1914:

> We received the most deadening, soul-racking order a soldier can receive – Retreat. We picked our way through the burning buildings, past the flaming oil tanks to the flaming pontoon bridge the engineers had built for us to cross and then destroy. On each side of the bridge stood hordes of refugees of every kind – children, women, nuns, priests. This was the bridge of sighs; they had been stopped so we could cross. The flare from the burning lit their faces, expressionless and hopeless, and we felt ashamed.[20]

On they rode. Next time you happen to be there, take a moment of still mental silence amidst the traffic of Holborn Viaduct or the chaos of Oxford Street to *jump back for a moment* and see the long lines of horsemen, faces a dark mix of detachment, anger and shame as they abandon the settlement and remaining towns-folk to the depredations of the natives, heading for the crossroads where Marble Arch now stands. There, by most interpretations, they swung right, onto Watling Street, the Edgware Road, and the ride back north in shame.

Other historians would have Paulinus march west from this point, accompanied by his Legions, an interpretation to which we will return, but that is not my reading of the sources; Paulinus turned north. I had cycled back the eleven miles to Elstree in his hoofprints after my hard ride to Marble Arch, through mile after mile of city, unnerving concrete flyovers, and a hundred red traffic lights, but suddenly at Stanmore, on Brockley Hill and then Elstree Hill, in the darkness of the woods, speeding through the twilight of the summer evening, London had gone, left behind in time and space, and I too was simply a tired man riding away from it in my urgent desire to be somewhere else.

I imagine all this still standing on London Bridge, having just completed Paulinus's journey, with my stiff flat white, and I walk down onto the Thames Path to follow the river. At Queenhithe I stumble across a mosaic set into a wall, unveiled in 2014, depicting the story of London. One of the first pictures is a chariot-mounted warrior queen, next to a depiction of a late face-horse Iceni coin, and an image of Londinium burning. AD 60 BOUDICCA SACKS LONDON, proclaims the legend. I walk on, along the Victoria Embankment, past the pock-marked shrapnel damage to Cleopatra's Needle, until Big Ben announces the proximity of another, greater depiction of the warrior queen.

Thomas Thornycroft's monumental bronze diorama of *Boadicea and Her Daughters* on the northern landfall of Westminster Bridge was raised in 1902, the final year of the Boer

War, the year after the death of Boudica's namesake monarch, Victoria, and seventeen years after the death of Thornycroft himself.

It is confusing that a half-page photograph in the *Illustrated London News* four years earlier, on 22 January 1898, shows the statue already in place, but a full-size plaster cast of the group was erected first to meet with public approval, which it clearly did. It undoubtedly met with royal approval too, for Prince Albert had been involved in the project from its beginnings in 1856, had influenced the design of the chariot, and loaned two of his own horses as models.[21] Thornycroft had worked on the Albert Memorial, as well as sculpting Victoria herself more than once.

The monument is a complex celebration of the legend of Boadicea as the Victorians perceived her, encapsulated in the legend inscribed on the tall, southern side of the high plinth, taken from William Cowper's *Boadicea: An Ode*:

REGIONS CAESAR NEVER KNEW
THY POSTERITY SHALL SWAY

Not a single well-educated Victorian or Edwardian schoolchild needed the verse finished for them . . . 'Where his eagles never flew, None invincible as they.' It was a clarion call to the destiny of Empire.

To most people, this is Boudica incarnate, Dio's description of the warrior queen writ large in three-dimensional splendour, a war goddess in bronze. Thornycroft left us an enduring monument to haunt us, a focus for future generations to contemplate the legacy of empires and the terrible folly of war, just as his grandson, a young fox-hunting man called Siegfried Sassoon, would do in a very different way and for a very different war.

Boadicea and her cubs survived the Zeppelins and Gothas raining death and destruction on the city in Sassoon's war, and a generation later the swastika Armageddon of Junkers and

Heinkels. Miraculously, no bomb fragments scar them like the wounded sphinx a few minutes away along the Embankment, or any number of pre-war buildings. If there is one image of the Blitz I could choose to see, it wouldn't be the dome of St Paul's silhouetted by the firestorm, but Boadicea, spear raised, majestic, defiant, immortal.[22]

Boadicea's statue is a masterful fusion of Victorian and classical forms. From the front, where the group is most easily if not most pleasingly viewed, we have a vision of Boudica as the Romans themselves might have portrayed her. Everything about the view is classical, from the robust figures to the style of chariot, from the rearing horses to the Romans' romantic ideal of the noble savage. Boudica's revolt mirrored many of the attributes that Rome liked to see in itself, of justice and nobility, tough, Spartan living, and never-say-die determination. The Roman retellings of the story are as much a criticism of effete contemporary Rome as a condemnation of the rebels. And that is what we have here, a justification, in the Roman spirit.

Here is Boudica leading a murderous revolt, and the violence isn't shied from. The scythes on the wheels, albeit dramatic licence, are enough to give any self-respecting Londoner a shiver, and those war horses, with flailing hooves and bared teeth, are not creatures I'd want to feed sugar lumps to, no matter how flat I kept my hand. But here too is the flogged Boudica and her violated daughters. Her raised spear could be replaced with the scales of justice without any loss of meaning. Not to suggest that anyone could actually mistake Boadicea for a genuine Roman statue, you could excavate her from the ash of Pompeii without too much *feeling* out of place.

But from the side we could be looking at a different statue entirely. This is Victorian, every inch of it; it is nearly art nouveau, and almost Pre-Raphaelite. Boudica is suddenly achingly feminine, and just as the Victorians liked to portray their women – Goddess-like, vulnerable and sacred, in stark contrast to their actual treatment of women: 'Oh woman! Masterpiece of creation, queen of humanity, mother of the human race . . . Take my boots off!'[23]

This could be Morgan le Fay, or the Lady of Shalott, or Guinevere, indeed any legendary female figure the Victorians latched onto. She could almost have been modelled by Elizabeth Siddal, the ill-fated artist, model and muse. Suddenly, and certainly though the Victorians would have denied it, this bronze Boudica is the perfect subconscious Victorian vision of womanhood, naturally elegant, with a noble purpose; she is a mother; she is silent; she is sexy.

The princesses intrigue me. The victims of bestial savagery, now at the moment of revenge, are they meant to be empowered or cowed, curling around their mother's legs like cats? Their expressions are otherworldly, mystical, wide-eyed, gazing upon something we cannot see, one with mouth half-opened as if in halted speech. Commenting on the daughters, Thornycroft claimed he made, 'One eager gaze forward, the other slinks back appalled at the battle cry,' but conceived them as, 'young barbarians who would regard their violation simply as an insult to be avenged.'[24]

These are not the almost prepubescent girls depicted in other contemporary portrayals such as those in Cardiff City Hall, or Brecon; it is only the comparison with their mother that confirms their youth. They are bare-breasted, a strange choice on Thornycroft's part. The Victorians certainly didn't shy away from classical nakedness, but it is not as if the girls really are naked, simply that their robes, revealing enough if Boudica's is anything to go by, have fallen away on both princesses to reveal their breasts, perhaps to symbolise their violation. The fact that they are only on the cusp of womanhood lends their semi-nakedness an innocence for, if Boudica had suffered the same wardrobe mishap, the exposure would have been deemed gratuitous. Remarkably, in side silhouette, the daughters almost disappear from view.

From behind the group takes on yet another form, more dynamic, the only view that gives a real sense of movement. The daughters suddenly emerge as an integral part of the whole, and the object of their attack and ferocity, the Palace of Westminster, the seat of Britain's imperial power, of both justice and injustice, is before them. The chariot almost seems to career away towards the objective. This image of female warriors storming parliament had an obvious appeal for the Suffragettes, who were using the statue as a rallying point by 1906. The Women's Social and Political Union quickly produced a beautiful silver brooch of the statue for sale in its shops.

Boadicea's statue is too high on its plinth to appreciate fully close-up, so one needs to step away and take the long view to drink in the full glory of the side profile. The high angle makes it difficult to meditate upon, and a devil to photograph successfully, but it does at least mean there's no endless queue of tourists climbing into the chariot for Boadicea selfies, however much I crave one myself.

Many have had the privilege. I have a 1937 press photograph showing three men cleaning the statue in preparation for the Coronation, two mounted on the horses, and a third on the queen's shoulder, having hung his wash bucket irreverently from her upraised hand. In 2009, female environmental protestors from Climate Rush climbed the plinth and occupied the chariot, draping the statue with banners proclaiming: DEEDS NOT WORDS.[25]

In 2005, Banksy, the elusive street artist, also ascended the plinth. Looking convincingly workmanlike in a high visibility jacket and carrying a ladder, he climbed up to the back of the group, and fixed a bright yellow wheel clamp to the chariot. 'The easiest way to become invisible,' he noted, 'is to wear a day-glo vest and carry a tiny transistor radio playing Heart FM very loudly.'[26] If I tried something like that, I'd be pistol-whipped and handcuffed before my foot hit the third rung of the ladder.

But in many respects, Boudica has been all but forgotten by this city that she still towers over. It doesn't surprise Banksy.

If you want someone to be ignored
then build a life-size bronze statue of
them and stick it in the middle of town.

It doesn't matter how great you were,
it'll always take an unfunny drunk
with climbing skills to make people
notice you.[27]

I search the souvenir stalls in vain for Boadicea tourist tat, even the one beneath her statue, which I crossly notice completely hides the inscription that tells you who she is. I have a few photographs and postcards from the 1900s showing a souvenir stall here from a gentler age. The white-bearded, homburg-hatted gentleman running the stall, constructed from, of all things, the tripod legs of an enormous brass telescope, *does* seem to be selling Boadicea tourist tat, the handwritten sign in one of the pictures advertising: HISTORY OF BIG BEN! BOADICEA! MAPS AND GUIDE. He sells Streimer's nougat and Fry's chocolate.

Clearly a well-known character in the first decades of the last century, he is referred to as 'the telescope man' in more than one caption. The telescope is sighted on Big Ben, and is a penny to look through. The stall is respectfully placed to one side so as *not* to obscure the proud legend on the front of the plinth, clearly legible in the photos, though too rarely seen today:

BOADICEA
(BOUDICCA)
QUEEN OF THE ICENI
WHO DIED AD 61
AFTER LEADING HER PEOPLE
AGAINST THE ROMAN INVADER

That a semi-permanent stall can be erected directly against this caption beggars belief, these essential words, which lend meaning and purpose to the whole, entirely lost from view. It pisses me off every time I walk past it. I don't blame the stallholders – fair play to them, it's a great location – but if the authorities of London can't give the statue the space it deserves, I'm sure the people of Norwich would gladly accept it as a gift and find a fittingly uncluttered spot for it in their own city.

I glance around the stall. One of the guys begins his sales patter.

'Do you have any souvenirs of the statue?' I ask, nodding towards the queen. He swings around and stares at the statue for a moment, and then turns back in triumph.

'Booodica,' he says proudly.

I nod enthusiastically. 'Do you have any souvenirs of *her*?'

He looks clean through me for a good five seconds, and then with a vague twinkle of humour and slight shake of the head says, 'No.' Conversation over, he turns to another tourist more likely to buy something.

I search other stalls for tourist tat in case I've missed something. No statuettes in miniature to use as a paperweight; no chariot-mounted warrior queen snow globes with red and orange particles to represent the swirling firestorm. No charms or tea towels, fridge magnets or T-shirts. Eventually I find a couple of postcards, not *of* her, but on which her horses are present in a photo of Big Ben or the London Eye. I feel unaccountably indignant, as if her honour could somehow be restored by my finding a keyring with a small brass Boadicea dangling beneath. Surely it is better this way, but someone is missing a trick. Can you name just three people in your world who *wouldn't* be thrilled with a Boadicea tea towel or keyring?

It feels entirely appropriate, as I leave this neglected icon of misplaced national pride, appropriated by minority activists from suffragists to environmentalists as a focus in the struggle against unjust power, that Parliament Square across the road is a sea of protestors, police, and a grotesque inflated blimp of Donald J. Trump wearing a nappy. By complete coincidence and great good fortune I have aligned my visit to Boadicea with The Donald's visit to Britain, and in the name of research I have the inestimable privilege of joining the protestors as they advance on Parliament, in the same spirit of women's equality and environmental outrage that have always latched on to *Boadicea and Her Daughters*.

Sadly, the procession is marching in the opposite direction to the British Museum, so I soon have to walk against the crowd, one of whom is a woman I instantly assume to be dressed as Boadicea, but then decide is probably Britannia – the distinction can be pretty slight, but the trident with red, white and blue ribbons suggests the latter. What a pity – Trump versus Boadicea would be something worth seeing, but failing that the woman behind Britannia in a red T-shirt proclaiming TRUMP IS A TWAT could definitely take him in a fight as well.

I am making a whistle-stop visit to the British Museum, always painful, as the wing I am visiting contains Lindow Man, the Snettisham Treasure, the Battersea shield, the Waterloo Bridge helmet . . . I could go on and spend all day there, but there are two artefacts within Room 49: Roman Britain, that I specifically want to see. Both are rather mangled pieces of metal, and it is time to tell their story.

The first is a damaged gladiator's helmet ploughed up from a field at Hawkedon in Suffolk in 1965, which dates to the mid-first century AD. If truth be told, it is an ugly piece, the dome from the front looking like a human cranium sliced horizontally through the eye orbits, and the flared neck protection is crude. But then it is what it is – hacking people to death, and avoiding being hacked to death, was a crude business, and much gladiatorial costume lacks the dandified affectation of the military. It would have had a protective mask to shield the face, with large segmented insect eyes and an overall impression of a fish face, or a grotesque, archaic diving helmet.

Made of bronze, it was originally plated with tin that would have given it a shining silver finish, so rather less crude than now, but no less horrifying to either the person wearing it, or the one staring back at it. Given its location and relatively early date, it is widely believed to have originated from Colchester, which leaves the intriguing question as to why and how it ended up in a field in Suffolk.

Graham Webster considered this helmet was 'probably' looted from Camulodunum by Boudica's rebels, perhaps even worn by one of them in battle, and then carried home,[28] which, if accepted, makes it almost unique as an associated item. I say *almost* because another helmet usually on display here, though not today, a first-century bronze auxiliary cavalry helmet from Witcham Gravel in Cambridgeshire, has also been suggested as Boudican loot.[29] Once more, it might be, but there is surely a limit to the number of stray Roman artefacts and petty thefts that we can try to pin on the Iceni and, like the gladiator helmet, it has to remain no more than a vague possibility.

More compelling, in a cabinet to the right, is a slightly larger than life bronze head, disembodied, but clearly once attached to a torso as the hacked remains of the neck attest. Indeed, from the angle of the neck it would appear that the head is not only missing a body, but also an underlying horse – the identifying personality of a monumental equine statue. This is officially known as the Alde Head, after the river Alde at Rendham in Suffolk in which it was found in 1907 by a boy playing in the river, but in popular archaeological literature it has always been the Alde Head of Claudius.

It may or may not be the head of Claudius – a strong case has also been made for it being a young Nero,[30] but either way, it would date the statue to the reign of Claudius or the earlier years of Nero, essentially the decade before AD 60. Stylistically, it is almost certainly Julio-Claudian (27 BC–AD 68),[31] and allowing for the inevitable discrepancies of artists at opposite ends of the empire who had probably never seen the emperor in the flesh, I can't help but see a striking resemblance between the

Alde head and the depiction of Claudius in the Aphrodisias rape sculpture.

More intriguing still is that a piece of a bronze horse's leg, of the same scale, but just thirty-five centimetres long, also violently hacked from a statue, was ploughed up at Ashill in central Norfolk in 1979,[32] thirty-eight miles to the north-west, which is now in the Boudica Gallery in Norwich Castle Museum. Roman Britain might have had more than one monumental equine statue, to be sure,[33] although at this very early date they would have been rare, and tests on the chemical composition of both pieces revealed a distinctive and unusual alloy with a low lead content. In short, it is likely that the decapitated head and the little bit of leg derived from the same continental bronze foundry[34] or, given the circumstantial evidence, the exact same statue.

Until Londinium began to flourish in the post-rebellion world of the later AD 60s and 70s, there can be little doubt that the place of origin of that statue was pre-rebellion Colchester, thirty miles south-west of where the head was found. Londinium may indeed have had some statuary by AD 60 – Professor Richard Hingley suggests that the town would have been 'well furnished' with bronze statues of emperors from the beginning,[35] somewhat tempered by London archaeologist Dominic Perring's assertion that early Londinium was 'a functional place with few frills', and, 'the buildings and symbols of Classical Rome had little social value'.[36]

Likewise, in 2014 Lacey Wallace noted that early Londinium lacked a 'symbolic and ideological package of monuments.'[37] Colchester, on the other hand, was a city with a monumental arch of victory for Claudius, a vast classical temple complex for Claudius, and may well have boasted the name of Colonia *Claudia* Victricensis, a place that the deified emperor himself had conquered. It would almost certainly have had big bronze equine statues of both Claudius and Nero, and they may well have sat bang outside the temple dedicated to Claudius, in the sacred temenos precinct.

Many have no doubt that this head was hacked from its statue during the storming of the Temple as war booty of the most powerful kind – the head of the emperor in whose name this citadel of alien power had been raised, or, perhaps, the ruling emperor Nero who was hated even more. As the adopted son and heir of Claudius, his statue would have been equally at home on display in the temple complex.[38] A recent study of the damage to the neck has attested to the extreme violence employed in the decapitation, most likely with an axe, after the statue had been toppled and was lying on its right side. The face seems to have been deliberately protected from damage, perhaps to increase its inherent trophy value.[39]

Incorporating the Ashill leg into the story, the remainder of the statue was dismembered, and pieces carried away for deposition, either ritually, or as keepsakes until these war souvenirs became too incriminating to keep. The fragment of leg was found fifty miles north of Colchester, in the heart of Icenian territory. A remote and lonely spot now, the square bank and ditch invisible beneath the ploughsoil may have been a ritual enclosure.

It is a hell of a tale. Like the strange rash of coin hoards suddenly appearing in Icenian lands at this time, I wonder if other fragments of this statue have been found by farmers, navvies or metal detectorists, but not recognised or reported, or if others still await discovery in key ritual locations. One more identifiable piece with that same alloy signature in another part of Norfolk or Suffolk would surely clinch it. Gazing into the empty black eye sockets of the bronze-green face whilst running this story and these images through your mind, of the violence and noise of its decapitation, the storming of the temple compound, and its long sleep in the slow waters of the Alde, can be intoxicating. I could pull up a chair and stare into them all day.

I go home with the image of the bronze head imprinted on my mind, perhaps splashing beneath the Alde even as Paulinus flew to Londinium's aid and Boudica's army stirred from its post-traumatic fug of weariness in the stinking ruins of Camulodunum and the Colne Valley. Bizarrely, as I travel home on the packed, stifling train, standing room only, I overhear a very tall young man, nicknamed Bambi, telling another passenger of the many attractions of Colchester, not least of which is the castle that, he explains, 'lies over the Temple of Claudius, which Boudica burnt to the ground.'

Paulinus had abandoned Londinium as Boudica's army approached, a half-deserted shell with a few frantic souls still wandering its alleyways or holed up in their homes, streams of exhausted refugees shuffling across the bridges, and overburdened ships lying midstream in the Thames. I now have to explore the London that he left to its fate, and the evidence for its destruction. The most appropriate way to do that is to follow Boudica's route to the town, and from Norwich there is a deceptively easy way to do that almost exactly, which hundreds do unwittingly every day. It's called the Norwich to Liverpool Street train.

If this sounds like a cop-out, it is worth following the rail line with your finger on the map, because it is astonishing how closely it follows the old Roman route, rarely more than two miles from it, and often only a couple of hundred yards. It stops at Colchester, crucially, and then runs directly by the road to the very edge of the Roman town. Given that the Iceni and Trinovantes must have swamped that road for hundreds or even thousands of yards to either side, then the train really does run through the swirling ghosts of AD 60, certainly from Colchester, and it is here where your imagination begins to reclaim the story. This was where Boudica's army was now stirring for the advance.

The last stands of the veterans and the Ninth Legion had been treasure troves for the Britons. For tribes long stripped of their armouries, the bounty of javelins, spears, shields and swords was snatched up, and mail shirts and helmets, only ever worn by the wealthiest of warrior nobles, must have been jealously fought over. The clunky segmented body armour was more alien, but undoubtedly coveted nonetheless for its incredible protection – its value even as scrap iron was stupefying.

The army that now swamped the line of the modern A12 and railway from Colchester to London was a different one, therefore, to that which had marched from Icenia to Camulodunum. Victorious, blooded and better armed, passions sated and renewed in slaughter, torture, drinking and plunder, and spiritually fortified by mass blood-sacrifice, there must have been a tangible aura of confidence and arrogance as thousands of decapitated heads were held aloft embedded on spear points. If the Colony of the Victorious, the stalwart veterans *and* the Ninth Legion could not stand before them, nothing could.

Both Tacitus and Dio refer to the atrocities carried out by this newly victorious army. Tacitus, true to his nature, is sober and undramatic:

> *The barbarians, who delighted in plunder and were indifferent to all else, passed by the fortresses with military garrisons, and attacked whatever offered most wealth to the spoiler, and was unsafe for defence. About seventy thousand citizens and allies, it appeared, fell in the places which I have mentioned. For it was not on making prisoners and selling them, or on any of the barter of war, that the enemy was bent, but on slaughter, on the gibbet, the fire and the cross, like men soon about to pay the penalty, and meanwhile snatching at instant vengeance.[40]*

This pitiless scene of fire, sword and gibbet is hardly to be wondered at, although the insinuation that they were avoiding stiff fights for plunder is rather belied by their recent military achievements of smashing into the stiffly defended temple complex and trouncing the battle group left to oversee the entire eastern half of the country. Dio makes darker claims that have come to haunt our mental image of the war:

> *Those who were taken captive by the Britons were subjected to every known form of outrage. The worst and most bestial*

> *atrocity committed by their captors was the following. They*
> *hung up naked the noblest and most distinguished women and*
> *then cut off their breasts and sewed them to their mouths, in*
> *order to make the victims appear to be eating them; afterwards*
> *they impaled the women on sharp skewers run lengthwise*
> *through the entire body. All this they did to the accompaniment*
> *of sacrifices, banquets and wanton behaviour, not only in all*
> *their other sacred places, but particularly in the grove of Andate.*
> *This was their name for Victory, and they regarded her with the*
> *most exceptional reverence.*[41]

I have never doubted that cruelties every bit as bad as these took
place, but atrocity stories, like silly speeches put into the mouths
of protagonists, are the details most likely to have been embel-
lished or fabricated to suit the specific needs of the target audience; even if based on original reports, nothing gains speed and
colour as it tears through an army by Chinese whispers like a
good atrocity story.

The question therefore is not whether such murder, torture and
mutilation took place – history, ancient and modern, from
Kalkriese to Kosovo to Kharkiv, sadly gives us every justification
in assuming that it did – but whether the explicit details related by
Dio are of significance. Certainly they are often taken at face
value by authors who are otherwise wary of Dio, and much has
been made of the clear sexual overtones of female mutilation
particularly, of sucking severed breasts, and lengthwise impale-
ment on skewers in simulated rape.

If these details are of possible ritual interest, however, or vengeance in kind, the fact that Dio specifically has the *noblest and*
most distinguished women hung up naked to be mutilated would
have had his upper-class Roman audience trembling with guilty
and dreadful delight. Perhaps most interesting is his mention of
the grove of Andate, surely a corruption of his previously
mentioned Andraste, and his assertion that *this was their name*
for Victory; was Dio getting his names and Celtic translations

mixed up? Goddess of Victory Andraste might have been, but *Boudica* was their actual name for Victory.

It would have been from the high ground at Brentwood, and then at Gallows Corner near Gidea Park station above Romford, where the rebel army first saw the haze of smoke along the great river valley that hailed their approach to Londinium, fifteen miles distant.

I leave the train at Stratford station, about four miles from the City, and gladly stretch my legs. It is another hot morning in this long summer of 2018, and I am walking the final stretch of Boudica's approach to Londinium, along the Roman route of Mile End Road and Whitechapel Road. I walk through areas where the extremes of affluence and poverty are side-by-side on the pavement, and diversity in the form of almost every type of national dress. There are languages I can't even identify let alone understand, swirling through the smells of exotic spices coming from the shops, and written words I cannot decipher; a cosmopolitan patchwork of rich and poor, old and new, the familiar and foreign. How similar it must have felt sometimes in early Roman London.

It was at Aldgate where Boudica's warriors encountered the first houses at the edge of the settlement and flooded across the Lorteburn Stream, a small valley delimiting the eastern edge of the town, though invisible now. Some of the buildings hereabouts were rich enough to have tiled roofs, and the ash and daub of their destruction has been found beneath the prow-like wedge of Landmark House at the Leadenhall–Fenchurch Streets junction.[42]

Those who had chosen to remain now saw the scale and fury of what was coming, as the first flames licked along the rooflines and screams rang along the streets. No one was going to buy their safety or be spared for having a British voice. Those who had affected the styles of a Roman provincial were done for, but many must still have worn their native trews, torn off anything foreign-looking, grabbed a spear and turned on their neighbours, hoping to pass themselves off as Boudica's warriors by joining in the slaughter.

Here the Roman and modern roads diverge, and I follow Fenchurch Street to the heart of the early Roman town, the so-called proto-forum, or marketplace, the huge gravelled area surrounded by large buildings that I speculated Paulinus might have temporarily requisitioned as his cavalry parade ground. It would have been deserted when the Britons burst across it, an open area with nowhere to hide, a trampled scatter of empty crates and sacks, broken amphorae and piles of horse dung. The eastern half of it now being dominated by Marks & Spencer, I pop in to get a sandwich for lunch.

Now, I didn't previously know this, but Marks & Spencer's Foodhall is on the lower ground floor, and at somewhere between four and five metres below ground. As such, this market of staples, essentials and exotic imports, from bread, milk and beer to spices, olives and wine, lies exactly where the early Roman one did, selling many of the same things and on about the same ground surface.

It is in such little discoveries that you can physically get down to the level of Boudica's Londinium in a way that often only archaeologists otherwise can. It was here, exactly where I stand amongst the other shoppers crowding the aisles, that Boudica's warriors flooded across the deserted gravel marketplace. The experience is crowned by something I spot in the drinks section. Sitting amongst the beers is a group of brown bottles with bright labels – *Boadicea Golden Ale*.

I glide back up the escalator and into the present day with my sandwich and beer souvenir, and hurry on along Lombard Street and Cheapside, past St Pauls and on to Holborn Viaduct to take in the Ludgate area of the settlement and its western edge. It would have been along this very road and another directly south of it, the final arteries leading out of the town, that the last and slowest of the refugees were overtaken. We can only assume that the rebel army swarmed in from the east, even if charioteers raced north of the town and horsemen who had swum their mounts across the river raced south of it, to cut off escape routes.

After ransacking the richer buildings of Aldgate and Cornhill, the tide would have washed on westwards across the Walbrook, smashing through the ribbon developments of homes, workshops and roundhouses along Cheapside and Newgate Street, and south of them at St Pauls and Ludgate Hill. Horsemen and charioteers could soon have mopped up the fugitives still flooding west beyond the Fleet. There had been no garrison. Half the population, and the fitter half able to flee at that, had gone, and there was no resolute core of ex-military settlers to organise a defence. The end of Londinium was simply a flame-lit massacre.

I know that I am not the first to wander these streets recreating these scenes in my head. The controversial Scottish folklorist Lewis Spence, in his extravagant and eloquent but otherwise rather dubious attempt at real history from 1937, *Boadicea: Warrior Queen of the Britons*, in recalling Dio's descriptions of live skewerings and mastectomies, wrote: 'Often as I have passed down Gracechurch Street or Cornhill the shrieks of these doomed women from sunny Italy have wrung in my ears, keening loud and shrilly above the tumult of the traffic.'[43]

Have we found any of these victims of Boudica in London? The famous Walbrook skulls, a bizarre phenomenon that has resulted in around three hundred jawless skulls being retrieved from the small Walbrook Valley over the years,[44] have traditionally been pushed as Londoners beheaded by Boudica's army, but they are highly unlikely to represent her victims. The Museum of London's archaeological unit has confirmed the skulls are more likely to have been washed into the stream from extensive Roman cemeteries to the north long after interment, for all that the processes are complex, possibly ritual, and not entirely understood.[45]

Some skulls with undeniable evidence of extreme violence are more likely to represent victims of the arena, or perhaps prisoners of war, dating to the second century.[46] A few disarticulated human bones of the right era, some with possible weapon scars, have been found alongside London Bridge, but the dead of Boudican Londinium are otherwise as lost to us as those of Camulodunum.[47]

I wander back into the City. A wedge-shaped development known as No. 1 Poultry occupies the acute angle between Queen Victoria Street and Poultry. It is a famous 1990s landmark, designed by James Stirling, which caused an understandable storm of controversy at the time due to the demolition of John Belcher's magical neo-gothic Mappin and Webb building to enable the development. The silver lining is that the destruction of the old resident allowed archaeologists in before the new build, and what lay beneath was a veritable portal back to Roman Londinium.

The line of the main east–west Roman road is lost within the City until it is picked up by Newgate Street. It crossed obliquely under Cheapside, and ran directly beneath No. 1 Poultry, on the western side of the Walbrook, where two minor roads also joined it. The site encompassed the full span of London's history, from the earliest demonstrable Roman feature, a boxed wooden drain laid down before the road, tree-ring dated to the winter of AD 47/48,[48] right through to the present, combined with excellent organic preservation due to the waterlogged conditions of the Walbrook valley. The archaeology of the later Roman city was truly magnificent, but it also preserved a snapshot of the more modest settlement of AD 60, and its violent destruction, in stunning detail.

The site exposed a plot of timber, wattle and mudbrick roadside buildings constructed on a series of low, revetted terraces to accommodate the slope of the Walbrook. The humdrum daily round and common task of the townsfolk in the days and months before destruction loomed could be picked out in the archaeological record. The road was patchily resurfaced at about this time,[49] and the tree rings within the timber from one roadside building betrayed its having been cut down during the winter of AD 59/60, utilised on the very eve of the war in this new build that seems to have incorporated both a stable and portico.[50] The clay floors and timber foundations all preserved the fierce burning of the destruction that quickly followed.

This same sad evidence was repeated across the site, of new or developing buildings razed by fire, leaving scorched floors, petrified mudbrick and blackened timbers, with a scatter of personal artefacts mixed in – brooches, pens, glass, an inkwell, a string of charred wooden beads. At the eastern end of the site was a tavern, where pieces of broken wine amphorae were concentrated, and the heavily used lavatory drains to the rear of the property were thick with olive stones, grape pips, nuts and fruit, the detritus of bar snacks, either dropped down the toilet or deposited via the bowels of the customers. The scorched oak timbers of the superstructure still lay where they had fallen in a great explosion of flame and sparks that terrible day.[51]

The most remarkable building lay just thirty metres away on the northern side of the main road, seemingly a roadside shop selling food and pottery.[52] A combination of burning, waterlogging and lack of later disturbance allowed a vivid glimpse back to its last moments. The clay floors were strewn with rushes, and flies infested the interior. Wooden shelves held pots of spices – mustard seeds, dill, fennel, celery seeds, coriander and black cumin, and a collection of bone spoons, either for sale or for serving the spices. A burnt wooden necklace lay on the floor.[53]

This room was probably the shop front, and behind lay a storeroom, with a hearth whose last fuel of wheat chaff was still present in the embers. A large quantity of stock was present in the room, represented by more than twenty-four kilograms of smashed pottery of various types, mostly imported, including decorated red samian tableware, a glazed flagon with beakers, and mortaria. A full-sized reconstruction of this building was displayed in the sadly temporary exhibition *High Street Londinium* at the Museum of London in 2000–2001.[54] How I wish it was still there.

Set into a doorway beneath the prow of the modern building is an entrance to Bank Station, one of several that dive down between four and five metres by stair, and then meet up in a warren of tunnels where the ground gently falls and rises, compounding the sense of disorientation that a simple country boy and most foreign tourists feel when descending into the bewildering incomprehensibility of the London Underground.

In those entrance tunnels, before the escalators dive to the great depths of the actual railways, you are once more walking close to the depth of Roman Londinium, through the cramped alleyways of those first roadside properties. The site of the tavern where Roman Londoners drank their wine and picked at olives, and the burnt pottery shop beyond, with the wooden necklace trampled into the dirt, lay only a few metres beyond the tiled walls.

Directly across the road from No. 1 Poultry is another modern construction, the Bloomberg site, whose redevelopment also allowed archaeologists access to the Roman layers, between 2010 and 2014. Unlike Poultry, this area had not been built on by AD 60, but archaeologists uncovered layers of accumulated detritus from the banks of the Walbrook, all beautifully waterlogged and perfect for preserving even the most delicate organic objects.

The stars of the assemblage were the large collection of 405 wooden writing tablets. These small sheets of wood,[55] slightly larger than a postcard, were sealed with a skim of coloured beeswax. A pointed metal stylus was used to write on the wax, exposing the lighter coloured wood beneath.[56] Once read, the wax could be scraped flat, or melted and the tablet reused. The wax has not survived the centuries, but the scratches on the underlying wood have, allowing Roman writing specialist Roger Tomlin to decipher about eighty of the original texts.

The majority of the tablets date to the decades after Boudica, a few even to her immediate aftermath, but incredibly twelve were written *before* the attack, including the first financial document from the British Isles, giving us the exact day it was written:

In the consulship of Nero Claudius Caesar Augustus Germanicus for the second time and of Lucius Calpurnius Piso, on the 6th day before the Ides of January [therefore 8 January AD 57]. *I, Tibullus the freedman of Venustus, have written and say that I owe Gratus the freedman of Spurius 105 denarii from the price of the merchandise which has been sold and delivered. This money I am due to repay him or the person whom the matter will concern . . .*[57]

The assemblage also contains the earliest reference to the name of Londinium, clearly scratched as *Londinio*, dating to AD 65–80. Other fragmentary letters give us the names of some of those living in the town before the attack. *Metello dabis* – 'you will give this to Metellus';[58] *dabis Grato Iuni filio* – 'you will give (this) to Gratus the son of Junius';[59] and a letter mentioning that 'they are boasting through the whole market that you have lent them money . . .' is addressed to *Tito*, Titus, and could even be referring to that lost marketplace on Fenchurch Street,[60] where those boasts, perhaps, still echo silently along the aisles of Marks & Spencer's Foodhall.

A little further along Walbrook is the entrance of the London Mithraeum. This remarkable installation is free to enter and contains many of the Bloomberg site artefacts. Displayed are some of the key writing tablets, including that AD 57 transaction, and the piece of wood with *Londinio* clearly scratched onto the surface. Styli, or the needle-like pens used to write on the tablets, are also displayed, as well as a breathtaking array of other artefacts – the big chunk of preserved wooden door that once hung in a first-century Londinium house is stunning. You then descend to view the remains of the later Roman temple of Mithras, a strongly male cult of soldiers and merchants, seven metres below ground surface, at the very level of the recent excavations.

Now housed in this purpose-built space, only twelve metres from its original location to preserve the in-situ foundations, the

London Mithraeum experience incorporates light, smoke and sound to create what has to be the closest that most of us will ever get to a ghostly time-slip experience at an archaeological site without the aid of non-prescribed drugs. If you can go when it is quiet, which I have fortuitously managed to do, so much the better – it can only add to the astonishing atmosphere, and I cannot recommend it highly enough.

What completes the experience is that you are not in a museum gallery, but down at the level of the Roman city, and almost on the spot where the Mithraeum stood, with the memory of the relict Walbrook stream flowing just beyond the far end of the temple. Even this has been incorporated into the development, at ground level, with two stunning artistic installations in bronze by artist Cristina Iglesias, with running water trickling over her tangled bronze interpretation of the Walbrook, called *Forgotten Streams*.

I cross London Bridge on its eastern side, closest to the line of the Roman bridge, and on to Borough High Street. It is remarkable how quickly the character changes from Cornhill to Southwark – the people are the same ones that have crossed the bridge with you, or are about to in the opposite direction, and yet there is no mistaking that you are out of the City, and the juxtaposition may have been just as striking in Londinium.

Comparatively, Roman Southwark has been poorly represented by excavation until relatively recently, when a major project was conducted during building works for the Underground, namely the construction of the new ticket hall at London Bridge Station.[61] This lay directly beneath Borough High Street alongside Borough Market, and exposed about sixty metres of the ribbon development along the Roman street. All in all this row of eight timber and mudbrick buildings, probably with yards at the rear, and gravel alleyways leading off, was not too dissimilar to much of

Roman Londinium or that exposed at No. 1 Poultry, but it was a neater row fronting more directly onto the road, with a mixture of thatch, shingle and ceramic tiled roofs.

All except one building, a smithy that had burnt down before AD 60, appeared to be domestic rather than commercial in character; these were people's homes.[62] Several houses contained the remains of a hearth, that magnetic pole of domesticity, with clay or plank floors, and a meagre scatter of artefacts. A dump of material between two of the buildings contained one of my favourite artefacts from Roman London, a tiny pottery oil lamp, just ten centimetres long, of a beautifully modelled human foot wearing a sandal, with a hobnailed base.

Probably produced in the Netherlands in an army workshop,[63] there is nothing particularly gender specific about the piece – to me the sandal is feminine in the extreme, but would not necessarily have seemed so to Roman eyes. The oil was poured through the ankle, and the wick emerged from the big toe, which is blackened by use. Not unique as a style of lamp, it is nonetheless something so evocatively Roman that the sight of it is quite mesmerising. It is on display in the Museum of London.

What these excavations showed was that the buildings fronting this first Borough High Street had all shared the same fate – in AD 60 they had been comprehensively destroyed by fire. The whole site was covered by a 30-centimetre-thick destruction layer of burnt clay, daub, charcoal and timber.[64] As if there could ever have been any doubt, the Iceni and Trinovantes had crossed the river and flattened Southwark.

At ground level all of this took place several metres below you, with the Roman road running adjacent to the Borough Market side of the road, almost exactly beneath the pavement. The houses of the ribbon development lay directly below the current road, in the space now occupied by the ticket hall. There is an entrance to the station from both sides of the road, one by stairs, the other by escalator, but either way you end up descending about seven metres below pavement level.

The large rectangular space you descend into, bisected by swinging ticket gates, lies a little below the first-century ground surface. The row of timber and daub houses fronting the road lay in a neat row the length of the ticket hall – as you hurry along to the escalator for the Northern and Jubilee Lines you are passing directly through them, perhaps at head or shoulder height, or, if you walk hard up against the left-hand wall, along their frontages. The road, that first-century Borough High Street, lies just beyond that wall.

The quotation that opens this chapter comes from the opening passage of Joseph Conrad's *Heart of Darkness*, as a group of friends await the turning of the tide aboard ship on the moonlit Thames estuary and listen to the tale related by their companion, Marlowe. The story was, of course, explosively updated to the Vietnam War in Francis Ford Coppola's 1979 masterpiece *Apocalypse Now*, which was my first exposure to the story in the mid-1980s, and left me with a passing interest in the Vietnam War, an appreciation of the Doors and Wagner, and an enduring fear of ever getting off the boat.

From then on I was dimly aware of the existence of the original story, but it was at a wedding many years later, telling a colleague of my wife what I did for a living, that it was brought sharply back into focus. He asked if I had ever read *Heart of Darkness*, and described the opening scene, of Marlowe's assertion that 'this also has been one of the dark places of the earth', as he ponders the experience of a young Roman sailing up the Thames, prefacing the tale of his own nightmare journey up the Congo.

I was encouraged to read the copy collecting dust on my shelf, and it expressed exactly what I had been trying to articulate myself for years. This familiar land upon which we live our daily lives, where you walk along the street, run to catch the tube, sit in the pub, or mow the lawn, was once, 'nineteen hundred years ago

– the other day . . .' a frontier landscape, of doomed native tribes and civilising conquistadors, heavily armed expeditions along uncharted rivers, isolated forts, war parties and slave raids, whooping war cries and the roll of distant drums throbbing along the valleys.

It can be difficult to visualise. In a city, it can be all but impossible. When I walk through Norwich, I see the gentle slope now occupied by the market square, and try to imagine it as pasture and meadow punctuated by copses, the smoke rising from isolated farmsteads along the valley, the lowing of distant cattle grazing on the water meadows straddling the river . . . and I can't. But strangely enough, in London, I can. Standing on London Bridge as the sun hangs low over Southwark, I can hear Marlowe beside me describing the 'utter savagery' surrounding us.

Like the stunned and silent fugitives lining the decks of boats moored midstream, I stare down at the Thames, eastwards, that same, endless flow, and I really can begin to visualise the sprawling Roman frontier town lying smouldering in the twilight, and almost smell the thick pall of smoke billowing across the river from hundreds of glowing ruins, the glare of the last ones still bright as they burn, all reflected in the dark water as the sun sets on it for the final time:

> The old river in its broad reach rested unruffled at the decline of day, after ages of good service done to the race that peopled its banks, spread out in the tranquil dignity of a waterway leading to the uttermost ends of the earth. We looked at the venerable stream not in the vivid flush of a short day that comes and departs for ever, but in the august light of abiding memories.

9

Ghost Town

A Funeral Pyre for Verulam

*Unsated by this butchery, the tribes now pressed
on to Verulamium, the last Roman city in this area
of the province . . .*

Lewis Spence, *Boadicea*, 1937

On a beautifully sunny Saturday morning at the beginning of September, Clare and I drive to Elstree. I had tracked Paulinus's retreat this far by bike, and it was, we can only assume, the route that Boudica's army took from smouldering Londinium to its next objective, Verulamium. Of course, we can never be certain of this – a warband could have fragmented away from the main army on the approach to London to deal with the little town, but Tacitus implies Boudica moving in a deadly *royal progress* from one to the next, and I shall not depart from that here.

It is also plausible that rather than following the road west from Londinium to the site of Marble Arch before turning sharp right, she simply cut north-west across country, colliding with Watling Street somewhere below Elstree. It is, therefore, the perfect place for us to pick up the march of the rebels.

We drive north. A few miles along, at Frogmore, glancing to the left to see only houses and trees, there was once a farmstead a few hundred yards to the west clearly visible from Watling Street, with the slope of the gentle hills directly south-west of Verulamium beyond. The farm is there no longer, the site lying within an area of old quarrying, but it was excavated in the 1940s ahead of gravel extraction required for the war effort. It goes by the rather grand name of Park Street Roman Villa, but in AD 60 it was a timber building with occupation extending back into the Iron Age. That farmstead is little understood, because the later stone version was built directly on top, and the earlier levels could only be observed patchily beneath the rooms of the latter.

One particularly impressive find from a pit dated to the time of the conquest, or a little before, was a slave chain, a manacle for wrist or ankle.[1] The preserved floors of the earlier farm also suggested it was rectangular rather than circular in the traditional British style. Whatever shape it was, and whoever inhabited it, the farm was clearly visible to Boudica's warriors, and the diminutive River Ver between the two did not save it. The burnt daub from its destruction littered the site.[2]

Dr Rosalind Niblett, an archaeological veteran of the St Albans area, has quite rightly pointed out that Boudica's involvement in the destruction here, and at another villa nearby, at Gorhambury, cannot be attributed 'with any degree of confidence'.[3] There is here, as elsewhere, a distinct desire to see Boudica's footprints in any layer of mid-first-century ash, and she simply cannot be blamed for all of them. Here, however, I am convinced of her involvement. The farm was on the line of march, was burnt about this time, and on the outskirts of a town that was certainly about to be attacked.

I believe the inhabitants escaped, having long evacuated with their possessions, for the new stone building that replaced it was built directly on the ashes of the old, which smacks of the same people returning to their hereditary farm and rebuilding it in a more modern and permanent style. In the first phase of the new stone farmhouse, one room contained a hearth set into the floor.[4] I wonder how long it was before the last tale of Boudica's attack was told around it to wide-eyed children at bedtime.

The layout and character of early Verulamium is much less understood than contemporary Camulodunum or Londinium, for all that it is doubtless more completely preserved. St Albans was not built on top of the Roman town, so it has not suffered the same barrage of later destruction and intrusions that the other sites have, and, although there has been significant excavation, there are comparatively few stories to be teased out of those elusive early layers.

Rik Mortimer Wheeler excavated here with his wife, Tessa Verney, in the 1930s, and it was she who was instrumental in founding the dedicated site museum. My copy of their excavation report[5] was owned by one of their excavation team, the distinctively named Cregoe D.P. Nicholson, who later inscribed it as a gift to a fellow archaeologist. It was published in 1936, the year of Tessa's untimely death at the age of forty-three.

More digs were carried out, particularly in the 1950s and 1960s under Sheppard Frere, and occasional, smaller interventions have continued – the site is not completely empty of development – the museum, car park, roads, church and some older houses all lie within. The flint wall that still surrounds much of the site was built in the early third century, originally three and a half kilometres long, over four metres high and enclosing an area of more than eighty-one hectares,[6] now almost all given over to public parkland. On this beautiful late summer Saturday afternoon, the people of St Albans are enjoying it to the full.

Verulamium in AD 60 was very much embryonic, still being laid out along gravel roads, but springing up fast. A large, central rectangular area, defined by a ditch and bank, and perhaps utilised as an early forum, predated the town and was clearly a place of importance in pre-Roman times. This lay on the valley bottom, close to the river, whilst actual settlement had always favoured the higher ground of the valley sides. This pattern was changing in the AD 50s, with settlers being attracted down to the site of the enclosure to build the new town.[7]

The later forum and basilica were built directly over this central enclosure, preserving the importance of the earlier site, which now lies beneath the church and grounds of St Michael's and its vicarage, and a little of the car park, all adjacent to the museum. Sheppard Frere's assumption that this central area contained an early fort, based on convincing circumstantial speculation at the time, has now been overturned by more recent excavation.[8]

It is thought that the central enclosure, with its deep ditch, was added to with another ditch and bank, north almost as far as the river crossing, and west as far as the site of the later theatre that still stands today, and it was perhaps this ditch that defined the settlement in AD 60, an overall area of ten or twelve hectares.[9] It seems, therefore, that unlike the other towns we have looked at, Verulamium alone had a defensive rampart to shelter behind, albeit utterly inadequate to ward off what was coming.

Clare and I arrive at Verulamium Museum, at the heart of that early settlement. It is somewhere here, between the museum and the theatre ruins across the road, that we must imagine Paulinus delivering his terrible news that the fall of Londinium was in progress, even as he spoke, that the smoke of its destruction was to be clearly seen twenty miles to the south, and that the inhabitants of Verulamium must abandon their homes.

The same wretched scene as in London must have been enacted for the benefit of his shame-faced troopers, for we know that he did not defend the town. Those who could, mounted their horses and joined him, others frantically packed bundles of possessions and followed after; the rendezvous with the Fourteenth Legion may have been imminent, or even have occurred, meaning the slower refugees on foot might yet find safety with the column.

Once more there may have been a sorry few who remained, but it is difficult to believe that anyone who could flee did not do so. Within a short time Verulamium would be deserted, a ghost town, with possibly a few wretched souls, the elderly and infirm, left to their fate, and a few chancers who couldn't resist the opportunity to loot the empty homes and shops, but I suspect that not even these few remained.

The museum is a wonderful creation that originally grew out of the need to house artefacts from excavations in the 1930s, and has now been substantially extended. It is beautifully presented and well worth an hour of your time, but you won't find much of Boudica within. She does have a small information panel with a picture of marauding rebels and a few lines of text, but modern St Albans and Verulamium make very little of Boudica's part in its story.

We would later find her on one or two of the information boards that punctuate the huge park outside the museum, but nothing at all in St Albans itself. It is astonishing that such a famous figure and event are not more exploited, when you compare it, for instance, to Nottingham's enthusiastic promotion of its dubious part in the mostly fictional story of Robin Hood. It was not always so.

The huge St Albans Pageants of 1907 and 1953 made great play of this story. Original Edwardian postcards of Boadicea's costume and chariot-mounted attack from the 1907 event are often to be found on eBay, and she dominates the colourful front cover of the souvenir programme for the 1953 pageant, with a full script, written by the Pageant Master, Cyril Swinson, inside.

After outlining the woes of herself and people, Boadicea's victory speech takes place after the meagre Roman defenders of the town have been overwhelmed:

BOADICEA:
Take all their jewels and gold;
Take all the corn and food
They have extracted from us.
Then set the town on fire
And let its ruins stand,
As symbol of the tyrants that ruled over us.

Men enter with torches, and soon smoke begins to rise from the town.

BOADICEA:
We have won a victory today,
But our enemy was weak and unprepared;
Much greater battles lie ahead.
But let this victory serve
As a token of our strong resolve:
Let Romans gather in their strength,
We will outnumber them,
Destroy them and never cease to battle
Until they depart for ever from this land.
Come then, we will seek out the enemy.
Let smoke and flames consume this town
And rise to heaven as a funeral pyre for Verulam.
If you are resolved to follow me, then let's away.

The people shout in triumph, and with Boadicea at their head, they march away.[10]

There is an occasional fragment of this 'weak and unprepared' town she destroyed hidden in the museum cabinets, but unmarked as such. I experience a little thrill of recognition as I spot a small piece of painted wall plaster that is illustrated in Rosalind Niblett's book *Verulamium*, that once graced the interior of an AD 50s bathhouse.[11]

There is something extraordinarily evocative about Roman painted wall plaster. It is often lying in bits on the floor, having fallen off the wall, and can therefore partially survive when the wall itself has long gone. It is not certain that this bathhouse existed pre-Boudica, but it was an early building that suffered fire close to the right time – certainly the original excavator believed it to have been damaged in AD 60.[12] This fragment of that bathhouse is small, only a few inches across, but stirs something far deeper than curiosity.

Like the little foot-shaped oil lamp from London, the decapitated bronze Alde head, or Iceni wolf gold coins, this little fragment of painted plaster sparks a flickering of the senses, like the wires of a torch being brushed against a battery terminal, as if the grunts and music, steam, sweat and perfumed oils of the bathhouse in the weeks before Verulamium's destruction are only just beyond perception.

Roman or Romanophile British eyes once glanced at these designs, orange and red, portraying a lyre, amongst other things more difficult to see, perhaps a bow and quiver. Eyes that looked up and saw these same colours and shapes were later the eyes of a fugitive who looked back at the finger of smoke on the horizon as Boudica's army razed this place to the ground. I wonder if the same eyes returned one day and gazed upon it again. There are many more wall paintings in the museum, some reconstructed across entire walls, but it is this one, small, lonely fragment that does it for me. It is possibly a rare part of that incredibly elusive early town that Boudica snuffed out, before the centuries of development and expansion that came after.

We leave the museum and pass through the quiet churchyard of St Michael's, on across the busy road whose widening and extension had given Sheppard Frere the opportunity to excavate here, and through the gateway to Verulamium Theatre. The small private road disappearing along the valley is, at this point, the original Watling Street – it then dives beneath farmland and rejoins the drivable section a mile on.

It is a beautiful spot overlooking the fields straddling the River Ver, the theatre itself a squashed and quartered circle with an open central space where plays and speeches would have been attended, and, perhaps, given its size, the odd gladiatorial fight, according to the information boards. Sadly, it post-dates Boudica by many decades, but beside it is a silent witness of AD 60, the floor plan of a row of shops that were burnt in the attack displayed at their original level.

Cyril Swinson's 1953 Pageant lines come to mind beside this sole visible survivor of Boudica's attack:

> And let its ruins stand,
> As symbol of the tyrants that ruled over us.

These roadside buildings fronting onto Watling Street were excavated by Frere between 1958 and 1960. They were always thought to have the whiff of the military about them,[13] causing much speculation about whether the legions had a hand in founding the town, but this is given less credence now. They consisted of a row of adjoining shops and workshops, all sharing the same continuous roof, which suggests a single owner renting out workspace to tenants.[14] They were timber-framed with wattle-and-daub walls, resting on sleeper beams that Frere saw as a building style introduced by the army, although it seems that it was also used locally by the indigenous people.[15]

We view the outline of the buildings from the top of a grassy bank. There is no sign specifically forbidding access to the building itself, although there is one for the unexcavated portion beside it that might apply, but either way walking the floor plan is certainly not encouraged and there is no obvious path to get down to it. As such, it is sadly understated and not given much of a glance by most visitors, who congregate around the theatre, or the more impressive stone-built footings of a later roadside building around the corner. There is no dedicated information board solely for the Boudican buildings, and most people must pass by without a clue of what they are meant to see here.

The shops would have presented a smart frontage to Watling Street, with a balustraded verandah or colonnade about eleven feet wide, smoothly daubed or plastered walls, an upper floor with windows overlooking the road, and neatly shingled or thatched roof. The backs of the properties were perhaps more typically ramshackle, as backyard spaces often still are today. The rooms fronting the verandah were generally about fourteen feet wide and nineteen feet deep, with slightly smaller rooms beyond, and with a combination of gravel, clay and plank floors.[16]

All of the shops shared the same fate, utterly destroyed by fire, although Frere, with his finely honed archaeological instincts, deduced that the fires had been started on the Watling Street frontage. The breeze, however, had blown the flames away from the rear of the buildings, the extremities of which had not been burnt, revealing an ephemeral detail otherwise impossibly lost to us – the day the rebels attacked, the wind had been blowing from the south-west.[17]

Standing on the bank it is easy to imagine the ancient wind at your back, and the flame and smoke curling and billowing away from you, across the road towards the river – 'And rise to heaven as a funeral pyre for Verulam.'

These shops and workshops seem to have been concerned with metalworking, particularly in bronze. The block was rebuilt after the war, and Frere recorded the presence of a small piece of bronze statuary, less than three inches long, clearly intended for re-smelting, which he suggested was from a statue ruined during the rebellion.[18] Prior to this rebuilding, however, Frere noted the poor preservation of Boudica's destruction layers, indicating that the ashes and daub had been carefully raked through when the inhabitants returned, either in search of lost possessions, or the remains of the dead.[19]

The townsfolk were probably drawn from the local population, rather than an influx of citizen colonists, as at Colchester, or the lively cosmopolitan mix attracted to a port and trading centre like London. As such it retained a pre-Roman power structure, as the amenable local leaders were naturally absorbed into the new system, but now in the Roman style and with Roman approval, a case of actively embracing the New Order.

The town may well have been a tempting and conveniently close target for the Iceni and Trinovantes to mop up and plunder after London, but one has to wonder if a deeper tribal, atavistic resentment had been tapped into, such as we can recall in recent history in Rwanda, the former Yugoslavia, or the hatred of occupied peoples in Europe against Nazi collaborators at the end of the Second World War. So little of AD 60 Verulamium has been exposed, sometimes hastily dug, only partially revealed and troublesome to interpret, but Tacitus tells us that after London *like ruin fell on the town of Verulamium*, and the evidence of its burning is present at the appropriate levels. There is little reason to suppose that its destruction was any less comprehensive or devastating than elsewhere.

It is a beautiful, hot day, and we stroll along the little road that was then Watling Street, away from the theatre, into open fields, hedges and pasture, where the Roman road invisibly diverges from the path and continues beneath those fields. This was the road, supposedly, that Paulinus and his men had travelled as they abandoned the town, and, as Clare points out, remove a few hedges, telegraph wires and fences, and the view might not have been too dissimilar back then.

Where we look to the east, towards the river, another large building had been excavated by Frere, of unusual posthole timber construction, about seventeen by twelve metres. Associated finds, of painted wall plaster, window glass and roof tiles suggest an impressive timber hall, built around AD 56–58, and inevitably destroyed in the attack. Frere regretted that more work could not be carried out on the structure, but resources were greatly stretched ahead of the road construction, and the building could only be partially exposed.[20]

From where we stand on Watling Street, the flames of its destruction would have been clearly visible a couple of hundred metres across the field. It now lies beneath the main road, the A4147. If you leave the theatre site, turning left at the gate, you drive directly through the space it occupied just a few seconds down the road.

This section of Watling Street was also, perhaps, the road that Boudica, her warriors and camp followers continued along as Verulamium burned behind them. We do not know this, and it is the story we will explore next. The traditional version of events suggests that Verulamium was the last victim before the armies clashed, but some believe otherwise. Archaeological excavation has revealed burnt layers dating to this era west of London, at Silchester, and Winchester. Were these places victims of Boudica's rebels? Or as Dr (now Professor) Miles Russell asked in 2010: 'Were the good citizens of these two towns simply careless with candles?'[21]

It is a good question. The problem lies in the dating of the deposits – the burning in question, particularly comprehensive at Silchester, cannot be dated to AD 60 as such. It falls within a date range of some twenty years or so.[22] This is sometimes also true within the towns where such deposits are unquestioningly accepted as Boudican, but those correspond exactly with the account of Tacitus. Fires were not rare in Roman towns. Given that Camulodunum, Londinium and Verulamium would all suffer major fires again within a hundred years of Boudica, is it reasonable to see a fire within twenty-five years of AD 60 as likely to relate to her war, in a part of the country that we have no historical reason to place her army?

It is certainly worth keeping an open mind on these things, but I can't quite embrace it myself. Certainly, local insurgents spurred on by news of rebellion could have been responsible for the fires, or even a marauding war party from the main army out on a jolly, but I see no reason to abandon the historical texts on such evidence, and move Boudica's army west. It is difficult to test Tacitus scientifically against archaeological data, but where such tests exist, he passes with straight A's.

The fact remains that this town of Verulamium, this spot, this little section of Watling Street, represents our very last historical glimpse of Boudica at a known location, a little like grainy black-and-white CCTV footage of the missing queen mounted in her chariot surrounded by marauding drunk people, before she flickers out of view.

The last known sighting.

From here her story continues, but the certain physical landscape and locations on which to project that narrative elude us. It is the hunt for that ultimate lost location, the site of her final confrontation with Paulinus, which has obsessed so many people since. Given the various narratives of Tacitus, archaeology, topography, place names, and folk tales we have followed thus far, is it even possible that such a bloodletting could disappear from landscape and memory alike and leave not a trace for us to find today?

'The people shout in triumph, and with Boadicea at their head, they march away.'

10

Thunderclap

Andraste's Scream

Boadicea: *Look where they stand, in yonder narrow pass,*
Hard by their fenced town of Verulam;
All that are left of them on Britain's earth;
Which burns the invader's foot . . . How few they seem!
Madoc: *Ten thousand, at the most.*
  Mrs Aylmer Gowing (Emilia Aylmer Blake), *Boadicea*, 1899

Emilia Aylmer Gowing was in her early fifties when she
published her play *Boadicea*,[1] in 1899. I don't know a great
deal about her, a late Victorian poet and novelist who married the
actor William Gowing, both largely forgotten today. *Boadicea – A
Play in Four Acts* is a shamelessly dramatic but not unenjoyable
romp through the story which, if shown today, could be ruined by
underacting. It demands exuberance and overemphasis.

Mrs Aylmer Gowing clearly used Tacitus as her main source of
inspiration, because she mentions a battle in a 'narrow pass', and
Boadicea ends her life by poison, both hallmarks of his account.
Also, Dio was less readily accessible then, and remains so, whilst
A.J. Church and W.J. Brodribbs' famous translation of *The
Annals* was widely available, and into its thirteenth reprint when
she wrote her play. My copy is the 1895 edition contemporary
with her writing of *Boadicea*. The quote from her play above is of
particular interest because she, neither historian nor archaeologist, has taken the simplest and most literal interpretation of the

text, without plotting rates of march or military dispositions on a map.

She has read Church and Brodribb and simply taken them, and Tacitus, at their word:

> *Like ruin fell on the town of Verulamium, for the barbarians, who delighted in plunder and were indifferent to all else, passed by the fortresses with military garrisons, and attacked whatever offered most wealth to the spoiler, and was unsafe for defence . . . Seutonius Paulinus had the fourteenth legion with the veterans of the twentieth, and auxiliaries from the neighbourhood, to the number of about ten thousand armed men, when he prepared to break off delay and fight a battle. He chose a position approached by a narrow defile, closed in at the rear by a forest, having first ascertained that there was not a soldier of the enemy except in his front, where an open plain extended without any danger from ambuscades.*[2]

To Aylmer Gowing's eyes this placed the battle hard by Verulamium, the final location of Boudica's army and the last place mentioned before Paulinus drew his forces together. The fact that the topography of the Ver Valley contains no such dramatic landscape feature as Aylmer Gowing's 'yonder narrow pass' did not concern the playwright – she may not have known – but it has troubled others, which means that few since have placed the battlefield quite so close to Verulamium. They have, however, placed it almost everywhere else.

If I can plunder a little of Emilia Aylmer Gowing's emotive spirit, the location of this lost battlefield has haunted me for decades. I remember a long coach journey back to Nottingham from London one night in the winter of 1990, alone, bored stiff and miserably hungover, staring through the misted window at the black landscape in the moonlight. Travelling up the M1, somewhere south of Leicester, I realised that the (then) number one candidate for the battlefield, Mancetter, near Atherstone in Warwickshire, lay only a few miles away in the direction I was staring. I convinced myself that I could see the silhouette of the distant ridge of Hartshill that rose above the battlefield as a timeless memorial.

In retrospect I almost certainly couldn't see it, but I wasn't bored any more, I was spellbound. The place where all the threads of the story were meant to come together was just across the rainswept fields in the darkness. The modern world was but a thin veneer; this was the landscape where it happened! I will never forget that moment.

It was another year or two before I actually got to visit Mancetter. I couldn't drive in my early twenties but my friend Rachel, newly licensed, drove us there one sunny day in her little car. There was no proof that the battle had been fought there, of course, but the greatest authority on Boudica at the time, Graham Webster, had located it there in his writings, initially in conjunction with classical scholar Donald Dudley,[3] and their speculation had become pretty close to definitive – after abandoning London, Paulinus and his cavalry had sped back north to meet the legions marching south.

Boudica had followed, and they finally clashed at Mancetter, seventy-five miles to the north. What the site lacked in archaeological evidence, it made up for with dramatic contours, sweeping vistas, and Dudley and Webster's combined professional gravitas. It was good enough for me. What I wanted was certainty, and here it was. All roads led to Mancetter, and now I was standing on that ridge, gazing across the battlefield. Once more, it is a moment I will never forget. It seared Mancetter into my mind as neatly as a branding iron.

As the years passed, I remained a Mancetter man. At Cambridge I worked with Grahame Appleby, and we argued the toss in various excavation site huts. Grahame was highly critical of Mancetter, preferring the theory of an increasingly fragmenting rebel force wanting to drift home after Verulamium, rather than doggedly pursuing a Roman force playing hard-to-get all the way up into the Midlands.

He had a point, but how could he so recklessly disregard Mancetter? Draw whatever lines you like on a map, and speculate the morale of the Iceni if you will, but we all know that, ultimately, the protagonists made their way to Mancetter. Didn't they? The thought that they didn't had never seriously occurred to me. Webster's arguments were so established, so simple, just so *final*. We hadn't really been sold a dead duck, had we?

Boudica had been playing second fiddle in my life for some years. Other historical interests and archaeological projects, as well as real life, love, marriage and childbirth, had knocked her out of prime position. In 2009, Grahame published his paper 'The Boudican Revolt: Countdown to Defeat',[4] proposing Arbury Banks, at Ashwell in Hertfordshire, as the battlefield, and was good enough to send me a copy. I was impressed, but still rather perplexed at the need to suggest another battlefield. We already had Mancetter.

In 2011, Grahame emailed me to say that he had been approached by Radio 4 to be interviewed about Arbury Banks. They also apparently needed someone to speak up for Mancetter, and asked if he could put my name forward. I was very glad for him to do so. It was for a series called *Punt P.I.*, in which comedian Steve Punt investigates real mysteries in a suitably irreverent manner. I was thrilled – Steve Punt had been a comedy hero of mine since his *Mary Whitehouse Experience* days, and standing in for the late Graham Webster to speak up for his theories would be a great privilege.

I thought I should brush up on the subject, extracted Webster's *Boudica* from the shelf, along with Tacitus, Grahame's Arbury Banks paper, and others, by Nic Fuentes and Martin Marix Evans, which proposed other sites. I went to the library and picked up copies of all the more recent Boudica titles. In my absence, the action had become known to some as 'The Battle of Watling Street', a name I didn't like and have never subsequently used. To me it had always been, and remains, 'The Great Battle'.

What I discovered, or rediscovered, was that there were other options open to Paulinus and Boudica than a set-to in Warwickshire which, as the crow flies, lies seventy-five miles away from their last known sighting at Verulamium, across and beyond the Chilterns and on through the forests of the Midland Plain. However you looked at it, it was a very long way to move the rebel army in a direction that held nothing but a battle at its end. I was inclined to agree with Grahame – the Icknield Way lay a few miles north of Verulamium, leading directly home to tribal lands. Whatever role it had yet to play, its presence would have dominated the planning and second-guessing of both commanders.

This mysterious ancient corridor along the chalk from Wiltshire to Norfolk,[5] which may well derive its name from the Iceni, is of uncertain origin; it has the potential to be of vast antiquity, but was certainly in use by the Roman conquest and was historically recorded in Saxon times. A natural artery along rolling, open downland that would mainline Boudica's army straight back to their homelands, its draw to these eastern tribes must have been like a giant bungee pulling at them. It is difficult to believe that Boudica could have shifted them beyond it northwards, and equally difficult to believe that Paulinus would want them getting anywhere close to it.

His greatest fear must have been of the rebel army disintegrating before he had a chance to smash it comprehensively in a single confrontation, otherwise he could be faced with another protracted guerrilla campaign, *another* endless nightmare on a front where the enemy could never be brought to battle in a decisive endgame. Straddling that route home somewhere like Arbury Banks would be one option, but it placed him in a difficult position from which to retire if the day did not go well. I doubted he would risk Boudica's army getting onto the Way at all.

In the end, neither I nor anyone else was required to speak up for Mancetter on national radio, perhaps because it was too far away from the other sites visited to include in the day's recording, which in itself speaks volumes about its distant location. The world had turned, it seemed, and Mancetter had had its day, but I was very impressed that Punt was every bit as keen as me to use the *Ladybird Book of Roman Britain* as a serious academic source. And Grahame got to make an excellent case for Arbury Banks, despite the indecision of the psychic mediums that Steve Punt had brought with him.[6]

A narrow defile opening onto a plain popularly conjures an image of a gorge – Emilia Gowing's 'narrow pass' – and a vast, flat expanse beyond, like the Midland Plain, but the gentlest of dry valleys could suffice militarily if it restricted the approach and opened onto reasonably clear ground. This wider interpretation opens up the number of possible battle sites in England from a few dozen, to a few hundred, and then a few thousand. It all hinges on the rather fluid interpretation of a single Latin word, *faucibus*,[7] which might variously be taken to mean a throat, neck, strait or chasm – a narrowing landscape feature that would channel the Britons.

I needed to look at the main contenders on their individual merits. It was time to get back out into the field.

On a clear-skied, beautiful day in early October, I drive to Mancetter in Warwickshire, to lay the ghost of this phantom battle there, in my own mind at least. I approach the crest of its surmounting ridge through the suburbs of Nuneaton, Camp Hill and Hartshill Hayes Country Park, a woodland on the eastern flank of the proposed battlefield.

I emerge from the woods where the map shows a viewpoint symbol, and what a view it is that meets the gaze. I don't know how far I can see across the plain into Leicestershire, but it looks like a good twenty or thirty miles. I follow the footpath along the ridge and down into the village of Mancetter, just above the River Anker, where Webster had his battle line.

Looking back up at the wooded ridge, I can see the draw of this place, with Watling Street the other side of the river and this flanking ridge behind, but by no interpretation of mine is there a *defile* that would satisfy Tacitus. In addition the River Anker bisects the main fighting ground, a dire obstacle over which both sides would ultimately have to fight, and Tacitus makes no mention of that either. Dudley and Webster wrote that anyone exploring the wooded hills north and west of the village would find defiles that would have given Paulinus, 'the rearward protection he needed'.[8]

Of the four translations of Tacitus I have, including Donald Dudley's own, two state that the Roman position was *in* a defile, and two that it was *approached by* a defile; the Latin could be read as Paulinus being *in front of* the defile,[9] but to do so would surely rob it of any tactical significance beyond constricting the Roman retreat if forced back into it. To place Paulinus in such a precarious position, and so far from Verulamium, there would have to be compelling other evidence to locate him there, and there is none. There is simply no reason to force the battle upon a distant landscape that struggles to match Tacitus, and the theory never convincingly answers the essential question of why the armies would have met here. It is a defile too far.

As I walk back up the hill, through the beautiful, barely autumnal woods of the country park, I remember the evidence that did so much to clinch this as the battlefield for me, and Webster, and so many others[10] – Mancetter is a time-worn echo of the Roman name for the fort and settlement here, *Manduessedum*, which itself is derived from its Celtic name. It means 'The Place of the War Chariots'.

Just occasionally place names can emerge from the landscape to chill and haunt us unexpectedly, and with a name like the Place of the War Chariots, you would have to be inhuman not to want Mancetter to be a corrupted, latinised memory of that day. Hold on to that magic. It clearly is an ancient memory of war chariots fossilised in the landscape, perhaps even of a great Iron Age battle on the plain, but from a society where chariots were so ubiquitous for hundreds of years, need it really be Boudica's chariot we think of? In this story only a fool would deny anything too strongly, but

I fear that the Place of the War Chariots is the site of Webster's Last Stand, not Boudica's.

I drive south-east. Ten miles along Watling Street lies that great strategical crossroads with the Fosse Way at *Venonae*, High Cross, another claimant for the battlefield crown. Here, just before the crossroads, the road runs down into a great dip, Smockington Hollow, as the road sign declares, and this is the defile chosen by John Waite in his book *Boudica's Last Stand*,[11] protecting Paulinus's rear like a gigantic defensive ditch. Waite's theory is well-argued, but this is still sixty-five miles north of Verulamium, a long way to kick a weary rebel army loaded down with plunder, and I cannot reconcile Smockington Hollow with the landscape described by Tacitus. I drive on.

Ten miles more and I arrive at Clifton-on-Dunsmore beside Rugby, another candidate on an impressive slope, a wonderful vantage point straddling Watling Street, proposed by Kerry Sullivan and Christopher Kinsella.[12] Once more, it is a perfectly good spot to defend, but the only defiles are gorges protecting the western flank and rear. As a nice touch, certain to appeal to me, the authors were apparently inspired upon their first visit to the site by seeing a hare sprint across the field, and took it as a good Boudica-related omen, although I would be much more convinced if they, or I, had instead impaled a walking boot on the rusty orange spike of a javelin-head protruding from the soil. Once more, a site that struggles to match Tacitus, and still fifty-seven miles north of Verulamium.

I continue along Watling Street, this road that has become the subject of such obsessive scrutiny by battlefield hunters and given the battle its unofficial name. There are, believe it or not, several more contenders along this next stretch alone, at Church Stowe,[13] proposed by John Pegg, which has an impressive defile, at last, but only a single piece of possible spear shaft to offer as evidence that, in an archaeologically rich landscape, is hardly compelling in itself.

Cuttle Mill by Paulerspury, near Towcester, proposed by military historian Martin Marix Evans,[14] is a gentler topography put forward with convincing gusto by its author. It does, however, require the Britons to attack from the wrong direction, and if you are looking for that elusive spread of battle artefacts, you are going to be disappointed. Again.

A site at Dunstable,[15] one of several possibles, is equally convincing and just as devoid of other supporting evidence, although it does have the advantage of being at the junction with the Icknield Way. Eighteen miles north-east along the Way is Grahame Appleby's proposed battlefield at Arbury Banks by Ashwell in Hertfordshire, which I had visited the day before, and was impressed by the open slope falling away from the Iron Age hillfort on the crest. William Foot, also supporting a blocking action across the Icknield Way, suggests a more distant site at Heydon in Cambridgeshire.[16] Deryk Cundy, in *The Vengeful Queen*,[17] heads west from Verulamium, suggesting another very plausible battlefield at Chivery Top, near Tring.

If you are beginning to experience a swelling sense of déjà vu in all of this, you are not alone. All of these sites are very good places to fight a battle, and each has had a strategic scenario and campaign timetable constructed to have the armies conveniently colliding at that location. And they all *claim*, to a greater or much lesser extent, to match Tacitus. What they also share is a complete lack of verified, artefactual evidence beyond a background noise of finds that would, alone, suggest nothing out of the ordinary had ever happened there. Without such evidence we are simply pointing at promising locations in the landscape, and I believe that there are hundreds of them.

Researcher Steve Kaye has tried to quantify the exact number of possible sites by subjecting landscape data to a Tacitus-based algorithm,[18] weighted with such things as access to the water supply that each army would require.

It is a fascinating piece of work worthy of close scrutiny, but any such system has an inherent problem built into it – if the landscape described by Tacitus is given a wide interpretation, it still opens up the number of possible candidates into the hundreds, potentially thousands, and tightening up the parameters risks filtering out the actual battleground long before a shortlist is reached. His own preference based on this work is at Ogbourne St George, in Wiltshire, favouring a Roman retreat *west* from London, a scenario shared by Nic Fuentes in 1984, who proposed Virginia Water.[19]

Paulinus needed a glorious victory that would resound across the empire, restore his own personal glory and reputation, and regain the province. His army would be itching for revenge and plunder. That required the rebel army to be both intact and willing to fight, or at least unable to refuse battle. In any case, Paulinus could not simply keep running. Continued retreat would be seen as little better than cowardice, and the loyalty of the Catuvellauni would be sorely tested not only by losing their coveted municipium of Verulamium, but also by the abandonment of their entire territory. The client tribes south of the Thames too would be appalled at being left to their fate.

There was only so much face that Paulinus could afford to lose before the allied tribes sniffed a change in the wind, and backed the new favourite. For me, this rules out continued retreat in *any* direction. Paulinus had retired from London and sacrificed Verulamium, as neither town was defensible, but he was not running scared.

The view from Boudica's camp may have looked very different indeed. With many tens of thousands of thirsty humans and animals it must have sprawled across a huge area along or straddling the River Ver. It contained a large number of non-combatants – including children – and vast numbers of animals for the wagons and carts in addition to the cavalry and chariots.

If staying close to the river kept the army's thirst at bay, it must have been almost impossible to feed it. Even if late enough in the summer for crops and fodder to be standing in the fields, the foraging parties would have had to scour the country for tens of miles, but the Roman army, having left its own campaign supply network far behind in northern Wales and outpaced its lumbering commissariat wagons, may have taken much of that harvest first and burnt what was left. Boudica's army had doubtless found sustenance at Camulodunum, but Paulinus almost certainly destroyed Londinium's grain stores before retreating, and likewise at Verulamium.

The dark spirits of sickness would be stalking the camp lines, too, seeking out the children, the old, the wounded and weak; the more so the longer the army stayed in any one location, as the camp ground and water sources became fouled with human and animal waste.

The lure of Camulodunum, Londinium, Verulamium and the scent of Paulinus had kept the vast tribal confederation together, and it had proved itself the equal of the Ninth Legion under Cerialis. It was still willing and able to fight, but that resolve must have been fast dissolving as the ancient route home along the Icknield Way, the *Iceni Way*, came within the orbit of the hungry scouts and desperate foraging parties. They were farmers, and that was the blessed trackway back to their farms.

Gazing back two thousand years at these events, nothing we say can ever be certain, but I do not believe that Paulinus and Boudica met seventy-five miles north in Warwickshire, or sixty miles west in Wiltshire, and I believe it unlikely that Paulinus allowed Boudica access to the Icknield Way. With his army dominating and blocking the Ver Valley, he had no reason to let Boudica's army ever leave it. He could end it here, and he could end it now.

If we wish to define an area in which to concentrate our search for that battlefield, we need to put our compass on the scale of an Ordnance Survey map and set the diameter to ten miles, and then stick the point into Verulamium Park and draw our circle. We need to identify a location within that circle that matches Tacitus, and preferably find some archaeology to back it up. If that search area is ever exhausted, then we can add another ten miles to the compass; but I suspect we don't need to.

The day before, when I had visited Grahame Appleby's impressive suggestion of Arbury Banks on the Icknield Way, I had detoured on the way home and pulled in at Verulamium Park. I walked uphill and out on to the fields to the south-west where some interesting Roman artefacts once turned up – the sort of nerdy hiatus to a journey that the families of archaeologists come to dread.

I drank in views and followed footpaths, traced contours with my finger on the map, thumbed an old archaeological report and a battered copy of Tacitus. There can probably never be a definitive confirmation of what we are looking for, but just as historians hang century-old battle footage onto the landscape of the Somme, I had to superimpose the narrative and archaeology onto this landscape to see if the horizons matched.

In 1987, a paper was published in the academic journal *Britannia* by Stephen Greep, entitled 'Lead Sling-Shot from Windridge Farm, St Albans, and the use of the Sling by the Roman Army in Britain'.[20] It detailed the discovery of over sixty oval lead slingshots, or bullets, found in a localised area by metal detectorists, and the knowledge that at least another fifty had been found in the past. They were mostly biconical in form, looking like small lemons or rugby balls, mostly around thirty-five millimetres long and weighing an average of forty or fifty grams. As sling ammunition, they were typical of first-century Roman army issue. Rather than randomly scattered, it seemed that the bullets had been found in small groups, but only a rough location could be ascribed to them.

With well over a hundred known slingshots (and more have been recovered since),[21] the original assemblage lying in the soil in the first century may have numbered thousands. It is not known what potential area of landscape the scatter occupied, for much nearby land has been built on, and the metal detecting was presumably a relatively random search. In addition, the known artefacts are those that have been reported – any number could have been found and not reported, and many more could have worked their way deep into the subsoil.

The sling is a remarkable weapon, weighing almost nothing, easily tied around the waist or stuffed inside a tunic, and nature often provided the ammunition in the form of pebbles. The Roman auxilia carried purpose-made lead shot, but would certainly use what lay on the ground too. Each shot merely required a bullet to be placed in the sling cup, and a single flick of the arm to loose it, enabling a huge rate of fire, ammunition permitting. Recent experiments have shown that the oval fifty gram lead bullets, typical of Windridge Farm, had a range of over two hundred metres, and only slightly less kinetic energy than a bullet shot from a .44 Magnum revolver.[22]

There are other explanations for the presence of slingshots, namely hunting, the casual losses or production detritus of a Roman camp, target practice, and buried hoards of recycled lead. The sheer quantity must rule out the first two, but the third is certainly an option – the location of a military practice range. This likelihood is overturned the moment you set foot on the fields of Windridge. Beneath your feet are million upon million of smooth, elongated pebbles, perfect slingshots. They are part of the natural geology, and you could fill a bucket in minutes.

If the army was practising slinging here, they would not be using their coveted lead shot but utilising what lay on the ground. Once fired, slingshots were effectively lost and unrecoverable. Experiments published in 2016 showed that lead bullets, even painted orange, are almost impossible to find once slung, normally burying themselves into the soil.[23] It is difficult to imagine the Roman army being quite that wasteful when plentiful, good quality ammunition lay at their feet.

The fourth option, that of hoarding, was suggested in the original report due to the groups of shot being found clumped together and the presence of a few small lead weights associated with them, clearly not slingshots, and therefore perhaps collections of lead for reuse. Whilst the most plausible interpretation at the time, the lead weights were mostly of a size and shape that would make them ideal sling ammunition. As some slingers may have been a specialist cadre in this era, it is easy to imagine them single-mindedly acquiring any pieces of lead they came across, either as ready-made ammunition, or to be melted down to make bullets; two of the weights were almost identical to the purpose-made ammunition, except for small suspension loops.

The clustering of the bullets, that initially supported the theory of hoards of lead being scattered by modern ploughing, becomes more intriguing when compared to evidence produced by the experiments published in 2016. This proved that a slinger required to fire quickly under stress will drop between 5 and 10 per cent of his bullets. Under battle conditions, most of those would remain unrecovered, a phenomenon of dropped ammunition observed on battlefields across the world.[24] The groupings found at Windridge, therefore, most likely represent the location of individual slingers or units in action.

Although this potential as a battle location was not noted in 1987, local archaeologist Rosalind Niblett suggested in 2001 that the bullets were more likely to represent a skirmish or battle taking place some time between the invasion of AD 43 and Boudica's war, and reiterated the point in 2006.[25]

The topography of the area around Windridge Farm is completely obscured on the Ordnance Survey map, the miniscule, pale orange contour lines entirely smothered by the built-up areas lying east and south. From up on the wide open ground of the plateau, with more than enough room to deploy an army of any size and backed by an ancient site that would have been as heavily wooded in antiquity as it is now, it was clear that the beginning of a narrow, shallow dry valley – a defile – ran south-east, still visible in the ploughed fields of the western side, and the eastern half swallowed by housing.

Follow the valley downhill, difficult today with any clear view of it, and it becomes deeper and wider. The valley bottom is eventually occupied by the A414 dual-carriageway, which runs along it to the large Park Street roundabout, the junction of that defile with – you guessed it – Watling Street, exiting directly into the face of Boudica's oncoming army.

A giant funnel couldn't have been better placed to catch them.

Verulamium is not an obvious place to look for the battlefield – Boudica destroyed it, and Paulinus had clearly left by the time she did. Even so, it is the last place that Tacitus names, and he hints that no great length of time or distance separated the sacking of the town and the meeting of the armies. This is the reason that the uncritical Emilia Aylmer Gowing placed the battle 'in yonder narrow pass, hard by their fenced town of Verulam'.

Tacitus was writing for a general, uncritical audience. He carried them with his story from Colchester, to London, to St Albans, and no further. He then declares that Paulinus *prepared to break off delay and fight a battle*, but does not say why.

After describing this sudden resolution to fight, Tacitus had one sentence in which to describe the topography of the battle, one short line in which to paint the canvas upon which that audience would project the mental image of his words. He had no need for the subtleties and complexities of landscape. The Britons, advancing from relatively clear ground, approached the Romans through some sort of narrowing valley with a forest behind. He doesn't say so, but if that defile led gently uphill to higher ground, which such defiles so often do, so much the better.

He doesn't tell us if the Romans had a line of retreat; it would be wise if they did. He doesn't mention all those fugitives that had accompanied and followed Paulinus from both Londinium and Verulamium, but they were presumably safe somewhere close by. He does tell us that, wherever this was, there was one hell of a fight once the Britons got through that defile, and as an archaeologist and ex-teenage metal detectorist with a fascination for artefacts, I have never believed for one moment that such a site would fail to produce battle detritus of some sort.

With the Roman army sitting on that high ground above Verulamium, Paulinus's rear and left were protected by forest and the extensive Iron Age earthworks of Prae Wood, a ready-made hilltop bastion anchoring his line; his right, potentially also heavily wooded, led to steeper and more broken ground beyond.

Paulinus had placed his army where Boudica could not pass it, could not refuse to fight it, and with only one corridor through which she could approach it. All Paulinus had to do was sit and wait:

> *His legions were in close array; round them, the light-armed troops, and the cavalry in dense array on the wings. On the other side, the army of the Britons, with its masses of infantry and cavalry, was confidently exulting, a vaster host than ever had assembled, and so fierce in spirit that they actually brought with them, to witness the victory, their wives riding in waggons, which they had placed on the extreme border of the plain.*[26]

Boudica's army would have camped on the raised ledge of ground bordering the Ver, around Park Street, the baggage wagons naturally following the contours of the higher ground parallel to the Ver, and the animals left to water themselves along the river. The camp may have spread across the lower lying ground and up onto the St Julian's spur.

This is all still fields, quiet and pleasant to walk, albeit bordered by housing and cut by roads and rail line. The army would have assembled in battle array to either side of Watling Street, centred exactly where the huge and thundering Park Street roundabout now stands. In launching their attack, the Britons would have flowed precisely from there into the opening of the valley, now directly along the first thousand metres of the A414 dual carriage-way and swamping the slopes to either side.

The Fourteenth Legion and part of the Twentieth, a mile up

that valley, were in a solid formation blocking the exit onto the wide open space of the heights, perhaps just below the pretty wooded road of Bedmond Lane. The auxilia, some with slings and bows, were deployed on the flanks, ready to pelt the oncoming tide with the leaden hail that still litters the hilltop to this day, exactly where Tacitus describes, to the side of the central legionary position.

At this point in the narrative, Tacitus allows himself a little free rein to fire up his audience with speeches – Boudica's a cry for liberty and freedom, Paulinus's a soldierly growl to forget looting, remember their drill, throw their javelins and win.

Finally, *Suetonius gave the signal for battle*:

> *At first, the legion kept its position, clinging to the narrow defile as a defence; when they had exhausted their missiles, which they discharged with unerring aim on the closely approaching foe, they rushed out in a wedge-like column. Similar was the onset of the auxiliaries, while the cavalry with extended lances broke through all who offered a strong resistance.*[27]

The Britons flooded on up the valley. After that first thousand metres of dual carriageway, the road drifts west up the defile side in a cutting, whereas the attack flowed on, always gently uphill, engulfing the ploughed fields beyond, and the modern estate streets of Netherway and Icknield Close. It would be around there, too, running close to the line of Bedmond Lane, that the solid line of legionaries awaited them, rank after rank, covering a front of around five or six hundred metres. Indeed, there is evidence that a Roman road ran directly across the top of the defile at this very point,[28] providing solid hard-standing and firm footing irrespective of ground conditions on the day, and a swathe of ground to either side already cleared of bush and undergrowth. A ready-made battle line.

The auxiliaries assembled to either side of the legionaries, presumably also along the road, the slingers adjacent to the buildings of Windridge Farm, where the slingshots were concentrated, and perhaps others a similar distance north-eastwards, where a corresponding scatter of lead shot may have been long lost to housing development. This would have covered the higher ground, and faced any Britons that brimmed the sides of the valley, but crowds flow like liquid, and the main thrust would have been along the lower ground. Even this minimal slope would have been tiring for battle-accoutred warriors on foot, the reason why most would have followed the defile, the gentlest potential incline, funnelled towards the legions as Paulinus had intended.

If the sides were clear ground, it was the mounted Britons and charioteers who would have attacked up and across them, where their opposite numbers in the Roman auxiliary cavalry, as well as archers and slingers, awaited them on the wings. At the head of the shallow valley, now between Park Wood and Tiberius Square, was where the attacking warriors would have picked up speed for the final charge as they neared the unbroken ranks ahead. By now the air would be hissing as slingshots, arrows, and the vicious steel-tipped bolts from *scorpio* catapults sought their victims in the packed mass. The front rank of legionaries with javelins held aloft stood silently awaiting their final order.

The devastation of that first volley of javelins would have been little different to the effect of machine guns opening up on them, the sky momentarily darkening with their flight. The moment of impact would have been clearly audible as an inhuman, inward-choking scream rising above the tumult as thousands of horses, men and women were simultaneously transfixed by the slim iron necks that punched clean through armour, shields, flesh and bone alike. The exhausted survivors flooded on, stumbling through a forest of javelin shafts and the tangled wreckage of smashed chariots, discarded shields and impaled horses and warriors, many felled but still alive, and then on into a second volley, and then a third.

Just as the defile promised to open up and release the deadly crush, where the beautiful country lane now runs directly across the slope, the path was blocked by the packed ranks of legionaries, immoveable and almost invulnerable behind their solid wall of shields. As the warriors were crushed against the shields, unable to swing their long swords, the short butcher's cleavers licked out at stomach height. Shoulder-barging with their shields and stabbing with their swords, the legionaries began their slow advance, trampling the dead and dying underfoot, and turning the tide back down the defile.

The few hundred metres below Bedmond Lane is where the main slogging match of hacking, stabbing and slaughter would have been done. It is a peaceful field now, ploughed on one side, and quiet estate roads on the other, but the violence that might once have been enacted here, and on such a scale, is almost beyond comprehension. A footpath crosses the field where the fighting would have culminated, as the Romans barged downhill and the Britons pushed up, just below Park Wood.

Walking the path, I see a tiny fleck of green, no bigger than a matchhead. It is a tiny shapeless nugget of copper alloy, green with corrosion, a few millimetres in diameter. It looks like a flattened air rifle pellet that has hit a wall. There is no way of dating it, and any archaeologist and metal detectorist would consider such a thing, in isolation and in the topsoil, of no diagnostic value and simply discard it. But here, it catches my attention. It could be of any date from prehistory to Victorian, but looking closely it is clearly a little flattened bronze rivet.

My instinct tells me to drop it, as I would if it was anywhere else, but not here. Almost everything a Roman soldier wore and carried was held together with little bronze rivets, from his belt and scabbard, to his armour and helmet, many, many dozens of them on every man. It is thin, presumably from leatherwork or a belt, if ancient, but having just visualised what might have occurred here, it is a curious scrap to have stumbled upon. It would have been somewhere here that the turning of the tide became a rout, and the fight carried quickly back down the valley, towards the British camp, families and baggage:

> *The rest turned their back in flight, and flight proved difficult,*
> *because the surrounding waggons had blocked retreat. Our*
> *soldiers spared not to slay even the women, while the very beasts*
> *of burden, transfixed by the missiles, swelled the piles of bodies.*
> *Great glory, equal to that of our old victories, was won on that*
> *day. Some indeed say that there fell little less than eighty thou-*
> *sand of the Britons, with a loss to our soldiers of about four*
> *hundred, and only as many wounded.*[29]

Eventually the Britons broke, the legionaries pushed on, slaughtering as they went, and the cavalry were unleashed to smash through the crowd, spitting and carving with lance and sword. The great slaughter as the fleeing warriors were crushed against their own baggage train and camp stuffed with their families must have been between the Park Street roundabout and the river.

After my long drive down Watling Street from Mancetter, visiting all of those other sites *en route*, I finally pull in by the fields of Windridge Farm, on Bedmond Lane, where I believe the Roman front line blocked the top of the defile, as a sanguineous sunset falls behind the black line of trees at the western end of Prae Wood. It is only twenty-four hours since that first exploratory visit, but I am now convinced that this is where my search for that battlefield should end, and whether I'm right or wrong, it reinforces the maxim of this book, that there is nothing like getting out of the library and walking a good landscape or two.

A few handfuls of Roman sling bullets alone cannot prove that this was the spot where the leaden sky of AD 60 came crashing down for the Iceni and Trinovantes, but Verulamium certainly punches above its weight with finds of early military origin, a conundrum, or even a 'problem' for a site that seems to have no founding fort.[30] As Rosalind Niblett points out, the Verulamium Museum contains an impressive collection of Roman military equipment, such as pieces of shield binding and decorative cavalry pendants.

Many come from metalworking contexts, signifying the reuse of scrap metal; a nearby battlefield would certainly provide plenty of that. Some small military items including buckles were recovered from the heights of Windridge itself, as well as early Roman coins, and a linchpin.[31] Verulamium has also produced a marvellous bronze Roman army helmet from an unknown (probably water-logged) context, with the owner's name, *Papirus*, scratched inside, and pieces of armour – part of a *segmentata* cuirass was found buried in a funerary context at Verulam Hills Field.[32]

It is a slowly mounting body of evidence that there was a military build-up or event of some kind near this seemingly non-military town. A mass grave would help, but so much of the field has already been developed, and none have come to light so far. There might never have been one. So many bodies would surely have been left to rot.

It is almost dark, only the vestigial glow behind the woods. The defile is still clearly visible, delineated by the lights of the houses nestled into its eastern side and the black line of trees down the centre. It is as good a spot as any to end this day of battlefield hunting, indeed, to end this journey in search of Boudica. Whether it was Boudica's warriors that died here in AD 60, or those of Caratacus in a forgotten rearguard stand as they retired west to the distant mountains in AD 43, the work of slaughter was once done in these fields, on this windy ridge, and the hiss of leaden shot was audible as the expert slingers plied their deadly trade.

There was, perhaps, a marching camp up here or in the mile or two north, where the men of Paulinus's army waited in the days before the battle, and returned to, blood-caked, in its wake. By occupying the heights and giving the Britons a free run of the valley bottom, Paulinus had sealed the fate of deserted Verulamium, which probably still burnt in the darkness. The south-westerly breeze, that Sheppard Frere had identified in the pattern of burning across his excavation, blew the pall of smoke away from them, far along the eastern valley side. But the inhabitants were safe, crammed with the hundreds of other refugees in their familiar old earthworks of Prae Wood.

As the failing light casts the hillside into a darkness twinkling with house, car and road lights, it is an atmospheric spot to stand and contemplate the aftermath of the fight. If the battle, this apocalypse, really happened here, this hillside, these woods, and the countryside for miles around must have been alive with fugitives, hiding, running, white-faced and disbelieving.

Tacitus tells us little enough about this fight and its aftermath, but he describes for us the postscript of another battle, Mons Graupius, a little over twenty years later in northern Britain, where Agricola, now the general, was equally victorious. It is unsettling to stand alone in this place and think of his words in the near darkness:

> *Then, indeed, the open plain presented an awful and hideous spectacle. Our men pursued, wounded, made prisoners of the fugitives only to slaughter them when others fell in their way . . . everywhere there lay scattered arms, corpses, and mangled limbs, and the earth reeked with blood . . . When, however, the enemy saw that we again pursued them in firm and compact array, they fled no longer in masses as before, each looking for his comrade; but dispersing and avoiding one another, they sought the shelter of distant and pathless wilds. Night and weariness of bloodshed put an end to the pursuit . . .*
>
> *Elated by their victory and their booty, the conquerors passed a night of merriment . . . The following day showed more fully the extent of the calamity, for the silence of desolation reigned everywhere: the hills were forsaken, houses were smoking in the distance, and no one was seen by the scouts.*[33]

This epilogue of battle is as old as war itself. The pursuit of a defeated enemy in such warfare was ever pitiless, but for all the wrenching sorrow and agony related in Tacitus's description of the wailing fugitives in the wake of Mons Graupius, the most biting line of all conveys the mournful emptiness of the landscape the following day, that *silence of desolation*, and the telling detail that *no one was seen by the scouts*.

That day at nightfall, 1958 years ago, this small valley, or one very like it not too far away, was heaped with the dead and dying, thousand upon thousand upon thousand of them. Dio states that 230,000 Britons were involved in this fight, surely a gross exaggeration in keeping with the rest of his account, that makes Tacitus's figure of 80,000 dead seem positively conservative. Eighty thousand is an extraordinary number of people, so many that none of us can visualise what it would look like, except in a stadium – the O2 Arena, for instance, seats around 20,000 at full capacity; Wembley can accommodate 90,000, but even that is somewhat beyond our comprehension to imagine on a battlefield.

If we are hugely cautious, and halve the number that Tacitus gives us, the deaths of 40,000 people would be twice the death rate for the other known bloodiest day in British history, 1 July 1916, in the mechanised, industrial slaughterhouse of the first day of the Somme, in which 19,240 British soldiers were killed and twice as many again wounded. The loss of that day still scars the national consciousness of Britain over a hundred years later; it is difficult to imagine the impact of twice or even four times that number on two or three Iron Age tribes.

For Paulinus's victorious army, as for Agricola's at Mons Graupius, it was *a night of merriment, elated by their victory and their booty*. The British army in the main killing ground had been slaughtered to a soul, *our soldiers sparing not to slay even the women*, but pity the fugitives rounded up and brought into the camp up here that night to be interrogated and beaten, tortured and enslaved, the women fought over by the soldiers, and executions for the wounded, maimed or defiant. *Elated by their booty* is the language of the victor, not of those unfortunate enough to become that booty themselves.

Roma Victrix! And to the victor the spoils, indeed.

The great triumphal columns in Rome celebrating victorious wars, Trajan's Column honouring the campaigns in Dacia (Romania, AD 101–2 and 105–6), and the Column of Marcus Aurelius marking the campaigns in Germania (AD 172–5 and, incidentally, the war recreated in the opening scene of *Gladiator*), vividly illustrate the Roman army on campaign and, disturbingly, its behaviour in victory.

The Romans were many things, but magnanimous and merciful in victory they were often not, and nor were they ashamed to advertise it. Julius Caesar was completely unabashed at sharing with his readers, in a work with the sole purpose of increasing his standing amongst the Romans, his annihilation of entire populations, the selling of hundreds of thousands of non-combatants into slavery, and even the lopping off of right hands *en masse*.

The Romans could be singularly bad winners, and the post-battle sections of the two famous columns are worth examining in a little more detail to get a flavour of the scenes going on in the vicinity of the Roman camp after the Great Battle. For all of their cinematographic qualities – both friezes spiral around the columns like cine film wrapped around a broom handle – it would be wrong to suggest that either column portrays accurate reportage of its respective campaign, or is contemporary with Boudica's war. They do, however, represent a universal truth surrounding the conduct of war on Rome's far-flung frontiers, and the fate of the barbarians they went up against.

Trajan's column, the more conservative and measured of the two, portrays the Roman army burning settlements, appropriating crops, butchering enemy livestock and looting in victory, and there is slaughter aplenty. Captives are bound and cowed. The violence, however, is rarely explicit, and is male-centric, females being rarely to the fore. Women and children do appear, mostly as fugitives, ambiguous figures, unarmed non-combatants either leaving their lands or returning to them, helpless and vulnerable either way. The dead, dying and captured, and the heads on spikes or proffered as trophies, are mostly clearly male, although not always adult. As a finale, the fugitive Dacian King, Decebalus, just manages to commit suicide before capture. His head, however, is decapitated, and presented to the Roman troops.[34]

By contrast, the Aurelian column is a monument to the horrors of war, conveying a 'pornography of violence',[35] and though it dates to the late second century, well over a hundred years after Boudica, the atrocities it conveys are really no different to those described or insinuated by Caesar over a hundred years before her. The abuse and horror depicted is shocking and upsetting to us, but was unlikely so to a Roman audience who were, after all, used to seeing barbarians herded into the city during triumphs as part of the booty, as well as watching them torn apart in the arena or crammed into cages at the slave market.

The body count is huge, indeed, more than one scene contains actual heaps of barbarian corpses; one view of victorious Romans shows barbarians being forced to behead their own comrades whilst the Roman troops look on. Another massacre scene portrays a group of captives being speared to death, including one whose mouth is open in silent horror, known chillingly as 'the screaming barbarian'.[36]

Other men, as well as women and children, are being led towards the place of slaughter, whether as witnesses or condemned is unclear, but we should not doubt that they are potential victims of the same treatment. A later scene certainly shows two women being killed by soldiers, whilst a third is dragged by the hair, and a fourth led forcibly by the arm.[37] In the ransacking of a farm, another woman fleeing from a hut looks as if she is about to be run through with a cavalryman's lance.[38]

A different burning village is the setting for what is generally accepted as showing the aftermath of rape. Although an actual rape would never be depicted on such a monument – even the Aphrodisias relief of Claudius mounting Britannia falls just short of that – the act is implicit at every turn. A German woman shown leaving the village has had her clothing upset, using one hand to hold the garment over her breasts and the other to hurry her child on its way.[39]

273

Other examples, also in ransacked villages, show another partially disrobed woman being dragged by the hair, her child still in hand, as the men of the settlement are executed and the emperor looks on; another young woman is shown resisting being dragged away by a lone soldier. These images would be no more ambiguous to the Roman viewer than they are to us, and it seems naive not to assume the worst of the situation.[40]

Like the Dacian king Decebalus, Boudica was not to long escape the field, and likely also died by her own hand. Tacitus claims she took poison; Dio that she died of illness. The illness, perhaps meant to be caused by wounds, certainly suggests an escape from the battlefield, but poison could have been administered at any point, and may only be a euphemism for the general act of suicide.

In the tumult of the final moments, as the slaughter reached the camp and wagon park, she might simply have cut her own throat, and those of her daughters, rather than risk capture in the pursuit. It is doubtful that Tacitus or Dio actually knew. In the days after the battle, when the bodies must have lain several deep over a huge area, strewn with the wreckage of the baggage train, carts and slaughtered oxen, were the Romans really likely to have found her corpse, or even recognised it?

We can only assume that Boudica and her daughters were never found, for Tacitus would surely have mentioned it, although Dio's assertion that the Britons gave her a *costly burial* is unlikely, as with so much of his account, for such burials were completely alien to Icenian lands. The intriguing possibility exists that she married into the Iceni from, perhaps, the Trinovantes or Catuvellauni, who certainly were known for such burials, but that is taking speculation too far. The chance of such a funeral taking place in this newly remilitarised zone, put into a state of martial law after the battle by an avenging army, seems forlorn indeed.

If the battle did take place here, it would be more likely that the few remaining splinters of her bone, or perhaps the more resilient enamel shells of her teeth[41] lie scattered in the fields between the Park Street roundabout and the winding River Ver.

The Black Year

To Spare the Conquered?

> They made a graveyard of the acres between what are now
> Bishopsgate and Thames Street. And when at last the sun of
> Boadicea had set and the victorious Romans returned to their
> Londinium, it must have been to find it a hecatomb of ashes
> bristling with charred bones. From that dreadful July day to
> the following spring, when the Roman administration had
> recovered sufficiently to commence the task of restoration,
> London must have lain silent as a charnel-house for the better
> part of a year.
>
> <div align="right">Lewis Spence, <i>Boadicea</i>, 1937</div>

The following day showed more fully the extent of the calamity, for the silence of desolation reigned everywhere . . .

At the first hint of dawn across the valleys to the east, the auxiliary cavalry would have been mounted and ready to scour the surrounding countryside for fugitives and any warbands that had gone to ground in the forests the previous day. Dog-tired and numb after the exertions and horrors of the fight, their little sleep had been plagued by the steady swell of groaning and crying rising out of the defile below them from the thousands of severely wounded and dying entangled with the dead. It was quietening now, and would continue to do so as the wretched survivors succumbed to their wounds, but some would cling on for days to come. The horsemen were undoubtedly relieved to be out on patrol, to leave the carnage and stench of the battlefield behind them.

We must assume that many tens of thousands of human and animal carcasses were strewn across the field of battle, some four hundred or so of them Roman. It is possible that Tacitus only refers to citizen legionary losses, the non-citizen auxilia being hardly worth the wordage to quantify, but I have never had the slightest problem with the apparent disparity of dead between the victors and the losers. It is simply what happens when one side plays to its strengths, and the other to its weaknesses.

These Roman dead would have been the priority in the immediate aftermath, to collect for decent burial or cremation. This would have taken place on the field, or close by, and the discovery of a cemetery or suitably inscribed funerary monument for these Roman soldiers represents the best chance we have of ever definitively locating the battlefield. As to the Britons, exactly what was a Roman general meant to do with forty thousand or more bodies? I strongly suspect he left them where they were, a spectacular and, briefly, stinking reminder of what happened to those who fucked with Rome.

A brief few weeks before, he had stood as the victor on some miserable holy island, having orchestrated a vast amphibious assault to crush resistance finally in the west and deal Druidism its killing blow, and the Fates had pissed on his boots. They weren't pissing now. Britannia had thrown the biggest rebellion it could muster at him, and half of the conquered province had stayed loyal to Rome. The other half lay in bits all around him.

There were too many to bury or to burn, so the abattoir became a bone field, a landscape ossuary. It must have been both a place of supernatural dread, and a physical and spiritual contaminant that the locals wanted rid of. As nature purified the liquefying corruption and evil air of the place, the farmers may slowly have cleared the bones to the edges of their old fields, burnt heaps of them, tipped cartloads into the river, or ploughed over them as the elements bleached and broke them, and the hooves of live-stock shattered and crushed them into the mud. If such was the process of disposal, there would be precious little of that mighty army to find today.

It is at least theoretically possible that such a localised drenching of the landscape with phosphates and minerals derived from human corpses might be chemically detectable in the subsoil. Physically, like so many graves archaeologists excavate in harsh conditions where the bones have long dissolved, the enamel tooth caps might survive, but even those, after two millennia in the dynamic, slow-spin-cycle grinding solution of the topsoil, could have been whittled down to microscopic fragments.[1]

Boudica's great army has probably returned to the earth as completely as it is possible for human remains to do.

Paulinus now had to concentrate his forces and obliterate any remaining resistance or dissent, but there was also the infrastructure of the shattered province to kick back into action. In the weeks and months following the battle, Londoners and merchants arrived back at the riverside boomtown to sift through the ashes and start again, many back within days, I believe, by riding out the destruction aboard ships on the Thames.

The archaeological evidence of this immediate return is not obvious, indeed, in most towns it has long been speculated that years passed before full redevelopment. Lewis Spence, opening this chapter, saw a year of desolation in London; Frere thought that fifteen years elapsed before his workshops were rebuilt at Verulamium, but the Bloomberg tablets confirm that reoccupation was rapid in both towns.[2]

Colchester, where destruction of both city and populace was probably the greatest, would have struggled. There was simply no one left to sift through the ashes. Nervous locals had undoubtedly crept through the still-smouldering wreckage in search of trinkets or out of simple curiosity, but they would have found it a wretched, haunted place, thick with decomposition.

When the first soldiers arrived, the story of the defence and massacre would have been written starkly in the makeshift defences of the temple precinct, the bodies littered across it in the running fight, and thickly clustered around the steps of the podium where the final stand was made, a dire visual memory committed to a military report and fossilised now in the account of Tacitus. Exposed to the weather and wildlife for the previous weeks, many of the bodies may have been partly skeletonised. Entering the temple itself, the hundreds of women and children heaped within, protected from the elements, would still have been in an advanced state of putrefaction. It was in sights such as this that much of the vengeance wreaked in the months to come must have found its origin.

There is an inherent danger in drawing too many parallels between events separated by 1800 years, but not, perhaps, in comparing the simple human reaction to almost identical psychological trauma. In 1857, another rebellion against imperial rule was blazing across the Indian subcontinent, when the sepoys of the East India Company rose in open revolt. The war is infamous for its descent into a catalogue of atrocities perpetrated by both sides, often on non-combatants, and for the British, the condensed horror of the Indian Mutiny was distilled into a single name: Cawnpore.

Cawnpore (Kanpur) in northern India lies on the river Ganges and the Grand Trunk Road. When the Indian garrison mutinied on 5 June 1857, the British there, about nine hundred people, the majority civilians, retired to an inadequate entrenchment with little water, food or shelter. After three weeks of siege and appalling suffering, the rebels offered the survivors safe passage by boat to Allahabad. The exhausted garrison and their families limped a gauntlet of abuse to the river and hauled themselves into the waiting boats, where a massacre ensued.

When the shooting spattered out, the survivors were rounded up, the men executed, and the remaining women and children crammed into a makeshift prison, the Bibighar. With a British relief force nearing Cawnpore, and reports of atrocities being carried out against Indian civilians by the various British columns, orders were given to slaughter the 200 British women and children by hand.

The relief column was led by Sir Henry Havelock. Upon hearing from a spy that the women and children were still alive, he had declared to his soldiers, 'By God's help, men, we shall save them, or every man of us die in the attempt!'[3] When the relief force arrived two days later, an advance party eagerly sought the women and children. What they found was the horror of the Bibighar, and a trail of blood and clumps of hair all the way to a nearby well.

'I have looked upon death in every form,' wrote one of the first unfortunates to reach the scene, 'but I could not look down that well again.'[4]

The British were out for vengeance.

The human reaction to this terrible episode had an Old Testament feel to it. General James 'Butcher' Neill, a homicidal Scot whose column had left a desolation of burnt Indian villages and civilian corpses in its wake, and who personally instigated the retributions, justified it thus: 'No one who has ever witnessed the scenes of murder, mutilation, and massacre can ever listen to the word "mercy", as applied to these fiends.'[5] He was true to his word.

Rebels were immediately hanged. Chief rebels or ringleaders (and it was up to them, impossibly, to prove their own innocence) were subjected to a deeper violence than the merely physical. Taboos relating to their caste were deliberately broken, and they were force-fed pork and beef. They were then taken to the Bibighar, still caked with dried blood. The blood was dampened, to soften it up, and the condemned men forced to lick the room clean before being kicked outside and hanged from a hastily erected gallows. Some were tied across the muzzles of cannon and vaporised, destroying the physical body in a direct assault upon Indian religious belief. A dark skin was enough to condemn a man.

The spirit of the moment was encapsulated in a piece of contemporary folklore, in which a group of Highlanders, finding a young woman's severed head, divided up the tresses of her hair, vowing to kill a mutineer for each strand.[6] An officer emerging from the Bibighar said simply, 'I have spared many a man in fight, but I will never spare another.'[7]

Somewhat hypocritical nineteenth-century British sentimentality with regard to the sanctity of women and children may not be directly comparable to the rather less mawkish first-century Roman mindset, but in the story of Cawnpore we can go some way towards peering into the minds of those first legionaries who, with wine- or vinegar-soaked neck scarves tied over their faces, had to enter the remains of the Temple of Claudius several weeks after the slaughter and pick through the many hundreds of bodies within. And we can begin to understand what it was like to be an eastern Briton who ran into them in the weeks and months to come.

One of the reasons for the paucity of human remains discovered at Colchester must have been this concentration of the bodies within such a confined area, which made collection and disposal an uncomplicated if sickening task. The prevailing burial practice in early Roman Britain was cremation. It seems inconceivable that the bodies were buried in a mass grave – consider the size of it – and there would have been little point in individually cremating such a vast number of anonymous, unrecognisable corpses.

I suspect a vast bonfire was lit, and the bodies fed into it *en masse* for several days, after which the ashes, or a token sample of them, were buried with a suitable monument on one of the roads leading out of the town. It may still await discovery, but without its monumental stone, which are so often missing, it is the sort of deposit that could potentially have been destroyed long ago without comment or notice.

The Ninth Legion was still lying somewhere along the Via Devana. As with the dead exposed in the temple precinct, depending upon the weather of the previous weeks, they might have been partly reduced to skeletons, but were probably still boiling with maggots, slowly liquefying and polluting the air for miles around. We have no record of the burial expedition, but Tacitus records the discovery of the lost army of Varus in the Teutoburg forest in Germany fifty years previously, which itself had been massacred, strung out on the line of march.

The Romans, led by the suitably named Germanicus, found the battlefield six years after the event:

> *In the centre of the field were the whitening bones of men, as they had fled, or stood their ground, strewn everywhere or piled in heaps. Near, lay fragments of weapons and limbs of horses, and also human heads, prominently nailed to trunks of trees. In the adjacent groves were the barbarous altars, on which they had immolated tribunes and first-rank centurions ... And so the Roman army now on the spot, six years after the disaster, in grief and anger, began to bury the bones of the three legions, not a soldier knowing whether he was interring the relics of a relative or a stranger, but looking on all as kinsfolk and of their own blood, while their wrath rose higher than ever against the foe. In raising the barrow Germanicus laid the first sod, rendering thus a most welcome honour to the dead, and sharing also in the sorrow of those present.*[8]

Once more, an event from more recent colonial history can shed the light of eyewitnesses on the actual human experience of discovering such a scene. Archibald Forbes and Melton Prior, Victorian war correspondents, wrote vivid pieces for the *Illustrated London News* about visiting the wreckage of the British camp at Isandlwana, overrun by the Zulus in 1879, where a similar number of British troops were likewise lost to an unexpected and well-orchestrated attack by an overwhelming tribal force.

It takes not the slightest effort to stand there now and superimpose these descriptions, in spectral palimpsest, over the rolling fields of the Colne Valley:

> In all the seven campaigns I have been in . . . I have not witnessed a scene more horrible. I have seen the dead and dying on a battlefield by hundreds and thousands; but to come suddenly on the spot where the slaughtered battalion . . . were lying . . . was far more appalling.
>
> Here, I saw not the bodies, but the skeletons, of men whom I had known in life and health, some of whom I had known well, mixed up with the skeletons of oxen and horses . . . showing how furious had been the onslaught of the enemy . . . individuals could only be recognised by such things as a patched boot, a ring on the finger-bone, a particular button, or coloured shirt or pair of socks . . . and this could be done with much difficulty, for either the hands of the enemy, or the beaks and jaws of vultures tearing up the corpses, had in numberless cases so mixed up the bones of the dead that the skull of one man, or bones of a leg or arm, now lay with parts of the skeleton of another.
>
> The lancers went about all over the field, often here and there quietly lifting the clothes off the skeletons, or gently pushing them on one side with their lances, to see what regiment they belonged to. I almost regretted to see this done, for it seemed like sacrilege. But this is a time of war.[9]

So wrote Melton Prior, an artist rather than a writer. Forbes, a hard man by nature and a wordsmith by trade, captured the eerie, aching sadness of the scene:

> In this ravine dead men lay thick – mere bones with toughened, discoloured skin like leather covering them, and clinging tight to them, the flesh all wasted away. Some were almost wholly dismembered, heaps of clammy, yellow bones. I forbear to describe the faces, with their blackened features and beards

blanched by rain and sun. Every man had been disembowelled. Some were scalped, and others subjected to yet ghastlier mutilation. The clothes had lasted better than the poor bodies they covered, and helped to keep the skeletons together. All the way up the slope, I traced by the ghastly token of dead men, the fitful line of flight . . .

It was like a long string with knots in it, the string formed of single corpses, the knots of clusters of dead, where, as it seemed, little groups might have gathered to make a hopeless, gallant stand and die . . . but on the slope beyond, on which from the crest we looked down, the scene was the saddest, and more full of weird desolation than any I had yet gazed upon. There was none of the stark, blood-curdling horror of a recent battlefield, no pool of yet wet blood, no raw gaping wounds, no torn red flesh that seems yet quivering – nothing of all that makes the scene of yesterday's battle so rampantly ghastly – shocked the senses. A strange dead calm reigned in this solitude of nature.[10]

Both Forbes and Prior, and Germanicus, were no strangers to the horrors of war, and yet there was clearly something about the discovery of an old massacre, something especially pathetic about the bones of comrades and the passing of time, the pathos, that got under their skins in a way that the immediacy of blood and gore never could. Such was the lot of those wandering in reverent silence through the tangled wreckage and *disjecta membra* of Legio IX Hispana, two thousand skeletal and putrefying bodies strewn across the Essex countryside, the hopeless last stands and attempts at escape written as clearly across the bluffs of the Colne as they had been to Forbes at Isandlwana.

The accounts in the *Illustrated London News* were accompanied by a stark double-page illustration and smaller sketches of the scene to upset many a Victorian breakfast. But seeing it in reality, as Forbes, Prior and Germanicus hint at, stirred something far deeper than pathos and curiosity. Burying the Ninth and entering the Temple of Claudius inspired so much more than simple horror.

We know that the Roman military machine was capable of slaughter, torture, rapine and enslavement on a vast and guiltless scale without the least encouragement, but I do not believe that we can truly appreciate the poorly understood aftermath of the revolt without looking to these deeper, atavistic layers of experience.

Tacitus gives a hint at what came next, but the archaeology is almost silent:

> *The whole army was then brought together and kept under canvas to finish the remainder of the war. The emperor strength-ened the forces by sending from Germany two thousand legion-aries, eight cohorts of auxiliaries, and a thousand cavalry. On their arrival the men of the ninth had their number made up with legionary soldiers. The allied infantry and cavalry were placed in new winter quarters, and whatever tribes still wavered or were hostile were ravaged with fire and sword.*[11]

The agony and horror concealed in the matter-of-fact brevity of Tacitus is encapsulated in those final words, *ravaged with fire and sword*, and it is here, perhaps, that the visual horrors of revenge we have in mind from the Indian rebellion should be kept near as we explore this terrible final chapter of the war. Examples from the nineteenth century should not be allowed to colour our imaginations too much – they were very different wars in very different times and places, but they were comparable mental traumas suffered by people bonded across the years by essentially similar shared experiences.

It is clear that the war did not end with the Great Battle, but far less certain whom the protagonists were, or where and how they fought – Tacitus speaks of *wavering or hostile tribes*, but not specifically the Iceni and Trinovantes. Barry Cunliffe believes that the war must have reduced eastern England to 'a virtual desert'.[12] There is, however, little physical evidence of fighting, settlement destruction or mass abandonment in Icenia, indeed, experts on Icenian metalwork and archaeology have argued that a close reading of the archaeological record alone supports no such assumption that the area was devastated post rebellion.[13]

If the archaeological evidence remains mixed and complex to interpret, Tacitus's claim is believable enough, knowing what we do of Paulinus and the Roman garrison of Britain – Paulinus would ultimately be removed from his command for the continued devastation he was wreaking on the province.

Subduing an area did not necessarily mean burning settlements, however, which might have left an archaeological trace, and anyhow, we have extensively excavated comparatively few settlements dating to this time in East Anglia. Even if the Roman army did not physically lay waste to these tribal territories, the losses of the Great Battle alone would have been cataclysmic to the peoples involved. Occupation of the Iron Age settlement at Spong Hill in central Norfolk seemingly continued unbroken, although there was a major change in layout after the revolt.[14] Excavations near Braintree in Essex have recently exposed a native settlement destroyed by fire in this period, but how, why and by whom are details more difficult to ascertain.[15]

The second hint that Tacitus gives us of the lingering devastation of the war concerns starvation:

Nothing however distressed the enemy so much as famine, for they had been careless about sowing corn, people of every age having gone to the war, while they reckoned on our supplies as their own.[16]

Here I must depart from my faith in Tacitus, just a little, and suggest that he was mistaken in the cause of the famine, for all that the end result was the same. I do not believe that the folk of Icenia, subsistence farmers one and all, could simply choose to ignore the timeless turning of the agricultural year any more than they could have chosen to live on the bottom of the sea. They were farmers and they did what farmers needed to do, reinforced at every turn by ritual and feast day, religion, superstition and folk tale, story, song and tradition.

The Iceni starved at the end of that war, I don't doubt it for a moment, but it was not for lack of planting their crops. It was that the labour-intensive task of bringing in the harvest after the Great Battle, which the whole community would be involved in, by necessity, now lacked the numbers – particularly the men and women in peak physical condition who would have done the greatest share of the hard work. In addition, the Roman army had undoubtedly done its share of crop-burning in retribution, and also of harvesting on their own account, to refill their depleted granaries.

Without a surplus, the Iceni couldn't sow an autumn crop or store seed-corn over the winter, and without their seed-corn, they couldn't sow the following spring. Roman swords and firebrands aside, the Iceni faced Armageddon. That great, heavy belly of East Anglian sky must have hung precarious and threatening above them; some might even have petitioned at their ruined shrines and splintered groves for it all to come crashing down, to end what they knew was to come.

At Sedgeford in north-west Norfolk, hard by Snettisham, a late Iron Age farm was completely abandoned at this time, to be replaced, after a hiatus, by a Romano–British farm with a 'radically new layout'.[17] The excavators have suggested their belief that this was a direct impact of the war, testimony of a 'contested landscape'.[18] Although this imposition of new layouts and alignments is hardly unique to Norfolk – later first-century dislocation of land use can be seen in the Addenbrooke's landscape in Cambridge[19] – it certainly represents a change in the wind at the right time, and given the historical background, the interpretation is undoubtedly broadly correct.

As the eminent archaeologist Tony Gregory stated of another Norfolk site:

No matter how objective and archaeologically based the reasoning, it is impossible to consider the Icenian tribal area in the third quarter of the first century AD without reference to Boudicca and the revolt of AD 60. To attempt to do so is self-deception . . . It will appear from our subconsciousnesses in any consideration of the period.[20]

The site of which Gregory was speaking, however, did not merely suggest the imposition of a new agricultural overlord, but a premeditated rebooting of the tribal soul – the physical and psychological deconstruction of local spiritual identity and power.

I know the A11 well, the main east–west artery in and out of Norfolk; when we first moved to Norwich for Clare's work, I commuted along it daily back to Cambridge for years. For most of that time I was unaware that twice a day, every day, as I followed the great bow of the Thetford bypass, I drove across one of the most enigmatic sites of the Iceni. It was a name I knew from books, a site somewhere near Thetford, but as I crossed the roundabout with a sign for the Fison Way industrial estate, I was daily skirting an ancient ritual site of huge importance.

The Fison Way site is not a visitor attraction, currently under pasture, and with related Iron Age activity undoubtedly spreading out beneath the bypass and the industrial estate. The only way to get a view of it, apart from a brief glimpse through the hedge as you drive down the bypass, is to pull into the estate, which lies on the high ground of Gallows Hill above Thetford. The site overlooks the rivers Little Ouse and Thet, marked by monumental Iron Age earthworks at the point of confluence. Turning off the roundabout and on to the estate we come to Howlett Way, and turning left takes us to one of the most unremarkable industrial estate dead-ends you will ever have the dubious pleasure of visiting.

Be not disheartened, for though a coach park lies to your right, and the tall corrugated metal walls of a factory to your left, directly ahead, fifty metres beyond the chain-link fence in the grassy field beyond, and invisible to the naked eye, lies the multi-ditched Icenian enclosure that still defies definite explanation to this day. In addition, if we shuffle over the grass verge, kicking the crisp packets and sweet wrappers to where the fence meets the corner of the factory, we are standing on the exact spot where the Thetford Treasure of late Roman gold and silver came to light, illegally metal detected in 1979.

Gallows Hill must have been an atmospheric spot before the industrial estate and bypass cut across it. With views down into the river valleys, and for many miles west across Suffolk, almost to the edge of the Cambridgeshire Fens, it is always a thrill to see the sun setting across the conifer forest of the Breckland and sinking beneath the distant marshes. The Fens are marsh no more, but the fact that the sun was seen to disappear beneath that watery threshold each day, the liminal borderlands of the tribal territory, must have been significant. If someone was to suggest that the site was special in ancient times for the quality and meaning of the sunsets you can observe from there, they would raise no argument from me.

It was the construction of the industrial units that led to the finding of the treasure hoard, and a rectangular cropmark in the adjacent field was assumed to be the Roman temple complex with which the treasure was related. As the field was earmarked for expansion of the estate, a rescue survey and excavation was carried out between 1980 and 1982 by Tony Gregory. It soon became clear that it wasn't Roman at all.

Gregory's team exposed a complex site that had been the focus of intense activity over a relatively short space of time, from the late Iron Age through to the latter half of the first century AD. Evolving out of a system of small plots with evidence of metalworking, around the time of the Roman conquest, a large, rectangular double-ditched enclosure was built with a single roundhouse in the central space. Many associated pits were interpreted as graves, although no bones had survived the acidic soil.

The central building was of such substantial and unusual construction that it appears to have been a two-storeyed roundhouse, a sort of roundhouse tower,[21] that would survive the complete reworking of its short-lived enclosure and the rapid construction of an even larger and much more complex one.

It is this final phase, which must date to the AD 50s – the height of Prasutagus and Boudica's rule – that is most enigmatic. The main roundhouse was joined by several more structures lying in one half of a rectangular ditched and embanked space, but this was only the centre of the complex. Thirty-five metres beyond, another ditch and bank completely surrounded the smaller enclosure, and this space was filled with row after row of narrow gullies a few metres apart, eight or nine in all, that marked the location of parallel timber screens or fences. These completely surrounded the inner enclosure, except for an entrance corridor approached through a massive timber gateway.

Nothing quite like it had been found before, and it was combined with a relatively small artefact assemblage of pottery, although many brooches were found. This paucity of domestic material would suggest that it was not a habitation site as such, unless kept scrupulously clean, but it was clearly a place of immense tribal importance, all lying in 'splendid isolation'.[22]

Graham Webster was the first to think outside the box. He suggested to Tony Gregory, very early in the excavation, that the site represented an artificial oak grove, something Gregory initially thought rather a great leap of reasoning, but increasingly accepted as the excavation and later analysis continued.[23]

Whatever Fison Way represents, whether an artificial sacred grove for religious rites, or a royal palace used for ceremonies of state, the inauguration of monarchs, and the receiving of ambassadors, it was clearly a ceremonial centre of some sort; Gregory likened the burials of the second phase being attracted there like the graves of kings to Westminster Abbey.[24] He also speculated that the surrounding timbers could have been left with their branches on to enhance the effect of a grove-like setting on what would have been treeless heath.[25] We simply do not know what the site represents, and I have always wondered if the narrow lanes between the concentric screens of timber were meant to be walked as a bizarre processional way.

The Fison Way enclosure would have been familiar to Prasutagus and Boudica; it is difficult to believe that they did not visit it on a regular basis, for affairs of state or religious ceremonies. As the possible location of great tribal meetings, Paul Sealey of Colchester Museum has speculated that this may have been the very spot that hosted the tribal conference that decided the rebellion.[26] One even has to wonder if this was where Boudica would naturally have received ambassadors, including the procurator's men, and was where the resulting atrocity therefore took place.

At some point in the latter half of the first century, the site disappeared. It was not burnt, and it was not left to rot; it was *removed*. The timbers were rocked back and forth to loosen them and were systematically pulled up. The ditches were partly backfilled.[27] We cannot ascribe this to a particular year or even to an exact decade, but as Tony Gregory has pointed out above, it is impossible not to consider the impact of the rebellion in such contexts.

A few stray fragments of Roman military equipment could have many explanations, but it has to be pondered if these represent a short-lived occupation by soldiers intent on eradicating the site from the face of the earth.[28] To burn it would be to leave a charred monument – they would simply remove it, every timber, ditch and trace of it, this focus of tribal power, ritual and memory. It has even been wondered if the Romans would have been so appalled by the desecration of their own most important temple in Camulodunum that they had found the Icenian equivalent and were paying them back in kind.[29]

But the Iceni did not forget. It seems that a much later Romano–British temple was founded at the site, beneath where the adjacent factory now stands, the aura of religious importance still tangible after more than three centuries had passed. Very close to the end of Roman rule in Britain, someone buried there a hoard of enormous wealth, where you can stand among the crisp packets and weeds beside the corrugated factory wall. One of the deities depicted on the metalwork, Faunus, was a woodland deity, an entirely appropriate god to conjure in memory of the artificial forest clearing that once occupied the treeless plateau,[30] that acidic, heathland hilltop where the sun could be seen to sink into the distant Fens beyond.

The memory did not last, but the physical rediscovery of the site in 1980 did, to some extent, rekindle the sense of importance. The area is now undergoing change again, to be incorporated in the imminent Kings Fleet development of five thousand new homes, but by my reading of the plans this field will be a green space, a heath, presumably an area of nature and walks, which will finally give public access to the site itself. There will be nothing much to see at ground level, but hopefully visitors will get what they currently lack – a good *from where you stand now* artist's reconstruction and heritage information board a suitable distance from it, and the opportunity to sit, imagine, and remember.

One day in the aftermath of the Great Battle, I believe a party of mounted men made their way out of Paulinus's camp, away from the cloying smoke of the endless cremations. They were bound for Isca, the vast legionary fortress of Legio II Augusta at Exeter, the peacekeeping garrison of the south-west, and they rode directly from the Governor, maybe members of his personal staff beefed up by senior centurions from the Fourteenth and Twentieth. Perhaps the twenty-year-old Agricola, speculated to be the absent senior tribune of the Second Legion,[31] was with them, sick to his stomach. It was a grim mission that was doubt-less accompanied by many mixed feelings.

They brought the Second Legion news of their monumental victory over the rebels, to the great and immortal glory of the units involved – the honorific titles that would be conferred upon them, *Valeria Victrix* for the Twentieth, and *Martia Victrix* for the Fourteenth, perhaps already being touted. They also brought a personal reprimand to the acting commander, in the absence of the legate or senior tribune – the *Praefectus castrorum*, or camp prefect, a middle-aged man called Poenius Postumus.

When Governor Paulinus had first received news of the rebel-lion on the rolling ridges above the Menai Strait, he would instantly have dispatched orders to each legionary base, either advising an immediate move to key locations, or an instruction to be prepared to march. Once he had a better grasp of what was happening, at Chester or Wroxeter, the orders to move would have been issued, probably to effect a concentration of the north-ern forces at that strategic Midland hub of High Cross.

The Second Legion, or a portion of it, was presumably ordered to march to a junction in the south-western road system, from where it could support Paulinus as future events dictated. Within a week or so, all those summoned legions and cohorts had scoured out the ditches of their vast marching camps at their respective assembly points; all except the Second.

The most likely circumstances must be that trouble had flared somewhere in the south-west, preventing the Second's march, or that the dispatch riders from Paulinus or Postumus had been intercepted and killed. Either way, Postumus held the Second at Isca, and in so doing disobeyed a direct order and plunged his legion into shame. The party of officers had not come to arrest the ill-starred prefect, but to impress upon him the necessity, and allow him the grace, to do the decent thing. He would have known that, whoever wielded the blade, he wasn't going to live long enough to argue his corner.

We can only wonder if Tacitus heard this story from Agricola himself:

> *Poenius Postumus, camp-prefect of the second legion, when he knew of the success of the men of the fourteenth and twentieth, feeling that he had cheated his legion out of like glory, and had contrary to all military usage disregarded the general's orders, threw himself on his sword . . .*[32]

The fresh-faced Agricola, possibly second-in-command of the legion, and the prefect's immediate superior, might have been guiltily considering that there, but for the grace of the gods, went he.

If the Second Legion was in its fortress in Exeter that day in AD 60, and it is a pretty good guess that it was, Postumus may well have retired to the *principia*, or headquarters complex, when informed of his general's great victory and fury at the Second's absence. Dismissing his staff and slaves, he might have said a few quiet words to his gods whilst reflectively draining the beautifully decorated cup of wine on his desk.

Drawing the eighteen inches of cold, razored steel of his gladius with its familiar, comforting rasp, from its scabbard, he felt delicately beneath his thin linen tunic for the base of the sternum. Pressing the point of the sword to the soft flesh beneath, he braced himself, and with a sudden explosion of force, thrust the sword upwards beneath his rib cage and into the heart. So ended the career, life and shame of Poenius Postumus, *Praefectus castrorum*, Legio II Augusta.

If you ever chance to find yourself in the centre of Exeter, in the vicinity of the crossroads where North Street, South Street, Fore Street and High Street all meet, roughly approximating to the site of the old *principia*, spare a thought for Poenius Postumus, whose life may have spilled out in a momentary rush of blood, agony and shame somewhere under the modern brick paving beneath your feet:

There, like the wind through woods in riot,
Through him the gale of life blew high;
The tree of man was never quiet:
Then 'twas the Roman, now 'tis I.

The gale, it plies the saplings double,
It blows so hard, 'twill soon be gone:
Today the Roman and his trouble
Are ashes under Uricon.[33]

Epilogue: Ashes and Dust

Journey's End

Some days in spring do you come back at will,
And tread with weightless feet the ancient ground?
O say, if not,
Why is this air so sacred and so still?

Frances Darwin Cornford

I drive to Thetford one muggy, overcast morning in late May. I walk the semi-circular ramparts of Thetford Castle, and then climb the central mound. I sit in the broken sunshine, try mentally to remove the castle mound, and wonder how this landscape has changed. The motte is Norman, every inch of it, but the huge surrounding earthworks are Iron Age, the remains of a promontory fort occupying a great bow in the course of the river where the Thet and Little Ouse converge by two fords. Dating to several centuries BC, this would have dominated the landscape when Boudica knew this place.

I follow the Little Ouse on its pretty, meandering, wooded course for about four miles, and then back along a busy country road to the Fison Way roundabout. I find my way off the road and on to the edge of a field on the south-western side, and look back along the line of my walk in the valley bottom below me.

I am sitting on a bank, the soil that was moved by bulldozers to create the raised and level ground for the roundabout forty years ago. It is overgrown with grass, a few wildflowers and, mostly, nettles, punctuated by molehills. As ever, I cannot resist the temptation of bare soil, and the small, weathered mounds are sandy with flint pebbles, but on top of the nearest is a little dark grey sherd of pottery, about two centimetres across. It is heavily abraded, and out of place, long and irretrievably removed from its original context, but from very close to where I sit; from somewhere on this once remarkable hilltop.

Tiny scraps of rough pot can be difficult to identify, but it looks to my eye to be Roman, so perhaps, *just* perhaps, dating to the time of the client kingdom; Prasutagus and Boudica's time. I hold it in my hand, this little survivor of another world, of the events that may have played out here in those crucial last decades of Iceni independence, a silent witness now of a world that was about to end.

In so much of this story there are details that we can never know, but we can let the landscape guide our thinking, and allow ourselves to wonder. I have long thought that the wide and gentle sides of this sheltered river valley, watched over by that enigmatic royal and ritual hilltop enclosure of Fison Way, in the southern borderlands of the Iceni, was where Boudica's war host gathered for the advance on Colchester. It is not just wishful thinking, a good logical case can be made for it.

The remarkable Iron Age archaeology and earthworks are not here by chance. This was a hub of land and river routes, with the conjoining rivers by the promontory fort, the source of the Waveney a few miles south-east, and that great ancient artery of the Icknield Way, the *Iceni* Way, fording the river by the fort. In addition, the line of Boudica's march to Camulodunum and the Colne Valley, almost due south, is a naturally fair and gentle route from here. Even if that army had averaged no more than five miles a day, they would have been there in a week. They would probably have made it in three or four days. Say what you like about wishful thinking. For me the rebellion started here, and in some small way, ended here too.

For the Iceni, the old world had gone. The glory days of wealth and power and freedom had ended a generation before, and the nominal liberty of the client kingdom had perished with Prasutagus. Boudica had offered a momentary glimpse of something else, but that had bled itself out on the javelins, short swords and slingshots of the Fourteenth and Twentieth Legions.

Roman historian and archaeologist Guy de la Bédoyère has said that Boudica had nothing to offer her followers but 'chaos, destruction and, ultimately, hunger'.[1] He is demonstrably right – chaos, destruction and hunger is exactly what she gave them, indeed, it is what most defeated commanders bequeath to their people, and the Iceni knew well enough what the costs of failure would be. However, no one sets out to fight a war convinced that they will lose it, and so, on the contrary, Boudica offered them everything, and the overwhelming of the great towns, the storming of the temple citadel and the massacre of the IX Hispana proved that she could give it to them.

The tragic inevitability of the outcome of the Great Battle is dependent upon our backward-glancing binoculars, for it was clearly not inevitable to the Britons who were there, or they would never have charged up that valley. Indeed, had the Iceni and Trinovantes been less confident of success, instilling caution, it is surely a battle they might have won. Whether they would have been better off had they won that battle, or, indeed, if they had never fought at all, it is beyond our vision to see. But their losses were apocalyptic.

As I look down into the valley where I like to think they camped, cupping that tiny nugget of Roman pottery in my hand, it is only human to wonder if the gamble was worth the price.

I gaze south-west across the Breckland, along the line of that ancient route to the Chilterns near Verulamium, as others must anxiously once have done from this same hillside, watching for the first hints of movement or dust kicked up in the distance. If Boudica's army had avoided battle with Paulinus, or beaten him, and made it onto the Icknield Way, it would have brought them to this very spot; a ghost road now for that vast army that never made it home.

But if Boudica had taken her beating and accepted the rape of her daughters, handed over the tribal treasury, watched her nobles lose their estates to belligerent colonists and her farmers made into slaves, and meekly slipped away to hide in the shadows, abandoning her people to their fate – what should we think of her now? Would we admire her?

I think that question answers itself.

I have before me a picture of Queen Boudica drawn by a nine-year-old boy. It is a good picture, and Tristan's history teacher has ticked the work and written: 'A great poster! She looks scary.' He drew it several years ago, and I remember him preparing for the associated school trip.

'We're going to Norwich Castle today to see the Boudica gallery,' he informed me. I already knew; I signed the permission slip. He was no stranger to the place, but it would be good for him to go with his friends.

'You'll have fun, but pay attention,' I said.

'It is a remarkable story. A sad, but remarkable story.'

Appendix 1

Casualty Figures in the Roman Conquest

Estimating the numbers of non-Roman participants in ancient battles, let alone the proportion of that uncertain number that might have fallen or been enslaved, is impossible in anything more than the vaguest terms, even when such numbers are offered in the surviving histories. What I offer here, therefore, is no more than a suggestion of possibility.

The Roman conquest of Britain, in its initial phase, lasted for exactly forty years, AD 43–83. In that period many, many dozens of battles were fought, in addition to prolonged periods of guerrilla warfare, for example in Wales throughout the AD 50s. Although heavy British casualties are often implied as a matter of course, including deliberate genocide in Wales, it is rare for actual figures to be given. These occur twice, in Boudica's final battle in AD 60, in which Tacitus proposes as many as 80,000 British dead, and at Mons Graupius in AD 83, where he gives a figure of 10,000.

It is widely considered that 80,000 British dead in Boudica's last battle is exaggerated, a caution shared by me, but given that 10,000 Romans participated – a figure that fits well with the known distribution of troops – and that it was a battle of deliberate annihilation, the British being slaughtered even down to the non-combatants and baggage animals, a figure of 40,000 dead would not seem excessive. The casualty figure given for Mons Graupius does not appear unreasonable, given the number of participants and the nature of the battle. Accepting these figures would account for 50,000 British lives in two battles – just two days of fighting in a forty-year period that included around thirty years of active campaigning.

David Mattingly, in his groundbreaking work *An Imperial Possession*, first published in 2006, suggests that between 100,000 and 250,000 Britons must have perished in this period. These are sobering figures, but I believe that the upper figure is perhaps the more likely, and still conservative, estimate.

Tacitus mentions devastating famine in the wake of Boudica's rebellion. Although he blames this on the Britons themselves failing to plant their crops – a detail of which I am sceptical, famine would have been the inevitable and ubiquitous legacy of every campaigning season on a fragile subsistence economy. Enumerating the losses and suffering of this aspect of the conquest period is impossible.

There is likewise no way to quantify the numbers of slaves taken in these years of conquest, but Plutarch, in describing Caesar's conquest of Gaul, states that around a million Gauls were killed and a like number enslaved – figures still widely touted. If a similar ratio was accepted for Britain, a further 250,000 could have disappeared into bondage, both for use within the province and to be shipped to the continent. Large numbers of young men would have been drafted or pressed into service in the auxilia, most to serve overseas and therefore unlikely to return if they survived their 25 years of service.

In addition to these losses must be added the large numbers of wounded who survived, often in a state of disability, as well as those, often non-combatants, who suffered the ubiquitous brutality of military occupation and martial law.

Appendix 2

Locating the Great Battle – Additional Considerations

In making the strategic case for a battlefield overlooking the Ver valley close to St Albans, and proposing a specific site that fits topographically and artefactually with the historical account, I hope that I have shifted at least some future scrutiny back to within the known geographical theatre of the war. I offer this short appendix in further support of the high ground to the south-west of Verulamium as the site of Paulinus's stand.

Just as this book was going to press, a new paper exploring the slingshots of Windridge Farm was published in *Britannia* (Reid, Müller & Klein, 2022). The paper is a timely and exciting piece of research, confirming the authors' (and this author's) belief, based upon Rosalind Niblett's original 2001 suggestion, that the spread of shot represents an early Roman battlefield. Isotopic analysis of the lead suggests that the source of the ore used was either Germany or Britain, with Germany the more likely.

Looking at the historical sources, the authors suggest that an action dating to Caesar's second British expedition in 54 BC, or to the Claudian invasion in AD 43, are the most likely contenders, and although Boudica's war is discussed, it is ultimately dismissed given that Verulamium had no military garrison in AD 60 to account for the shots, and the Ninth Legion must have gone into action closer to Colchester. Boudica's Great Battle was not considered as a candidate action.

The potential source of the lead does not provide any strong clue towards date – if the ore is accepted as German, it must be noted that the Roman army undoubtedly brought much continental lead with it, including crates of slingshots, which might have continued in service throughout the first century AD. The authors point out that both the Fourteenth and Twentieth Legions came to Britain from garrisons on the Rhine, very close to one of the main sources of German ore, and Caesar's legions had also campaigned there a hundred years previously. The authors reasonably suggest, however, that the later the date of the shot, the more the expected source of ore would be Britain.

The authors assume that the action was one in which Roman slingers were the attackers, as would likely have been the case in either 54 BC or AD 43, and suggest a direction of attack – from the south-west – based upon the topographic exclusion of other directions. The south-east approach – along the defile – is excluded because it leads down to the marshy ground of the River Ver, although one of the major arterial routes of early Roman Britain – Watling Street – itself traversed the river margin here, and lay at the end of the defile. If the initial assumption is reversed, and the slingers were defending the plateau as part of Paulinus's army upon Boudica's approach in AD 60, an attack from the south-east, along the defile from Watling Street, would become the likely direction of approach by the attacking force.

The new study of the Windridge ammunition is a stimulating reassessment of the evidence combined with new data and a fresh consideration of the potential historical candidates, to which this book adds the final, and perhaps most compelling, contender.

Windridge Farm in a military context

The Iron Age earthworks and settlement of Prae Wood, immediately behind the proposed Roman position at Windridge Farm, would almost certainly have been heavily wooded in antiquity as it is now – Julius Caesar describes such places as being invariably densely wooded, and was speaking of sites local to this area when he did so (Caesar, *Gallic War*, V.21.1; Cunliffe, 2005, p. 161).

The earthworks themselves are enigmatic in their later phases. Effectively protecting the hilltop and Paulinus' left flank from the direction of Verulamium and the northerly Ver Valley, the Wheelers considered them poor as a defensive structure, having little military value (Wheeler & Wheeler, 1936, p. 11) but found that at the end of their useful life, in the mid first century AD, the western portion was suddenly converted into a definitely military defensive work with the addition of an outer ditch and palisade, to meet some sort of 'emergency' (ibid., pp. 22, 48). The basal finds dated the work to the mid first century, and the Wheelers naturally linked it to the conquest of 43.

The interpretation of the Wheelers, and the phasing and nature of the earthworks are still open to debate but, whenever they were re-fortified, this conversion would have provided a bastion on which to anchor Paulinus's left wing, as well as protecting refugees sheltering in the old Prae Wood settlement; could it not have been his troops that re-fortified it?

There was also the original continuation of the Iron Age ditch system that blocked the entire north-eastern scarp of the plateau. Had the Britons attempted to split their force and attack simultaneously from the north, their exhausting uphill slog, probably through woods, would have been met by an earthwork on the crest suddenly bristling with troops.

As to the water source that a Roman army of that size would require, the Iron Age settlement of the heights would doubtless have had watering holes for livestock, and possible shafted wells were attested to by the Wheelers. The River Ver, directly below and partially surrounding the position from the south-east to the north-east, would only have been denied to them for the day, or few days, when the Britons took control of the vale.

The Roman road that crossed the hilltop, running directly north of Windridge Farm, was an early route linking Verulamium with Silchester to the south-west, and with a linking route to Akeman Street north of it. Any force occupying the hilltop might have abandoned direct access onto (but not necessarily control over) Watling Street, but had instead secured access onto (and control over) the south-western arterial network – a particularly valuable asset for a general awaiting aid from the Second Legion garrisoned in that direction. It would, of course, also provide a line of retreat towards allied tribal territories, the south-western military zone and associated supply infrastructure, and the southern coast.

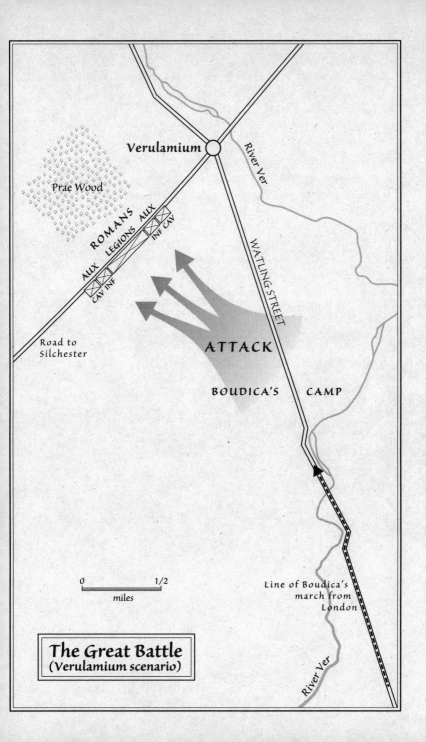

Verulamium

Prae Wood

ROMANS
AUX LEGIONS AUX
CAV INF   INF CAV

River Ver

WATLING STREET

ATTACK

Road to
Silchester

BOUDICA'S CAMP

0   1/2
miles

Line of Boudica's
march from
London

River Ver

The Great Battle
(Verulamium scenario)

Acknowledgements

The longest-suffering and most deserving of thanks are my wife Clare and son Tristan, as well as Jojo, who witnessed much of the story first-hand and suffered the neglect of the parts they did not with patience and acceptance. Without their love and support of every kind, there would be no book to write an acknowledgement for.

Emma and Jonny Tabor took part in the journey at a difficult time in their lives and went on to read the first draft. Their comments were hugely helpful and reassuring. Iris Beadsmoore too provided numerous instances of welcome hospitality, grand-son supervision and dog care. Edgar Harden, Ghislaine Wood, Lesley Bowker and Kneale Metcalf are all omnipresent in the narrative without ever being named. During the time of writing the book (2016–2019) they were my constant support network at weekends and on holidays, deflecting my protestations that 'I should be working' to force good food, strong drink and kind comradeship upon me, much to my physical and mental benefit. Adam and Judith Haworth suffered me admirably on holidays during which I determinedly wore Roman army caligae in the name of research. My siblings Mandy, Penny, Ally and Melanie, and our mum Daphne, all took a great interest in the book, and helped patch together the story of Sydney from vague family memories to concrete research. It was fated that neither Mum nor Dad should get to read the book, but I hope they would have liked

307

it. The more recent trials of rewriting in the topsy-turvy world post-2019 were greatly eased by the encouragement and interest of John and Jackie Beadsmoore, Emily Carey, Andy Snelling and Nick and Mel Watson.

I credit Grahame Appleby with drawing my myopic gaze away from Mancetter and convincing me of the importance of the Icknield Way. His choice of battlefield may differ to my own, but I hope that our contenders now complement, rather than contradict, each other. Suffice to say that all the mistakes in the book remain entirely my own.

It was a piece of extraordinary good fortune that my manuscript should land, very early on, on the desk of Jim Gill at United Agents who, with Amber Garvey, helped transform the book and ultimately found it a home.

My editor Rupert Lancaster guided the metamorphosis of the narrative from rambling manuscript to readable book. He and the team at Hodder & Stoughton, especially Ciara Mongey and Tom Atkins, have steered a novice through the maze with patience and kindness.

Finally, I owe a great debt of gratitude to a multitude of archaeologists past and present, some old comrades, and many not. This really is a story that could not have been told without the labours of generations of excavators, patiently exposing the stories of the past with fortitude and passion. I doff my cap to them all. We all should.

Bibliography

Ancient sources

Cicero, Marcus Tullius, *Letters to Atticus*. Translator Evelyn S. Shuckburgh, 1912. London: George Bell & Sons.

Dio, Cassius, *Roman History*. Translator Earnest Carey, 1925. LOEB.

Frontinus, Sextus Julius, *The Stratagems*. Translator Charles E. Bennett, 1925. LOEB.

Livy, Titus Livius, *The History of Rome*. Translator Daniel Spillan, 1853. London: Henry G. Bohn.

Lucan, *Pharsalia*. Translator Sir Edward Ridley, 1905. London: Longman's, Green & Co.

Suetonius, Gaius (Tranquillus), *Lives of the Twelve Caesars*. Translator J.C. Rolfe, 1913, LOEB.

Tacitus, Cornelius, *The Agricola*. Translators A.J. Church & W.J. Brodribb, 1876. New York: Random House.

Tacitus, Cornelius, *Annals*. Translators A.J. Church & W.J. Brodribb, 1895. London: Macmillan & Co.

Tacitus, Cornelius, *Histories*. Translators A.J. Church & W.J. Brodribb, 1873. New York: Random House.

Tertullian, *De Spectaculis*. Translator T.R. Glover, 1931. LOEB.

Modern sources

Alcock, J.P., 2011, *A Brief History of Roman Britain*. London: Constable & Robinson.

Aldhouse-Green, M., 2006, *Boudica Britannia*. Harlow: Pearson Education.

Alexander, J. & Pullinger, J., 2000, 'Roman Cambridge: Excavations on Castle Hill 1956–1988'. *Proceedings of the Cambridge Antiquarian Society* LXXXVIII for 1999.

Anon., 1974, 'Colchester', *Current Archaeology* 43, pp. 237–43.

Anon., 2008, 'Chester: Dark Secrets of the Arena Revealed', *Current Archaeology* 224, based on information supplied by Dan Garner & Tony Wilmott, pp. 18–25.

Appleby, G., 2009, 'The Boudican Revolt: Countdown to Defeat', *Hertfordshire Archaeology and History*, Vol. 16, pp. 57–65.

Arthur, M., 2002, *Forgotten Voices of the Great War*. London: Ebury Press.

Attenborough, D., 1993, 'The Shadow of the Hare', *Wildlife on One*, Easter special television documentary, BBC. Aired 12/04/1993.

Babington, C.C., 1883, *Ancient Cambridgeshire: or An Attempt to Trace Roman and Other Ancient Roads that Passed Through the County of Cambridge*. Second Edition. Cambridge: Cambridge Antiquarian Society.

Baddeley, C., 2013, *Roman Mancetter*. Atherstone: Atherstone Civic Society.

Banksy, 2006, *Wall and Piece*. London: Century.

Bayliss, A., 2005, 'Radiocarbon Dating', in Malim, T., *Stonea and the Roman Fens*. Stroud: Tempus.

BBC, 1978, *Living in the Past*, documentary series. Aired 23/02/1978–11/05/1978.

BBC, 2001, *Surviving the Iron Age*, documentary series. Aired 2001.

BBC, 2008, *Living in the Past*, 'What Happened Next?', documentary. Aired 20/05/2008.

Beard, M., 2009, *Pompeii: The Life of a Roman Town*. London: Profile Books.

Beard, M., 2013, *Confronting the Classics: Traditions, Adventures and Innovations*. London: Profile Books.

Beard, M., 2016, *Mary Beard's Ultimate Rome: Empire Without Limit*, BBC/Lion Television, documentary series. Aired April–May 2016.

Benario, H.W., 1986, 'Legionary Speed of March before the Battle with Boudica', *Britannia* XVII, pp. 358–62.

Binyon, L., 1927, *Boadicea: A Play in Eight Scenes*. London: Ernest Benn Ltd.

Birley, A.R., 2004, 'Petilius Cerialis [Pitillius Cerialis Caesius Rufus], Quintus', *Oxford Dictionary of National Biography* online, accessed 05/07/2017.

Birley, R., 1999, interview in *The Roman War Machine*, television documentary, A&E Television Networks.

Blake, E.A., 1899 – *see* Gowing, A., 1899.

Bibliography

Bowden, W., 2012, 'The Iceni Under Rome – Excavating Caistor St Edmund', *Current Archaeology* 270, pp. 28–35.

Bowden, W., 2017, 'The changing view of *Venta Icenorum*', in *A Town of the Iceni? 10 years of research at Venta Icenorum*, conference abstract. Caistor Roman Project.

Bowden, W., 2020, *Venta Icenorum – A Brief History of Caistor Roman Town*. Norwich: Norfolk Archaeological Trust.

Bowman, A.K., 2008, *Life and Letters on the Roman Frontier: Vindolanda and its People*. London: British Museum Press.

Bowsher, D., 1997, 'An Evaluation of the Roman Road at Brockley Hill, Middlesex', *Transactions of the London and Middlesex Archaeological Society* 46, pp. 45–57.

Braund, D., 1996, *Ruling Roman Britain: Kings, Queens, Governors and Emperors from Julius Caesar to Agricola*. London: Routledge.

Browne, D.M., 1974, 'An Archaeological Gazetteer of the City of Cambridge', *Proceedings of the Cambridge Antiquarian Society* 65 (1973–4), pt. 1.

Buckler, G., 1876, *Colchester Castle: A Roman Building and the Oldest and the Noblest Monument of the Romans in Britain*. Colchester: Benham & Harrison.

Burke, J., 2000, 'Dig Uncovers Boudicca's Brutal Streak', *Observer*, 3 December 2000.

Camulos website (www.camulos.com), 2018.

Carroll, K.K., 1979, 'The Date of Boudicca's Revolt', *Britannia* X.

Castle, I., 2010, *London 1917–18: The Bomber Blitz*. Oxford: Osprey Publishing.

Catling, C., 'The Riddle of the Lake – Llyn Cerrig Bach and Iron Age Anglesey', *Current Archaeology* 273, pp. 26–33.

Chadburn, A., 1996, 'Iron Age Coins', in Jackson, R.P.J. & Potter, T.W., *Excavations at Stonea, Cambridgeshire 1980–85*. London: British Museum Press.

Chadburn, A., 2006, 'The Currency of Kings', *British Archaeology* 87, March–April 2006.

Chimirri-Russell, G., 2003, 'Changing Artistic Perspectives on Celtic Coins', in C. Alfaro Asins, C. Marcos Alonso & P. Otero Moran (Eds.), *XIII Congreso internacional de numismatica, Madrid: Actas-proceedings-actes*, pp. 441–5. Madrid: Ministerio de Cultura, Dirección General de Bellas Artes y Bienes Culturales, Subdirección General de Museos Estatales.

Church, A.J. & Brodribb, W.J., 1882, *Tacitus*, Classical Writers series edited by Green, J.R. London: Macmillan & Co.

Church, A.J. & Brodribb, W.J. (Trans.), 1895, *Annals of Tacitus*. London: Macmillan & Co.

Codrington, T., 1918, *Roman Roads in Britain*, Third Edition. London: SPCK.

Cornford, F., 1948, *Travelling Home*. London: Cresset Press.

Cottam, E., de Jersey, P., Rudd, C. & Sills, J., 2010, *Ancient British Coins*. Aylsham: Chris Rudd.

Creighton, J., 2000, *Coins and Power in Late Iron Age Britain*. Cambridge: Cambridge University Press.

Crummy, N., 2001, 'Iron', in Lucas, G., *Excavations at Vicar's Farm, West Cambridge*, CAU Report 425. Cambridge: Cambridge Archaeological Unit/University of Cambridge.

Crummy, N., 2015, 'The Fenwick Treasure: The Jewellery', in *Colchester Archaeologist* 27, pp. 22–7.

Crummy, N., 2015b, 'The hoard and what it reveals', in Crummy, P. & Wightman, A., 'The Fenwick Treasure', *Current Archaeology* 308.

Crummy, N., 2016, 'A Hoard of Military Awards, Jewellery and Coins from Colchester', *Britannia* 47, pp. 1–28.

Crummy, N., 2017, 'The small finds', in Wightman, A. & Crummy, P., *An Archaeological Excavation and Watching Brief at Fenwick Colchester (formerly Williams & Griffin), 147–151 High Street, Colchester, Essex*, CAT Report 1150. Colchester: Colchester Archaeological Trust.

Crummy, P., 1977, 'Colchester: The Roman Fortress and the Development of the Colonia', *Britannia* VIII, pp. 65–105.

Crummy, P., 1984, *Colchester Archaeological Report 3: Excavations at Lion Walk, Balkerne Lane, and Middleborough, Colchester, Essex*. Colchester: Colchester Archaeological Trust.

Crummy, P., 1986, *In Search of Colchester's Past*. Colchester: Colchester Archaeological Trust.

Crummy, P., 1997, *City of Victory: The Story of Colchester – Britain's First Roman Town*. Colchester: Colchester Archaeological Trust.

Crummy, P., 2002, 'Britain's first town wall', *The Colchester Archaeologist* 15, pp. 19–21.

Crummy, P., 2013, 'The current state of knowledge', in Gascoyne, A. & Radford, A., *Colchester: Fortress of the War God – An Archaeological Assessment*. Oxford: Oxbow Books.

Crummy, P., 2015, 'Colchester and the Boudiccan War of Independence', in *Colchester Archaeologist* 27, pp. 28–31.

Cundy, D., 2015, *The Vengeful Queen: The Timeless Struggle of a People Against Invasion, Subjugation and Oppression*. Wales: Cambria Books.

Cunliffe, B., 1997, *The Ancient Celts*. London: Oxford University Press.

Cunliffe, B., 2005, *Iron Age Communities in Britain*. Fourth Edition. Abingdon: Routledge.

Curl, J., 2017, 'Human bone from the Fenwick Colchester site (2014) and a summary of the bone from the Telephone Exchange Excavation (1966)', in Wightman, A. & Crummy, P., 2017, *An Archaeological Excavation and Watching Brief at Fenwick Colchester (formerly Williams & Griffin), 147–151 High Street, Colchester, Essex*, CAT Report 1150. Colchester: Colchester Archaeological Trust, pp. 228–32.

Cuttler, R., Davidson, A. & Hughes, G., 2012, *A Corridor Through Time: The Archaeology of the A55 Anglesey Road Scheme*. Oxford: Oxbow Books.

Cutts, E.L., 1853, *Colchester Castle Not a Roman Temple: Being a Review of 'A Lecture on Colchester Castle, by the Rev. H. Jenkins, B.D.' Reprinted (with Additions) from the 'Essex and West Suffolk Gazette' of January 7th and September 9th, 1853*. London: George Bell.

Dando-Collins, S., 2005, *Nero's Killing Machine*. Hoboken: John Wiley & Sons.

Dannell, G.B. & Wild, J.P., 1987, *Longthorpe II – The Military Works-Depot: An Episode in Landscape History*, Britannia Monograph Series No. 8. London: Society for the Promotion of Roman Studies.

Davies, H., 2011, *Roads in Roman Britain*. Stroud: The History Press.

Davies, J., 1999, 'Patterns, Power and Political Progress in Iron Age Norfolk', in Davies, J. & Williamson, T. (Eds.), *Land of the Iceni: The Iron Age in Northern East Anglia*. Norwich: Centre of East Anglian Studies.

Davies, J., 2008, *The Land of Boudica: Prehistoric and Roman Norfolk*. Oxford: Oxbow Books.

Davies, J. (Ed.), 2011, *The Iron Age in Northern East Anglia: New Work in the Land of the Iceni*, BAR British Series 549. Oxford: Archaeopress.

Davies, J., 2011a, 'Closing Thoughts', in Davies, J. (Ed.), *The Iron Age in Northern East Anglia: New Work in the Land of the Iceni*, BAR British Series 549. Oxford: Archaeopress.

Davies, J., 2011b, 'The role of museums in the study of Iron Age Norfolk', in Davies, J. (Ed.), *The Iron Age in Northern East Anglia: New Work in the Land of the Iceni*, BAR British Series 549. Oxford: Archaeopress.

Davies, J., 2011c, 'Boars, Bulls and Norfolk's Celtic Menagerie', in Davies, J. (Ed.), *The Iron Age in Northern East Anglia: New Work in the Land of the Iceni*, BAR British Series 549. Oxford: Archaeopress.

Davies, J. & Robinson, B., 2009, *Boudica: Her Life, Times and Legacy*. Cromer: Poppyland Publishing.

Davies, J. & Williamson, T. (Eds.), 1999, *Land of the Iceni: The Iron Age in Northern East Anglia*. Norwich: Centre of East Anglian Studies.

de Jersey, P., 2014, *Coin Hoards in Iron Age Britain*. London: Spink/The British Numismatic Society.

de la Bédoyère, G., 2001, *The Buildings of Roman Britain*. Stroud: Tempus.

de la Bédoyère, G., 2003, *Defying Rome: The Rebels of Roman Britain*. Stroud: Tempus.

de la Bédoyère, G., 2015, *The Real Lives of Roman Britain*. London: Yale University Press.

Delamarre, X., 2012, *Noms de lieux celtiques de l'europe ancienne*. Arles: Editions Errance.

Dimbleby, D., 2010, 'The Age of Conquest', episode in *Seven Ages of Britain*, BBC documentary series, aired 31/01/2010.

Dodwell, N., 1998, 'Human Remains', in Evans, C. & Knight, M., *The Butcher's Rise Ring-Ditches: Excavations at Barleycroft Farm, Cambridgeshire 1996*, CAU Report 283. Cambridge: Cambridge Archaeological Unit/University of Cambridge.

Dodwell, N., 2001, 'The human remains', in Lucas, G., *Excavations at Vicar's Farm, West Cambridge*, CAU Report 425. Cambridge: Cambridge Archaeological Unit/University of Cambridge.

Dodwell, N., 2004, 'The human skeleton in pit F229', in French, C., 'Evaluation survey and excavation at Wandlebury Ringwork, Cambridgeshire, 1994–7', *Proceedings of the Cambridge Antiquarian Society* XCIII.

Drummond-Murray, J., Thompson, P. & Cowan, C., 2002, *Settlement in Roman Southwark: Archaeological Excavations (1991–8) for the London Underground Limited Jubilee Line Extension Project*, MoLAS Monograph 12. London: Museum of London Archaeology Service.

Drury, P.J., 1984, 'The Temple of Claudius at Colchester Reconsidered', *Britannia* XV, pp. 7–50.

Dudley, D.R. & Webster, G., 1962, *The Rebellion of Boudicca*. London: Routledge & Kegan Paul.

Dunnett, B.R.K., 1971, 'The Telephone Exchange Site', in *Transactions of the Essex Archaeological Society* Vol. III (Third Series), Part I, pp. 7–37.

Dunwoodie, L., 2004, *Pre-Boudican and Later Activity on the site of the Forum: Excavations at 168 Fenchurch Street, City of London*. London: Museum of London Archaeology Service.

Ellis, P., 2012, *Wall Roman Site*. London: English Heritage.

Evans, C., Lucy, S. & Patten, R., 2018, *Riversides: Neolithic Barrows, a Beaker Grave, Iron Age and Anglo-Saxon Burials and Settlement at*

Trumpington, Cambridge. New Archaeologies of the Cambridge Region (2). Cambridge: McDonald Institute for Archaeological Research.

Evans, C., Mackay, D. & Webley, L., 2004, *Excavations at Addenbrooke's Hospital, Cambridge: The Hutchison Site*, CAU Report 609. Cambridge: Cambridge Archaeological Unit/University of Cambridge.

Evans, C., Mackay, D. & Webley, L., 2008, *Borderlands: The Archaeology of the Addenbrooke's Environs, South Cambridge. New Archaeologies of the Cambridge Region (1)*. Cambridge: Cambridge Archaeological Unit/ Oxbow Books.

Evans, C. & Ten Harkel, L., 2010, 'Roman Cambridge's Early Settlement and Via Devana: Excavations at Castle Street', *Proceedings of the Cambridge Antiquarian Society* XCIX, pp. 35–60.

Evans, M.M., 2001, 'Boudica's Last Battle', *Osprey Military Journal*, Vol. 3, issue 5, pp. 25–33.

Evans, M.M., 2004, *The Defeat of Boudicca's Rebellion*. Towcester: Gemini Press.

Ferris, I., 2003, *Enemies of Rome: Barbarians Through Roman Eyes*. Stroud: Sutton.

Ferris, I., 2009, *Hate and War: The Column of Marcus Aurelius*. Stroud: The History Press.

Fincham, G., 2004, *Durobrivae: A Roman Town Between Fen and Upland*. Stroud: Tempus.

Firstbrook, P., 2001, *Surviving the Iron Age*. London: BBC.

Fitzpatrick, A., 1992, 'The Snettisham, Norfolk, hoards of Iron Age torques: sacred or profane?', *Antiquity* 66, issue 251, pp. 395–8.

Foot, W., 2019, 'AD 60, Boudica: Unlocated Battle', *British Archaeology* 165, March/April, pp. 26–9.

Forbes, A., 1879, 'Isandhlwana Revisited', *Illustrated London News*, No. 2091, Vol. LXXV, 12 July, pp. 37–8.

Fox, C., 1923, *The Archaeology of the Cambridge Region*. Cambridge: Cambridge University Press.

Fox, C., 1923a, 'Excavations in the Cambridgeshire Dykes. I. Preliminary Investigation; Excavations at Worstead Street', *Proceedings of the Cambridge Antiquarian Society* XXIV 1921–22, pp. 21–7.

Fox, C., 1946, *A Find of the Early Iron Age From Llyn Cerrig Bach, Anglesey*. Cardiff: National Museum of Wales.

Fox, C., 1958, *Pattern and Purpose: A Survey of Early Celtic Art in Britain*. Cardiff: The National Museum of Wales.

Fraser, A., Robertshaw, A. & Roberts, S., 2009, *Ghosts on the Somme: Filming the Battle, June–July 1916*. Barnsley: Pen & Sword.

French, C., 2004, 'Evaluation survey and excavation at Wandlebury Ringwork, Cambridgeshire, 1994–7', *Proceedings of the Cambridge Antiquarian Society* XCIII, pp. 15–65.

Frere, S., 1972, *Verulamium Excavations*, Vol. I. Oxford and London: Oxford University Press and the Society of Antiquaries.

Frere, S., 1983, *Verulamium Excavations*, Vol. II. London: Society of Antiquaries and Thames & Hudson.

Frere, S., 1991, *Britannia: A History of Roman Britain*. Third Revised Edition. London: Pimlico.

Frere, S. & St. Joseph, J.K., 1974, 'The Roman Fortress at Longthorpe', *Britannia* V, pp. 1–129.

Fryer, V., 2017, 'Charred plant macrofossils and other remains', in Wightman, A. & Crummy, P., *An Archaeological Excavation and Watching Brief at Fenwick Colchester (formerly Williams & Griffin), 147–151 High Street, Colchester, Essex*, CAT Report 1150. Colchester: Colchester Archaeological Trust.

Fuentes, N., 1984, 'Boudicca re-visited', *London Archaeologist* 4, pp. 311–17.

Gascoyne, A., 2013, 'The Roman legionary fortress, AD 43–49', in Gascoyne, A. & Radford, A., *Colchester: Fortress of the War God – An Archaeological Assessment*. Oxford: Oxbow Books.

Goldsworthy, A., 2015, *The Complete Roman Army*. London: Thames & Hudson.

Gowing, A. (Blake, E.A.), 1899, *Boadicea: A Play in Four Acts*. London: Kegan Paul, Trench, Trübner & Co. Ltd.

Greaves, A., *Isandlwana*. London: Cassell & Co.

Green, M., 1986, *The Gods of the Celts*. Gloucester: Alan Sutton.

Greep, S.J., 1987, 'Lead Sling-Shot from Windridge Farm, St Albans and the use of the Sling by the Roman Army in Britain', *Britannia* XVIII, pp. 183–200.

Gregory, T., 1991, *Excavations in Thetford, 1980–1982, Fison Way*, East Anglian Archaeology Report No. 53. Dereham: Norfolk Museums Service.

Hall, J. & Swain, H., 2000, *High Street Londinium: Reconstructing Roman London*. London: Museum of London.

Hanson, N., 2009, *First Blitz*. London: Random House.

Harlow, N., 2021 *Belonging and Belongings – Portable Artefacts and Identity in the Civitas of the Iceni. BAR* 664. Oxford: BAR.

Haverfield, F., 1914, 'The Battle Between Boadicea and Suetonius', *The Antiquary*, November 1914, pp. 439–40.

Hawkes, C.F.C. & Crummy, P., 1995, *Colchester Archaeological Report 11: Camulodunum 2*. Colchester: Colchester Archaeological Trust.

Hawkes, J., 1984, *Mortimer Wheeler: Adventurer in Archaeology*. London: Sphere.

Hebditch, M., 1971, 'Excavations on the South Side of the Temple Precinct at Colchester, 1964', *Transactions of the Essex Archaeological Society*, Vol. III, Third Series, pp. 115–30.

Hill, J.D., 1999, 'Settlement, Landscape and Regionality: Norfolk and Suffolk in the Pre-Roman Iron Age in Britain and Beyond', in Davies, J. & Williamson, T. (Eds.), *Land of the Iceni: The Iron Age in Northern East Anglia*. Norwich: Centre of East Anglian Studies.

Hill, J. & Rowsome, P., 2011, *Roman London and the Walbrook Stream Crossing: Excavations at 1 Poultry and vicinity, City of London*. London: Museum of London Archaeology.

Hind, J.G.F., 1989, 'The Invasion of Britain in AD 43 – An Alternative Strategy for Aulus Palutius', *Britannia* XX, pp. 1–21.

Hingley, R., 2018, *Londinium: A Biography – Roman London from its Origins to the Fifth Century*. London: Bloomsbury Academic.

Hingley, R. & Unwin, C., 2005, *Boudica: Iron Age Warrior Queen*. London: Hambledon and London.

Hopkins, K. & Beard, M., 2011, *The Colosseum*. London: Profile Books.

Horne, B., 2014, 'Did Boudica and Paulinus Meet South of Dunstable?', *South Midlands Archaeology*, No. 44, pp. 89–93.

Hoselitz, V., 2015, *Imagining Roman Britain – Victorian Responses to a Roman Past*. Woodbridge: Boydell Press.

Hughes, B., 2017, 'Boudica's Revenge', episode in *Eight Days that Made Rome*, Channel 5 documentary series. Aired 24/11/2017.

Hughes, M., 2014, *On Boudica's Trail: Innovative Research*. Abstract and summary of conference held on 29 June 2013 at University of Warwick, for Atherstone Civic Society.

Hughes, M., 2020, *Boudica At Mancetter*. Atherstone: Atherstone Civic Society.

Hull, M.R., 1958, *Roman Colchester*. Oxford: Society of Antiquaries of London/Oxford University Press.

Hunt, R., 2003, *Queen Boudicca's Battle of Britain*. Staplehurst: Spellmount.

Hutcheson, N.C.G., 2004, *Later Iron Age Norfolk: Metalwork, landscape and society*, BAR British Series 361. Oxford: British Archaeological Reports.

Hutcheson, N., 2011, 'Excavations at Snettisham, Norfolk, 2004: Re-investigating the past', in Davies, J. (Ed.), *The Iron Age in Northern East Anglia: New Work in the Land of the Iceni*, BAR British Series 549. Oxford: Archaeopress, pp. 41–8.

Hutton, R., 1991, *The Pagan Religions of the Ancient British Isles: Their Nature and Legacy*. Oxford: Blackwell.

Hutton, R., 2014, *Pagan Britain*. London: Yale.

Huws, G.P. & Beggs, T., 2004, *The Menai Strait*. Ceredigion: Gomer Press.

Jackson, K., 1979, 'Queen Boudicca?', *Britannia* X, p. 255.

Jackson, R.P.J. & Potter, T.W., 1996, *Excavations at Stonea, Cambridgeshire 1980–85*. London: British Museum Press.

Jenkins, H., 1853, *Colchester Castle Built by A Colony of Romans as a Temple to their Deified Emperor, Claudius Caesar. The Substance of a Lecture Delivered Before the Colchester Archaeological Society*. London: William Edward Painter.

Jenkins, H., 1869, *Colchester Castle Shewn to Have Been The Templed Citadel Which the Roman Colonists Built at Colonia Camulodunum to Their Deified Emperor Claudius*. London: John Russell Smith.

Johnson, M., 2012, *Boudicca*. London: Bristol Classical Press.

Jones, R.C., 2011, *Crossing the Menai: An Illustrated History of the Ferries and Bridges of the Menai Strait*. Wrexham: Bridge Books.

Kaye, S., 2010, 'Can Computerised Terrain Analysis Find Boudica's Last Battlefield?', *British Archaeology* 114, Sept/Oct., pp. 30–3.

Kaye, S., 2015, *Finding the Site of Boudica's Last Battle: Multi-Attribute Analysis of Sites Identified by Template Matching*. Unpublished essay at http://independent.academia.edu/SteveKaye.

Lang Jones, H., 1913, *Songs of a Buried City*. London: J.M. Dent & Sons Ltd.

Lawson, A.K., 1986, 'A Fragment of Life-Size Bronze Equine Statuary from Ashill, Norfolk', *Britannia* XVII, pp. 333–9.

Lepper, F. & Frere, S., 1988, *Trajan's Column*. Gloucester: Alan Sutton.

Lucas, G., 2001, *Excavations at Vicar's Farm, West Cambridge*, CAU Report 425. Cambridge: Cambridge Archaeological Unit/University of Cambridge.

Luff, R., 1984, 'The human remains from the legionary ditch', in Crummy, P., *Colchester Archaeological Report 3: Excavations at Lion Walk, Balkerne Lane, and Middleborough, Colchester, Essex*. Colchester: Colchester Archaeological Trust.

Lynch, F., 1991, *Prehistoric Anglesey: The Archaeology of the Island to the Roman Conquest*, Second Edition. Llangefni: The Anglesey Antiquarian Society.

Macdonald, P. & Young, T., 2007, 'Field Survey at Llyn Cerrig Bach', in Macdonald, P., *Llyn Cerrig Bach: A Study of the Copper Alloy Artefacts from the Insular La Tène Assemblage*. Cardiff: University of Wales Press.

Bibliography

Macdonald, P., 2007, *Llyn Cerrig Bach: A Study of the Copper Alloy Artefacts from the Insular La Tène Assemblage*. Cardiff: University of Wales Press.

Mackay, D., 2001, *Land Around Homerton Street, Cambridge: An Archaeological Evaluation*, CAU Report 423. Cambridge: Cambridge Archaeological Unit/University of Cambridge.

Mackay, D., 2001a, *The Old Cattle Market, Cambridge: An Archaeological Evaluation*, CAU Report 437. Cambridge: Cambridge Archaeological Unit/University of Cambridge.

Mackay, D., 2001b, *An Archaeological Investigation at Homerton Street, Cambridge*, CAU Report 448. Cambridge: Cambridge Archaeological Unit/University of Cambridge.

Madgwick, R., 2017, 'Statement on $^{87}Sr/^{86}Sr$ and $õ^{18}O$ isotope analysis of human remains', in Wightman, A. & Crummy, P., *An Archaeological Excavation and Watching Brief at Fenwick Colchester (formerly Williams & Griffin), 147–151 High Street, Colchester, Essex*, CAT Report 1150. Colchester: Colchester Archaeological Trust, pp. 233–5.

Malim, T., 2005, *Stonea and the Roman Fens*. Stroud: Tempus.

Manley, J., 2002, *AD 43: The Roman Invasion of Britain*. Stroud: Tempus.

Margary, I.D., 1967, *Roman Roads in Britain*. London: John Baker.

Marsden, P., 1987, *The Roman Forum Site in London*. London: HMSO.

Marshall, R., 1994, *Storm From the East*. London: Penguin Books/BBC.

Mason, D.J.P., 2003, *Roman Britain and the Roman Navy*. Stroud: Tempus.

Mattingly, D., 2007, *An Imperial Possession – Britain in the Roman Empire*. London: Penguin.

Millett, M., 1992, *The Romanization of Britain*. Cambridge: Cambridge University Press.

Milne, G., 1985, *The Port of Roman London*. London: Batsford.

Mortimer, R. & Regan, R., 2001, *Chesterton Lane Corner, Cambridge: Archaeological Excavations at Anglia Water sewage shaft M5*, CAU Report 420. Cambridge: Cambridge Archaeological Unit/University of Cambridge.

Mortimer, R., 1997, *The Marion Close Enclosure: Excavations at 138 Huntingdon Road, Cambridge*, CAU Report 203. Cambridge: Cambridge Archaeological Unit/University of Cambridge.

Nash Briggs, D., 2010, 'Reading the Images on Iron Age Coins 3. Some Cosmic Wolves', in *Chris Rudd List 110*, auction catalogue, pp. 2–4.

Nash Briggs, D., 2011, 'The Language of Inscriptions on Icenian Coinage', in Davies, J. (Ed.), *The Iron Age in Northern East Anglia: New Work in the Land of the Iceni*, BAR British Series 549. Oxford: Archaeopress.

Niblett, R., 1985, *Sheepen: An Early Roman Industrial Site at Camulodunum*, CBA Research Report 57. London: CBA.

Niblett, R., 2001, *Verulamium: The Roman City of St Albans*. Stroud: Tempus.

Niblett, R., 2006, 'Images of Boudicca', *Britannia* XXXVII, pp. 489–92.

O'Neil, H.E., 1945 (1946), 'The Roman Villa at Park Street, Near St. Albans, Hertfordshire: Report on the Excavations of 1943–45', *Archaeological Journal* CII, pp. 21–110.

Oddy, W.A. & Craddock, P.T., 1986, 'Report on the Scientific Examination of the Fragment of Horse's Leg', in Lawson, A.K. 'A Fragment of Life-Size Bronze Equine Statuary from Ashill, Norfolk', *Britannia* XVII, pp. 333–9.

Owen-Jones, E., 2012, 'A Remarkable Find at Valley', in Steele, P., *Llyn Cerrig Bach – Treasure from the Iron Age*. Llangefni: Oriel Ynys Môn.

Peach, L.D.G. & Kenney, J. (Illus.), 1959, *Ladybird Book of Julius Caesar and Roman Britain*. Loughborough: Wills & Hepworth.

Peddie, J., 1997, *Conquest: The Roman Invasion of Britain*. Stroud: Alan Sutton.

Pegg, J., 2010, *Landscape Analysis and Appraisal, Church Stowe, Northamptonshire, as a Candidate Site for the Battle of Watling Street*. London: craft:pegg.

Percival, J., 1980, *Living in the Past*. London: BBC.

Perring, D., 1991, *Roman London*. London: Seaby.

Perring, D. 2022, *London in the Roman World*. Oxford: Oxford University Press.

Pollard, N. & Berry, J., 2016, *The Complete Roman Legions*. London: Thames & Hudson.

Prior, M., 1879, 'Isandhlwana Revisited', *Illustrated London News*, No. 2091, Vol. LXXV, 12 July, p. 37.

Punt, S., 2011, 'The Battle of Watling Street', Episode 4, Series 4 of *Punt PI*, BBC Radio 4. Aired 31/12/ 2011.

Radford, D., 2013, 'The early Roman colonia, AD 49–61', in Gascoyne, A. & Radford, A., *Colchester: Fortress of the War God – An Archaeological Assessment*. Oxford: Oxbow Books.

Radford, D., 2013a, 'Camulodunon in the late Iron Age, c50 BC–AD 43', in Gascoyne, A. & Radford, A., *Colchester: Fortress of the War God – An Archaeological Assessment*. Oxford: Oxbow Books.

Radford, D., 2013b, 'The later Roman town, AD 61–410', in Gascoyne, A. & Radford, A., *Colchester: Fortress of the War God – An Archaeological Assessment*. Oxford: Oxbow Books.

Bibliography

Rainbird Clarke, R., 1954, 'The Early Iron Age Treasure from Snettisham, Norfolk', *Proceedings of the Prehistoric Society* XX, Part 1, pp. 27–86.

Ranieri, S. & Telfer, A., 2017, *Outside Roman London: Roadside Burials by the Walbrook Stream*. London: Museum of London Archaeology.

Reid, J., 2016, 'Bullets, Ballistas, and Burnswark: A Roman Assault on a hill-fort in Scotland', *Current Archaeology* 316, July, pp. 20–6.

Rickett, R., 1995, *The Anglo-Saxon Cemetery at Spong Hill, North Elmham, Part VII: The Iron Age, Roman and Early Saxon Settlement*. East Anglian Archaeology 73.

Rivet, A.L.F. & Smith, C., 1981, *The Place-Names of Roman Britain*. London: BCA.

Roberts, A. & Oliver N., 2015, *The Celts: Blood, Iron and Sacrifice*. BBC documentary series. Aired October 2015.

Robinson, B., 1996, *Chasing the Shadows: Norfolk Mysteries Revisited*. Wicklewood: Elmstead Publications.

Robinson, J., 1997, *Angels of Albion: Women of the Indian Mutiny*. London: Penguin.

Ross, A., 1974, *Pagan Celtic Britain*. London: Cardinal.

Ross, A., 2004, *Druids: Preachers of Immortality*. Stroud: Tempus.

Rudd, C., 2000, 'The Face That Launched 80,000 Deaths', *Coin News*, October 2000, pp. 23–4.

Rudd, C., 2015, 'The Fakenham Hoard', *Coin News*, September 2015, pp. 39–40.

Rudd, C., 2018, *Chris Rudd List 157*, auction catalogue. Aylsham: Chris Rudd.

Rudd, C., 2018a, 'The Deal the Dog Made', *Coin News*, May 2018, pp. 36–9.

Russell, M., 2010, *Bloodline: The Celtic Kings of Roman Britain*. Chalford: Amberley Publishing.

Russell, M. & Laycock, S., 2011, *UnRoman Britain: Exposing the Great Myth of Britannia*. Stroud: The History Press.

Russell, M. & Manley, H., 2013, 'A case of mistaken identity? Laser-scanning the bronze "Claudius" from near Saxmundham', *Journal of Roman Archaeology* 26, pp. 393–408.

Sealy, P.R., 2010, *The Boudican Revolt Against Rome*. Oxford: Shire Publications.

Sellar, W.C. and Yeatman, R.J., 1930, *1066 And All That*. London: Methuen & Co. Ltd.

SHARP/Faulkner, N., Robinson, K. & Rossin, G. (Eds.), 2014, *Digging Sedgford: A People's Archaeology*. Cromer: Poppyland Publishing.

Shimmin, D., 2013, *An Archaeological Evaluation at 97 High Street, Colchester, Essex*, CAT Report 701. Colchester: Colchester Archaeological Trust.

Spence, L., 1937, *Boadicea: Warrior Queen of the Britons*. London: Robert Hale Ltd.

Stead, I.M., 1991, 'The Snettisham Treasure: Excavations in 1990', *Antiquity*, Vol. 65, No. 248, pp. 447–64.

Stead, I.M., 1998, *The Salisbury Hoard*. Stroud: Tempus.

Stead, I.M., 2006, *British Iron Age Swords and Scabbards*. London: British Museum Press.

Straker, V., 1987, 'Carbonised cereal grain from first century London: a summary of the evidence for importation and crop processing', in Marsden, P., *The Roman Forum Site in London*. London: HMSO.

Sutcliff, R., 1978 (1984), *Song For A Dark Queen*. Sevenoaks: Knight Books.

Sutcliff, R., 1954 (1980), *The Eagle of the Ninth*. Harmondsworth: Puffin.

Swain, H. & Williams, T., 2008, 'The Population of Roman London', in Clark, J. et al, *Londinium and Beyond: Essays on Roman London and its Hinterland for Harvey Sheldon*, CBA Research Report 156. York: Council for British Archaeology.

Swinson, C., 1953, 'Episode 1, Queen Boadicea: The Battle against the Romans, AD 61' in *The St Albans Pageant, Masque of the Queens, Verulamium, June 22–27 1953 Souvenir Programme*. St. Albans: Gainsborough Press.

Symonds, M. & Redfern, R., 2014, 'Roman headhunters in London? The Mystery of the Walbrook skulls', *Current Archaeology* 288, pp. 38–41.

Talbot, J., 2017, *Made for Trade: A New View of Icenian Coinage*. Oxford: Oxbow Books.

Talbot, J., 2018, 'The Die is Cast: Investigating Icenian Coinage', *Current Archaeology* 341, August 2018, pp. 32–8.

Tannahill, R., 1995, *Sex in History*. London: Abacus.

Taylor, A., 2000, 'Discussion and Conclusions', in Alexander, J. & Pullinger, J., 'Roman Cambridge: Excavations on Castle Hill 1956–1988', *Proceedings of the Cambridge Antiquarian Society* LXXXVIII for 1999.

Tomlin, R.S.O., 2016, *Roman London's first voices: writing tablets from the Bloomberg excavations, 2010–14*, Mola Monograph 72. London: Museum of London Archaeology.

Tranströmer, T. (trans. Robin Fulton), 1997/2011, *New Collected Poems*. Hexham: Bloodaxe Books.

Bibliography

Wacher, J., 1978, *Roman Britain*. London: J. M. Dent & Sons Ltd.

Waite, J., 2007, *Boudica's Last Stand: Britain's Revolt Against Rome AD 60–61*. Stroud: Tempus.

Waite, J., 2011, *To Rule Britannia: The Claudian Invasion of Britain AD 43*. Stroud: The History Press.

Walker, F.G., 1910, 'Roman Roads into Cambridge', *Proceedings of the Cambridge Antiquarian Society* LVI, pp. 141–76.

Wallace, L.M., 2014, *The Origin of Roman London*. Cambridge: Cambridge University Press.

Ward, A., 2004, *Our Bones Are Scattered: The Cawnpore Massacres and the Indian Mutiny of 1857*. London: John Murray.

Ward, C., 2016, 'Gender and precious metal jewellery', in Crummy, N., 'A Hoard of Military Awards, Jewellery and Coins from Colchester', *Britannia* 47.

Webster, G., 1993, *The Roman Invasion of Britain*. London: Batsford.

Webster, G., 1993a, *Rome Against Caratacus*. London: Batsford.

Webster, G., 1993b, *Boudica*. London: Batsford.

Webster, G., 2002, *The Legionary Fortress at Wroxeter: Excavations by Graham Webster 1955–85*. London: English Heritage.

Webster, G. & Dudley, D.R., 1973, *The Roman Conquest of Britain*. London: Pan.

Wells, H. G., 1895 (2012), *The Time Machine*. London: Penguin.

Wheeler, R.E.M., 1920, 'The Vaults Under Colchester Castle: A Further Note', in the *Journal of Roman Studies* X.

Wheeler, R.E.M., 1921, 'The Balkerne Gate, Colchester', in *Transactions of the Essex Archaeological Society* 15, pp. 179–89.

Wheeler, Sir M., 1956, *Archaeology from the Earth*. Harmondsworth: Penguin.

Wheeler, Sir M., 1958, *Still Digging: Adventures in Archaeology*. London: Pan Books.

Wheeler, R.E.M. & Laver, P.G., 1919, 'Roman Colchester', in the *Journal of Roman Studies* IX.

Wheeler, R.E.M. & Wheeler, T.V., 1936, *Verulamium: A Belgic and two Roman Cities*. Oxford and London: Oxford University Press and the Society of Antiquaries of London.

White, R. & Barker, P., 1999, *Wroxeter: Life and Death of a Roman City*. Stroud: Tempus.

Wightman, A. & Crummy, P., 2017, *An Archaeological Excavation and Watching Brief at Fenwick Colchester (formerly Williams & Griffin)*,

147–151 High Street, Colchester, Essex, CAT Report 1150. Colchester: Colchester Archaeological Trust.

Wild, J.P., 1984, 'The textiles', in Crummy, P., *Colchester Archaeological Report 3: Excavations at Lion Walk, Balkerne Lane, and Middleborough, Colchester, Essex*. Colchester: Colchester Archaeological Trust.

Wilson, D.R., Wright, R.P., Hassall, M.W.C & Tomlin, R.S.O., 1975, 'Roman Britain in 1974', *Britannia* VI.

Wood, M., 1980, *In Search of Boadicea*, BBC television documentary. Aired 11/03/1980.

Wood, M., 1981, *In Search of the Dark Ages*. London: BBC.

Source Notes

Preface: AD 60 and All That

1 Hawkes, 1984, p. 78; Wheeler & Laver, 1919, pp. 146–7; Wheeler, 1920, pp. 87–9; Radford 2013, p. 79.
2 Tacitus, *Annals*, XIV: 32.
3 Wheeler, 1956, p. 13.
4 Hanson, 2009, pp. 237–42; Castle, 2010, pp. 36–42.
5 See Fraser et al, 2009, the related documentary *Battle of the Somme – The True Story* (Yap films, 2006), the Imperial War Museum DVD of *The Battle of the Somme 1916*, and *How I Filmed the War* by Geoffrey Malins.

Chapter 1: A Far-Flung Isle

1 See Appendix 1.
2 de la Bédoyère, 2015, p. 30.
3 Beard, 2016, episode 3.
4 Burke, 2000.
5 BBC, 1978.
6 Percival, 1980.
7 Firstbrook, 2001.
8 ibid., p. 123.
9 Tacitus, *The Agricola*, 21.
10 Creighton, 2000, p. 101.
11 Strabo, *Geography*, 4.5.2.
12 Davies, 2008, pp. 109, 127; Davies, 2011a, pp. 103–5.
13 Cunliffe, 2005, pp. 146–7.

14 Nash Briggs, 2011, pp. 83–102.
15 See Cottam et al, 2010, pp. 88, 90; Chadburn, 2006, pp. 27–9.
16 Jackson, 1979, p. 255.
17 Beard, 2013, p. 152.
18 Braund, 1996, p. 70.
19 Cottam et al, 2010, pp. 24, 78, 87; Rudd, 2018, p. 11; Rudd, 2018a, pp. 36–9.
20 Nash Briggs, 2011, pp. 98–9; Rudd, 2018a, pp. 36–9.
21 Cottam et al, 2010, p. 78.
22 Rainbird Clarke, 1954, p. 30; Robinson, 1996, p. 2.
23 Rainbird Clarke, 1954, pp. 28–31.
24 Stead, 1998, p. 145.
25 ibid., p. 146.
26 Stead, 1991, pp. 450–1. The figures are all taken from Stead's original paper. The exact figures, for both numbers and torc dates, may be revised in the long-anticipated definitive British Museum report (Joy, J. & Farley, J. (eds), forthcoming *The Snettisham Hoards. Research Publication 225.* London: British Museum Press) which was sadly still delayed and yet to be available at the time of going to press.
27 Stead, 1998, pp. 147–8.
28 Cunliffe, 2005, p. 570; 1997, p. 196.
29 Rainbird Clarke, 1954, p. 70.
30 Stead, 1991, p. 463.
31 de Jersey, 2014, pp. 310–29.
32 Talbot, 2017, pp. 109, 223–4; certainly at least conquest period: de Jersey, 2014, pp. 317–26.
33 Hutcheson, 2004, p. 25.
34 Hutcheson, 2011, pp. 41–8.
35 or potentially both; see Fitzpatrick, 1992.
36 for example, Cunliffe, 2005, p. 197; Davies, 2008, pp. 101–3.
37 Davies, 2008, pp. 94–106.
38 SHARP, 2014, pp. 47–9.
39 Talbot, 2017, pp. 91–2.
40 Ross, 1974, p. 279; Rudd, 2000, pp. 23–4; Cottam et al, 2010, p. 16.
41 Described by Talbot, 2017, pp. 91–2, and credited originally to Chimirri-Russell, 2003.
42 Talbot, 2018, p. 35.
43 Talbot, 2017, p. 92.
44 ibid., pp. 143, 147.

45 Nash Briggs, 2010, pp. 2–4; 2011, p. 98.

46 Cottam et al, 2010, p. 131; Nash Briggs, 2011, p. 98 after Rainer Kretz.

47 arguably – the Cantiaci may have produced one, Cottam et al, 2010, p. 37, coin 258; p. 94, coin 1788, Lincolnshire Wolf.

48 Davies, 2011, pp. 59–68.

49 ibid., p. 65.

50 SHARP, 2014, p. 49.

51 Rudd, 2015, p. 40.

52 Hutton, 1991, p. 155.

53 Sturluson, *Heimskringla*, Saga of Hákon the Good.

54 Talbot, 2017, p. 86.

55 Creighton, 2000, pp. 41–53.

56 Hutcheson, 2004, p. 99.

57 Davies, 2008, p. 110.

58 Davies, 2011b, p. 5 ; Cunliffe, 2005, p. 197.

59 Cottam et al, 2010, p. 78.

60 Creighton, 2000, pp. 22–6; Hutcheson, 2004, p. 96.

61 Fox, 1958, p. 139.

62 Sutcliff, 1954, p. 98.

63 Ross, 1974, pp. 236–7; Green, 1986, pp. 140–1.

64 For hints of IA settlement see Davies, 2008, p. 120; Davies, 1999, pp. 35–6. However grand the Roman town was yet to become, it was slow to develop and seemingly never reached its full potential. Like so many societies across the world, the aftermath of imperial conquest and subjugation involved the adoption of the invader's material culture, religion and urbanisation. Archaeologically, this can appear to be a successful metamorphosis. The associated impoverishment, agony and social dislocation of the process can be more difficult to identify.

65 Hill, 1999, pp. 189–92; Davies, 2011a, p. 103.

66 Bowden, 2012, p. 29; 2017, p. 2.

67 Davies, 2008, pp. 120, 151.

68 Bowden, 2020, pp. 18–20.

69 Lang Jones, 1913.

Chapter 2: The Eagle Has Landed

1 Tacitus, *The Annals*, II: 23.

2 ibid, II: 24.

3 Manley, 2002, p. 84.

4 Dio, *History*, LX: 19.

5 Webster, 1993, p. 96.

6 Peddie, 1997, p. 41.

7 Wacher, 1978, p. 29; Webster & Dudley, 1973, pp. 41–7.

8 Dudley & Webster, 1973, p. 40; Webster, 1993, p. 95; Frere, 1991, pp. 48–9; Peddie, 1997, pp. 60–5; Waite, 2011, pp. 131–7.

9 Hind, 1989, pp. 1–21; Manley, 2002, pp. 31–6; Russell, 2010, pp. 96–9.

10 Pollard & Berry, 2016, pp. 85, 95.

11 ibid., p. 102.

12 Cottam et al, 2010, p. 135.

13 Dio, *History*, LX: 19.

14 Manley, 2002, p. 90.

15 ibid., p. 62.

16 Frere, 1991, p. 192.

17 Hawkes & Crummy, 1995, p. 59; Crummy, 1997, pp. 34–6.

18 Dio, *History*, LX: 22.

19 Gascoyne, 2013, p. 68.

20 Suetonius, *The Twelve Caesars*, X: 4.

21 Millett, 1992, p. 55.

22 Tacitus, *Annals*, XII: 31.

23 Ross, 2004, pp. 161–3.

24 Malim, 2005, p. 56.

25 ibid., pp. 60–7.

26 ibid., pp. 43, 73–4, 82.

27 ibid., pp. 82, 86; Jackson & Potter, 1996, p. 42.

28 Malim, 2005, p. 82.

29 ibid., p. 84.

30 Jackson & Potter, 1996, p. 44.

31 Davies & Robinson, 2009, pp. 54, 91–2.

32 Wood, 1981, p. 21.

33 Malim, 2005, pp. 75–7.

34 Malim, 2005, pp. 70–1.

35 Bayliss, 2005, pp. 94–5.

36 Malim, 2005, pp. 69–70, 80.

37 Tacitus, *Annals*, XII: 31.

38 ibid, XVI: 15.

39 Cunliffe, 2005, p. 542.

40 Braund, 1996, p. 133.

41 Tacitus, *Annals*, XII: 32.

42 See Bowman, 2008, p. 103. He translates the term loosely as 'wretched Britons', and notes its contemptuous nature, p. 93. Soldiers being soldiers, and given the atmosphere of first-century Britain and comparisons from more recent history, I think even *fucking little Britons* is probably a rather mild rendition of the spirit of its usage.

43 Tacitus, *Annals*, XIV: 31.

44 Crummy, 1997, pp. 53–4.

45 Crummy, 1984, pp. 94–7; Luff, 1984, pp. 97–8.

46 Cicero, *Letters to Atticus*, 4: 16.

47 Beard, 2016, Episode 3; Dimbleby, 2010; Hughes, 2017.

48 Braund, 1996, p. 5.

49 Cunliffe, 2005, p. 221.

50 Radford, 2013, p. 78.

51 Millett, 1992, pp. 58–9.

52 Hutcheson, 2004, p. 95, for a short précis of sources.

53 Talbot, 2017, pp. 60, 75, 84.

54 Davies, 2008, p. 139; Davies, 2011c, p. 65; Aldhouse-Green, 2006, p. 69.

55 Sealey, 2010, p. 49.

56 Davies, 2008, p. 139.

57 Hutcheson, 2004, p. 96.

58 Rickett, 1995, p. 148.

59 Russell and Laycock, 2011, pp. 58–9.

60 Very small indeed. Imported einkorn grain has been found carbonised in AD 60 layers in London (Marsden, 1987, pp. 71, 97; Straker, 1987, pp. 151–3), perhaps suggesting a need to import grain, but, as de la Bédoyère (2003, p. 59) has pointed out, shipping grain to London from the continent may have been a good deal easier than transporting it from inland. Be that as it may, Britain should have been a major *exporter* of grain (Mason, 2003, p. 87).

61 Tacitus, *Annals*, XIV: 31.

62 ibid.

63 Aldhouse-Green, 2006, p. 154.

64 Sutcliff, 1978, p. 83.

65 Dio, *History*, LXII: 2.

66 ibid.

67 Dudley & Webster, 1962, pp. 144–5; Tomlin, 2016, pp. 55–6.

68 Carroll, 1979, pp. 197–202; Talbot, 2017, p. 120.

69 Aldhouse-Green, 2006, pp. 144–71; Cunliffe, 1997, p. 191.

70 Aldhouse-Green, 2006, p. 132.

71 ibid., pp. 152, 154.

72 Talbot, 2017, pp. 117–19, 150.

73 ibid., p. 150.

74 Hutcheson, 2004, p. 93.

75 Chadburn, 1996, p. 273; numerous hoard listings in de Jersey, 2014.

76 Talbot, 2017, pp. 121–2.

77 ibid., pp. 117–18.

78 Cottam et al, 2010, p. 84.

79 Talbot, 2017, p. 89; 2018, p. 36.

80 Talbot, 2017, pp. 47, 150.

81 ibid., pp. 119–21.

82 Russell, 2010, pp. 121–2.

83 Chadburn, 2006, pp. 27–9.

84 ibid.

85 Cottam et al, 2010, p. 90.

86 Stead, 2006, p. 197, no. 217; Davies, 2008, p. 93.

87 Stead, 2006, p. 176, no. 103.

88 Hill, 1999, p. 203, n. 4.

89 Rudd, 2018a, p. 39.

90 Hill, 1999, pp. 201, 203, n. 4.

Chapter 3: Till in Her Ashes She Lie Buried

1 Jenkins, 1853.

 2 ibid., p. 24.

 3 Hoselitz, 2015, p. 121.

 4 Jenkins, 1853, pp. 17–18.

 5 quoted in Hoselitz, 2015, p. 121.

 6 Cutts, 1853, p. 3.

 7 ibid., p. 14.

 8 Jenkins, 1869, pp. 7–8.

 9 Buckler, 1876.

10 Crummy, 2013, p. 170.

11 Niblett, 1985, pp. 43, 115, 124, 168, microfiche B12.

12 anon, 1974, p. 240.

13 Wheeler, 1958, pp. 53–4.

14 Wheeler, 1921, p. 80.

15 Wheeler, 1958, p. 48.

16 Wheeler, 1921, pp. 180–3.

17 Crummy, 1984, pp. 121–3.

18 Crummy, 1997, p. 60.

19 ibid., p. 87.

20 Wheeler, 1921, pp. 187–8; Crummy, 2002, p. 19; Crummy, 1997, pp. 86–9; Radford, 2013b, pp. 107–8.

21 Crummy, 2002, p. 20; Radford, 2013b, p. 107.

22 Wheeler, 1921, p. 187.

23 Tacitus, *Annals*, XIV: 32.

24 Dio, *History*, LXII: 1.

25 Crummy, 2013, p. 98; Radford, 2013b, p. 116.

26 Crummy, 2013, p. 97; Radford, 2013b, p. 116.

27 de la Bédoyère, 2001, p. 104.

28 Tacitus, *Annals*, XIV: 32.

29 ibid.

30 ibid, XIV: 31.

31 Crummy, 1997, pp. 59–60; Radford, 2013b, pp. 142–3.

32 Crummy, 1997, p. 60.

33 Tacitus, *Annals*, XIV: 41.

34 Crummy, 1997, p. 60.

35 Crummy, 1997, p. 64.

36 ibid., p. 75.

37 Crummy, 1977, pp. 85–6; Drury, 1984, p. 22.

38 Wightman & Crummy, 2017, p. 251, fig. 118.

39 see the marvellous Walk the Wall Trail on www.Camulos.com.

40 Crummy, 1984, pp. 5–9.

41 Beard, 2009, pp. 9–10.

42 Crummy, 1984, pp. 40–2.

43 ibid., pp. 42–4; Wild, 1984, pp. 44–7.

44 Beard, 2009, p. 89.

45 Dunnett, 1971, p. 8; Crummy, 2015, p. 31.

46 Crummy, 2015, p. 31; Wightman & Crummy, 2017, pp. 250–1.

47 Wightman & Crummy, 2017.

48 Madgwick, 2017, p. 235.

49 Curl, 2017, pp. 228–31.

50 Wightman & Crummy, 2017, p. 32.

51 Fryer, 2017, pp. 220–7.

52 A small unstratified hoard of 27 coins found in a pot, burnt, and of the correct era, was found in 1926–7 in the garden of St Martin's House; Hull, 1958, p. 104.

53 Crummy, N., 2015b, p. 22.

54 Ward, 2016, pp. 19–20.
55 Crummy, N., 2015b, p. 27. Sadly, having forced a reproduction of one of these earrings through my twenty-year-unused earring scar, and walking, swaying and jerking, I have failed to make it rattle. The pearl on a thin wire, however, does *look* like a rattle.
56 ibid.
57 Crummy, N., 2016, p. 9.
58 Crummy, N., 2015b, p. 29; 2016, pp. 9–11.
59 Wightman & Crummy, 2017, p. 34; Crummy, N., 2017, pp. 116–17.
60 Shimmin, 2013, p. 1.
61 Hebditch, 1971, pp. 121–3; Radford, 2013, p. 143; Drury, 1984, pp. 24–5.
62 Radford, 2013, p. 143.
63 ibid., pp. 142–3.
64 Drury, 1984, pp. 11–12.

Chapter 4: Paths of Glory

 1 Tacitus, *Annals*, XIV: 48.
 2 Frere & St. Joseph, 1974.
 3 Dannell & Wild, 1987.
 4 Goldsworthy, 2015, pp. 54–5.
 5 Frere & St. Joseph, 1974, pp. 61–3.
 6 Fincham, 2004, pp. 21–5.
 7 Dannell & Wild, 1987, p. 67.
 8 Frere, 1991, p. 98.
 9 Tacitus, *Agricola*, 19.
10 Alcock, 2011, p. 286.
11 Millett, 1992, pp. 56–7.
12 Frere & St. Joseph, 1974, p. 30, Building x.
13 Bowman, 2008, p. 51.
14 Frere & St. Joseph, 1974, pp. 61–2, no. 77.
15 Birley, 2004.
16 Tacitus, *Histories*, 5: 21.
17 ibid, 4: 71.
18 www.romaninscriptionsofbritain.org.
19 Walker, 1910, p. 161; Codrington, 1918, p. 118.
20 Mortimer, 1997.
21 Evans & Ten Harkel, 2010, p. 57; Alexander & Pullinger, 2000, pp. 28–34; Taylor 2000, p. 77.

22 Taylor, 2000, p. 77.

23 Malim, 2005, p. 137.

24 Babington, 1883, pp. 26–9.

25 Mortimer and Regan, 2001.

26 Walker, 1910, pp. 166–7; Browne, 1974, p. 5 & Map 26.

27 Mackay, 2001; Mackay, 2001b; Evans, Mackay & Webley, 2004, p. 94; Evans, Mackay & Webley, 2008, p. 133.

28 Mackay, 2001a, pp. 10, 24; Walker, 1910, p. 167; Fox, 1923, p. 176.

29 Evans, Mackay & Webley, 2004; 2008.

30 Evans, Mackay & Webley, 2008, p. 137. Or, indeed, have been casualties of the fighting against the Romans in AD 43.

31 French, 2004.

32 Dodwell, 2004, pp. 57–9.

33 ibid.

34 Cunliffe, 2005, p. 552.

35 Tacitus, *Annals*, XIV: 32.

Chapter 5: The Eagle of the Ninth

1 Alcock, 2011, p. 155.

2 Greaves, 2001, p. 74.

3 Davies, H., 2011, pp. 60–2.

4 Fox, 1923, pp. 129–31; 1923a.

5 Rudyard Kipling, *The Way Through the Woods*, 1910.

6 https://www.darwinproject.ac.uk/letter/?docId=letters/DCP-LETT-60. xml;query=babington;brand=default accessed 1/7/17.

7 Babington, 1883, p. 34.

8 Walker, 1910, p. 162.

9 ibid, p. 149.

10 Codrington, 1918, pp. 182, 193.

11 Margary, 1967, pp. 212–13.

12 ibid., p. 211.

13 Bowman, 2008, p. 148.

14 Birley, 1999.

15 Lucas, 2001.

16 Dodwell, 2001, p. 74, Skeleton F2058.

17 Crummy, 2001, p. 78.

18 see Hutton 1991, p. 236 & 2014, pp. 264–5.

19 Dodwell, 2001, p. 82.

20 Lang Jones, 1913, p. 28.

21 Attenborough, 1993.

22 Dodwell, 1998, p. 55.

23 Tacitus, *Histories*, 4: 77.

24 The eagle would probably only have been carried by the complete legion.

25 Tacitus, *Annals*, XIV: 33.

26 Dando-Collins, 2005, pp. 214–15.

27 Frere & St Joseph, 1974, pp. 38–9.

28 I am pleased to record that Emma was to make a quick and full recovery.

29 Sutcliff, 1954, pp. 126–7.

30 Reported after the destruction of the Chinese city of Chung-tu in 1215 when the population was massacred and the city burnt by Genghis Khan's Mongol army. An Islamic ambassador recorded that the streets were greasy with human fat and littered with carcasses; Marshall, 1994, p. 35.

Chapter 6: Enemy Coast Ahead

1 Webster, 1993a, p. 30.

2 Tacitus, *Annals*, XII: 39.

3 Tacitus, *Agricola*, 14.

4 Frere, 1991, p. 70; Webster, 1993b, p. 87; other locations were possible – see Mason 2003, p. 92.

5 Frere, 1991, p. 70.

6 Tacitus, *Annals*, XIV: 29–30.

7 Jones, 2011, pp. 53, 92.

8 Mason, 2003, p. 91.

9 ibid., p. 78.

10 ibid., pp. 46–7.

11 Dio, *History*, LX: 19.

12 Frontinus, *Stratagems*, I: iv.

13 Huws & Beggs, 2004, pp. 89–91.

14 *Ancient Assassins* documentary series, Episode 2, 2016.

15 Lynch, 1991, p. 321.

16 Tacitus, *Annals*, XIV: 30.

17 Ross, 2004, p. 22.

18 ibid., p. 120.

19 Tacitus, *Annals*, XIV: 30.

20 Lucan, *Pharsalia* III.

21 The photograph is reproduced in Macdonald, 2007, plate 1.

22 Fox, 1946, p. 1; Owen-Jones, 2012, p. 10; Catling, 2012, p. 28.

23 Macdonald, 2007, p. 1.

24 Fox, 1946, p. 59.

25 ibid., pp. 61–4.

26 See Macdonald, 2007, pp. 152–5.

27 ibid., pp. 156–7.

28 ibid., p. 173.

29 Aldhouse-Green, 2006, pp. 155–6.

30 Macdonald, 2007, p. 173.

31 Macdonald & Young, 2007.

32 Macdonald, 2007, p. 174.

33 Frere, 1991, p. 70.

34 Macdonald, 2007, pp. 171–2.

35 ibid., p. 169.

36 Cuttler, Davidson & Hughes, 2012.

37 Tacitus, *Annals*, XIV: 30.

Chapter 7: London Calling

1 Tacitus, *Histories*, 2: 31.

2 ibid., 2: 25.

3 Dudley & Webster, 1962, pp. 49, 150, n. 12.

4 Tacitus, *Annals*, XIV: 33.

5 Dio, *History*, LXII: 8.

6 Benario, 1986, p. 359.

7 Haverfield, 1914, pp. 439–40.

8 Church & Bodribb, 1882, p. 92.

9 Benario, 1986.

10 Appleby, 2009.

11 Dudley & Webster, 1962, pp. 69–73; Carroll, 1979, pp. 199–201.

12 Tacitus, *Annals*, XIV: 33.

13 Benario, 1986, p. 359.

14 Hunt, 2003, p. 96.

15 Fuentes, 1984, p. 312.

16 Kaye, 2010, p. 32.

17 Dudley & Webster, 1962, p. 59; Webster, 1993a, p. 71; Webster, 1993b, p. 87; Frere, 1991, p. 70.

18 Hopkins & Beard, 2011, p. 135.

19 anon, 2008, pp. 18–25.

20 Tertullian, *De Spectaculis*, XII.

21 Webster, 2002, p. 80.

22 White & Barker, 1999, p. 9.

23 Delamarre, X., 2012, p. 273. I have so far been unable to inspect a copy of this book to verify the reference.

24 Webster, 1993a, p. 76; Webster, 2002, pp. 80–2; Frere, 1991, p. 61; Ellis, 2012, pp. 16–17.

25 Tacitus, *Annals*, XIV: 33.

26 Bowsher, 1997.

27 Wallace, 2014, pp. 44–5.

28 Perring, 2022, p. 79; Mattingly, 2007, p. 274.

29 Wood, 1980.

Chapter 8: Apocalypse Now

1 Perring, 2022, pp. 49–70.

2 Tacitus, *Annals*, XIV: 33.

3 Wallace, 2014, p. 155.

4 Milne, 1985, p. 7.

5 Wallace, 2014, pp. 98–9.

6 ibid., p. 101.

7 Swain & Williams, 2008, p. 39; Hingley, 2018, p. 27.

8 Wallace, 2014, pp. 111–14.

9 ibid., pp. 143–4.

10 ibid., p. 92.

11 ibid., pp. 81–2, 84.

12 ibid., pp. 84–8.

13 ibid., pp. 49, 109–11.

14 ibid., pp. 115–16.

15 ibid., p. 144.

16 Tacitus, *Annals*, XIV: 33.

17 Milne, 1985, p. 98.

18 Dunwoodie, 2004, p. 15; Marsden, 1987, p. 21.

19 Tacitus, *Annals*, XIV: 33.

20 quoted in Arthur, 2002, p. 41. Sergeant Richard Tobin, Hood Battalion, Royal Naval Division.

21 Hingley & Unwin, 2005, p. 162.

22 See the front cover of Cundy, 2015!

23 Nineteenth-century French cartoonist Paul Gavarni, quoted in Tannahill, 1995, illust. 19.

24 quoted in Hingley & Unwin, 2005, p. 163.

25 Johnson, 2012, pp. 123–4.

26 Banksy, 2006, p. 237.

27 ibid., p. 208; Johnson, 2012, p. 123.

28 Webster, 1993b, p. 126.

29 Hingley & Unwin, 2005, p. 101.

30 see Russell and Manley, 2013.

31 ibid.

32 Lawson, 1986, p. 333.

33 one of Nero is probably attested to at Chichester c.AD 58; Cunliffe, 2005, p. 221.

34 Oddy and Craddock, 1986, p. 339.

35 Hingley, 2018, pp. 43, 55.

36 Perring, 1991, p. 14.

37 Wallace, 2014, p. 102.

38 Russell & Manley, 2013, 'conclusions'.

39 Russell & Manley, 2013, 'damage sustained'.

40 Tacitus, *Annals*, XIV: 33.

41 Dio, *History*, LXII: 7.

42 Wallace, 2014, sites 56 & 73. See also sites 44, 53, 82.

43 Spence, 1937, p. 231.

44 Ranieri & Telfer, 2017, p. 121.

45 ibid., pp. 120–7; Hingley, 2018, pp. 54–5.

46 Symonds & Redfern, 2014, p. 38–41.

47 Perring, 2022, p. 110.

48 Hill & Rowsome, 2011, p. 24.

49 ibid., p. 38.

50 ibid., pp. 22, 46–7.

51 ibid., Building 11, pp. 61–2, 291–3.

52 ibid., pp. 294–304.

53 ibid., pp. 54–8, 294.

54 ibid., p. 294, fig. 277, p. 300, fig. 281; Hall & Swain, 2000.

55 Tomlin, 2016, pp. 25–6.

56 ibid., p. 15.

57 ibid., pp. 152–5.

58 ibid., pp. 60–1.

59 ibid., pp. 62–3.

60 ibid., pp. 120–3.

61 Drummond-Murray, Thompson & Cowan, 2002.

62 ibid., p. 49.

63 ibid., pp. 31, 218.

64 ibid., p. 48.

Chapter 9: Ghost Town

1 O'Neil, 1945, pp. 65–6.
2 ibid., p. 36.
3 Niblett, 2001, p. 67.
4 O'Neil, 1945, p. 39.
5 Wheeler & Wheeler, 1936.
6 Niblett, 2001, p. 122.
7 ibid., pp. 42–3.
8 ibid., p. 56.
9 ibid., pp. 61–2, 66.
10 Swinson, 1953, p. 13.
11 Niblett, 2001, colour pl. 8.
12 ibid., p. 65; Wilson et al, 1975, p. 258.
13 Frere, 1972, pp. 10–11.
14 ibid., p. 12.
15 Niblett, 2001, p. 64.
16 Frere, 1972, pp. 13–19.
17 ibid., p. 14.
18 ibid., p. 11.
19 ibid., p. 9.
20 Frere, 1983, pp. 102, 105–7.
21 Russell, 2010, p. 12.
22 ibid., p. 138; Russell & Laycock, 2011, pp. 61, 234, n. 40.

Chapter 10: Thunderclap

1 Gowing, 1899.
2 Tacitus, *Annals*, XIV: 33–4.
3 Dudley & Webster, 1962.
4 Appleby, 2009.
5 see Evans, Lucy & Patten, 2018, p. 424.
6 Punt, 2011.
7 Hughes, 2014, pp. 14–16.
8 Dudley & Webster, 1962, p. 74.
9 Hughes, 2014, p. 15. The seemingly endless quest for suitable defiles at Mancetter is also taken up by Baddeley, 2013, and by Hughes again in 2020.
10 Rivet & Smith, 1981, pp. 411–12.
11 Waite, 2007.

12 Hughes, 2014, pp. 42–6; 2020, pp. 220–2. Sadly the original paper by Kinsella and Sullivan has proved strangely elusive up to the time of writing.

13 Pegg, 2010; Punt, 2011.

14 Evans, 2001; 2004; Punt, 2011.

15 Horne, 2014.

16 Foot, 2019, pp. 26–9.

17 Cundy, 2015.

18 Kaye, 2010; 2015.

19 Fuentes, 1984.

20 Greep, 1987.

21 noted on the Portable Antiquities Scheme database.

22 Reid, 2016, p. 25.

23 ibid., pp. 24–5.

24 ibid., p. 25.

25 Niblett, 2001, p. 55; 2006, p. 492.

26 Tacitus, *Annals*, XIV: 34.

27 ibid, XIV: 37.

28 Margary, 1967, p. 180, Road 163; Niblett, 2001, p. 55.

29 Tacitus, *Annals*, XIV: 37.

30 Niblett, 2001, p. 57.

31 ibid., p. 55.

32 ibid., p. 58.

33 Tacitus, *Agricola*, 37–8.

34 See Lepper & Frere, 1988.

35 Ferris, 2009, p. 97.

36 ibid.

37 ibid., pp. 115–17.

38 ibid., pp. 117, 118.

39 ibid., pp. 118–19.

40 Ferris, 2003, pp. 94–5.

41 There is a fascinating post querying such a potential survival by Steve Kaye, from 25 April 2012, post 144, on the Roman Army Talk Forum thread, 'Calling All Armchair Generals'.

Chapter 11: The Black Year

1 See previous note.

2 Tomlin, 2016, p. 158. A tablet dated 21 October AD 62 mentions 20 loads of provisions to be brought from Verulamium to Londinium.

3 Ward, 2004, p. 399.

4 Robinson, 1997, p. 126.

5 Ward, 2004, p. 454.

6 Robinson, 1997, p. 128.

7 Ward, 2004, p. 437.

8 Tacitus, *Annals*, I: 62–3.

9 Prior, 1879, p. 37.

10 Forbes, 1879, pp. 37–8.

11 Tacitus, *Annals*, XIV: 38.

12 Cunliffe, 2005, p. 229.

13 Hutcheson, 2004, p. 97; Harlow, 2021, pp. 212–13.

14 Rickett, 1995, pp. 148–50.

15 *Current Archaeology*, March 2021, No. 372, p. 11.

16 Tacitus, *Annals*, XIV: 38.

17 SHARP, 2014, p. 55.

18 ibid., p. 56.

19 Evans, Mackay & Webley, 2008, p. 89.

20 Gregory, 1991, p. 190.

21 ibid., p. 194.

22 ibid., p. 196.

23 ibid.

24 ibid., p. 199; Aldhouse-Green, 2006, pp. 161–4.

25 Gregory, 1991, p. 199.

26 Sealey, 2010, p. 12.

27 Gregory, 1991, pp. 98, 111.

28 ibid., pp. 199–200; Sealey, 2010, p. 42.

29 Aldhouse-Green, 2006, pp. 163, 170, n. 65.

30 Gregory, 1991, p. 199; Aldouse-Green, 2006, pp. 163–4.

31 Webster, 1993, p. 16.

32 Tacitus, *Annals*, XIV: 37.

33 A.E. Housman, *A Shropshire Lad*.

Epilogue: Ashes And Dust

1 de la Bédoyère, 2015, p. 30.

Index